Unconditional Care

Unconditional Care

Relationship-Based, Behavioral Intervention with Vulnerable Children and Families

John S. Sprinson
Ken Berrick

2010

OXFORD
UNIVERSITY PRESS

Oxford University Press, Inc., publishes works that further
Oxford University's objective of excellence
in research, scholarship, and education.

Oxford   New York
Auckland   Cape Town   Dar es Salaam   Hong Kong   Karachi
Kuala Lumpur   Madrid   Melbourne   Mexico City   Nairobi
New Delhi   Shanghai   Taipei   Toronto

With offices in
Argentina   Austria   Brazil   Chile   Czech Republic   France   Greece
Guatemala   Hungary   Italy   Japan   Poland   Portugal   Singapore
South Korea   Switzerland   Thailand   Turkey   Ukraine   Vietnam

Copyright © 2010 by Oxford University Press, Inc.

Published by Oxford University Press, Inc.
198 Madison Avenue, New York, New York 10016

www.oup.com

Oxford is a registered trademark of Oxford University Press

Library of Congress Cataloging-in-Publication Data

Sprinson, John Scott, 1950–
Unconditional care : relationship-based, behavioral intervention
with vulnerable children and families / John S. Sprinson, Ken Berrick.
p.   cm.
Includes bibliographical references and index.
ISBN 978-0-19-973303-3
1. Behavior therapy for children.   2. Problem children—Behavior modification.
3. Family counseling.   4. Counselor and client.   I. Berrick, Ken.   II. Title.
RJ505.B4S67 2010
618.92'8914—dc22
2009023033

Printed in the United States of America
on acid-free paper

This book is dedicated to the extraordinary children and families of Seneca Center.

Acknowledgments

This project was originally conceived by Ken Berrick, founder and CEO of Seneca Center. I have been enormously fortunate to participate in the growth and development of this wonderful organization. When Ken hired me in 1986 he had already articulated the agency's commitment to the practice of unconditional care that is at the heart of this book. He has led Seneca from a very tiny agency with a handful of staff to a very large organization that continues to serve the most traumatized and vulnerable children in California. I am very grateful to have had Ken as a colleague for all these years and to have been part of the collaboration that is Seneca. He deserves specific credit for conceiving this project, making the time and resources available for its completion, and always understanding the importance of unconditional care.

Neil Gilbert, chairperson of the Seneca Board of Directors and professor in the School of Social Welfare at the University of California at Berkeley, was very generous with his time, read several drafts, and ultimately gave us an introduction to Oxford University Press. Jill Duerr Berrick, also a professor of social welfare at Berkeley, read the manuscript and provided encouragement.

Seneca is absolutely blessed to have many, mostly very young, staff members who work every day and every night with passion, curiosity, and amazing energy. They engage our clients and their families with great respect and love and give them the gift of "holding them in their minds." Without them, the agency could not do the work it does and this project could not have happened.

Tony Stanton, the consulting psychiatrist of the Seneca Center Residential Program, has been my most valued intellectual collaborator and very good friend for many years. His thoughtfulness and curiosity together with his unwavering commitment to a relational approach in the face of regular pressures to rely on medication have been mainstays of my professional life for more than 20 years. I am enormously grateful to have him as a friend and a colleague. His thinking is threaded through the very best parts of this book. He conceived the original format of the Table of Life Events many years ago and prepared the sample table that accompanies the first case illustration in Chapter 8. Tony also contributed the section of Chapter 5 titled "Underlying Assumptions in Two Diagnostic Models."

Morgen Humes, Director of Training and Research at Seneca, has been a critically important support throughout the writing of this book. This project would never have been completed without her oversight. She has kept me focused, offered encouragement, read drafts, and provided any resource I requested. Her intelligence and calm good humor have been greatly appreciated. The entire Training Department at Seneca has provided assistance to this project. Megan McQuaid, Associate Director of Training and Research, read drafts and made many useful comments; Rebecca Mitchell and Vanessa Phillip provided administrative support; and Jenny Grantz stepped in at the last minute to provide superb editorial assistance. Mary Ager helped with editing and organizing several versions of the manuscript. In the final months of polishing the manuscript Darci Powell helped with library research at the University of California, Berkeley, and found many lost references.

Several program directors at Seneca have read drafts, made suggestions, and always been available for discussion and exchange of ideas. Leticia Galyean deserves special mention for her contribution of the second case illustration in Chapter 8. With very short notice she put in many hours pulling this material together. Julie Hess, Scott Osborn, Daren Dickson and Alan Sherman have all read drafts and offered thoughtful input. Kevin Conboy and Mike Mertz, who have been with Seneca from the very beginning, have always been especially generous with time and ideas and are among my most valued colleagues. They contributed significantly to the discussion of organizational values at the end of the book.

Finally, I must acknowledge the patience and support of my family. They have always provided unconditional care. My wife Laura, who also happens to be a program director at Seneca, read many drafts with great care, listened to my doubts, and has always been my most important collaborator. My older daughter, Rebecca, has been away at college for most of this process but has, thanks to the Internet, been able to assist with research and encouragement. My younger daughter, Susanna, has lived with this process through much of her adolescence. When I have been distracted, she has been tolerant; and when I have been discouraged, she has enlivened me with her humor. I am very grateful for their love and support.

John S. Sprinson

In the final analysis, this is a book about two profoundly simple and yet endlessly complex ideas: love and learning. In order to make such abstract concepts accessible we rely on terms such as attachment theory and behavioral theory. But make no mistake, the core concepts are simply love and learning.

In keeping with the premise of this work, there are many to whom I am indebted for offering and sustaining a community of love and learning. First and foremost, I want to acknowledge the first author of this book, John Sprinson. John, supported by the superb organizational skills of Morgen Humes and Megan McQuaid, is the author of every word in this book save those written in this acknowledgment. It is only through his grace in recognizing over 20 years of work together that I am included as a second author.

Implicit in my inclusion as an author is recognition of the extraordinary work of the entire staff at Seneca Center. Their commitment, courage, and compassion populate the pages of this work, and their cumulative contribution is immeasurable. Their partnership, along with the experiences of the children and families that we have been privileged to know, is at the core of this book. Some of my colleagues are mentioned below, but many are not. In acknowledging those listed it is my intention that they represent the whole of our efforts.

My friend and co-founder of Seneca, Chris Stoner Mertz, must be mentioned for hers is the heart of Seneca. Michael Mertz, Kevin Conboy, Alfred Gales, Larry Liebman, Kim Wayne, and a host of others have had enormous influence on the formation of our programs and the translation of theory to action. Special acknowledgment also goes to Dr. Tony Stanton, Dr. George Stewart, Dr. John Whalen, and Amy Shell FNP for crafting psychiatric and medical policies that are consistent with our organizational values.

Katherine West is the person who makes Seneca run and hence makes this work possible. Her relentless commitment to our values and mission are at the center of this effort. Gina Plate, Jill Mason, Daren Dickson, and Scott Osborn have all made significant contributions to the structure of our programs and the implementation of these ideas, while Shane Patterson, Mac Young, and departed friend Richard Meyers understood that place makes a powerful statement about compassion.

Professor Neil Gilbert, Seneca's Board Chair and my friend, convinced us that this work could and should be published and has led our Board of Directors, whom I also acknowledge here, to support this effort.

Finally, I want to thank my wife, Jill Duerr Berrick, for teaching me the definition of intellectual integrity and for what she and our children, Sierra and Elias, have taught me about the foundations of this book: love and learning.

Ken Berrick

Contents

Afterword

A Note Regarding Values 229

Appendices 235

Introduction

At the age of 7, Maureen and her 5 year-old half sister were found alone in a small apartment with no food. The children reported that they had not seen their parents in several days. Needles and other drug paraphernalia were found on the kitchen table. Both children were quickly placed in a county foster home. This initial attempt to protect Maureen was the first step in a long series of failed efforts to provide her with safety and some sense of security. While her sister seemed to thrive in a new setting, Maureen's behavior became both increasingly disorganized and increasingly sexualized. With no additional support, the foster mother was quickly overwhelmed by her rageful tantrums, constant demands for attention, and startling seductive behavior that few adults would ever imagine they might encounter in a 7 year old. Within only 2 months the foster mother found herself calling Maureen's county worker and requesting that she be moved.

Over the next 7 years, Maureen was to make her way through more than 20 placements. Some were very brief—just several nights in an emergency shelter placement. Others were longer—nearly 1 year in a group home where she seemed to make gains in controlling her behavior and connecting with staff. Her abrupt discharge from this setting followed a burst of sexual and aggressive acting out that occurred after a series of visits from her mother and stepfather. Several placements were on inpatient child psychiatry units where Maureen was rapidly assessed, given a series of increasingly grave diagnoses and placed on a bewildering variety of powerful psychotropic medications. Ultimately and tragically, the efforts of the child protection, mental health, and special education systems that sought to serve Maureen came to be an additional, unintended source of her difficulties. Never landing in a setting where her behavior could be addressed and where she might come to feel held and contained, Maureen came to see herself as crazy, bad, and repellant to others.

In contrast to the many books that would assist clinicians, teachers, and parents of challenging children and adolescents, this book presents a model for engaging the most challenging children and families who are served by the child welfare, mental health, juvenile justice, and special educations systems. These children, like Maureen, are among the most troubled and troubling clients that treatment programs will ever encounter. They are the children who have found ways to fail and be failed by every adult, every treatment modality, and every system of care that they encounter. Like Maureen, these are the children whose behavior invites every adult who comes in contact with them to abandon them at the first opportunity. Ultimately, all too many of them fail through a series of placements until whatever system of care is responsible for them is forced to place them in the most intensive, the most expensive, and the most restrictive setting available.

Such children present numerous challenges to those who would seek to engage or reengage them in a program of support or intervention. These children will direct a barrage of highly provocative behaviors at adults that may include aggression, defiance, sexual acting-out, or extreme disorganization. The reactions of those who are the targets of this behavior may include startled retreat, frightened dismay, or angry retaliation. While the development of children who are lucky enough to grow up in benign settings is driven forward by the pleasures of mastering new skills and by a variety of external rewards, these most vulnerable clients often seem unmoved by such inducements to growth. In fact, it will often seem as though they have set a course to actively and pointedly defeat the efforts of therapists, teachers, and counselors with an insistent demand that, once again, they be found too difficult, too dangerous, or simply too bad. When distressed, frightened, or hurt many of these vulnerable children are unable to make use of an adult's attention or soothing in a straightforward way that brings relief or comfort. Instead, they may never solicit such attention or they may pursue it in a way that is equivocal or even alienating. Their parents, some of whom grew up in regular contact with the same agencies that are working unsuccessfully to serve their children, have come to the task of parenting with few resources and little support. Their struggles as parents often have roots in their own early experiences of loss and trauma. Repeated interventions by child welfare, educational, mental health and juvenile justice systems have left them feeling blamed, discouraged, and discounted.

It is precisely this group of highly challenged and vulnerable clients and families that many agencies and clinicians now find themselves struggling to serve. *Unconditional Care* presents both a theoretical model and practical guidelines for working with this most difficult group of children. This model is unique in that it incorporates ideas from two intellectual traditions that are not usually discussed together: attachment theory and learning theory. While seeming to speak somewhat different languages and to attend to phenomena in different ways, these two approaches to development, family interaction, and what is generally referred to as "psychopathology" provides conceptual schemes and methods that can work in concert.

Attachment theory and learning theory have been, in both academic psychology and in applied settings, approaches that have not had much to say to each other and are not usually found in any sort of explicit collaborative relationship. Attachment theory had its origins in psychoanalysis, evolutionary theory, and ethology, while learning theory and its clinical wing, behavior modification, arose from empirical work done in university-based psychology departments and was derived from the theorizing and observations of Pavlov, Watson, and Skinner. In more current clinical applications attachment theory has influenced the development of a variety of interventions aimed at supporting the parents of young children as well as the general field of psychoanalytic psychotherapy (see, for example, Wallin, 2007, or Beebe and Lachmann, 2005). Learning theory, and its more modern incarnations, social learning theory and cognitive behavior therapy, has also had broad clinical influence in work with disabled individuals, chronically suicidal borderline adults (Linehan, 1993), interventions with high-risk families (Reid, Patterson, and Snyder, 2002) and school-based approaches to work with developmentally delayed and behavior-disordered children (Bambara and Kern, 2005).

It is quite possible, particularly for those familiar with both behaviorism and attachment theory, that this effort to integrate or demonstrate the overlap between behavioral and attachment based ways of thinking will seem like an incongruous and jarring combination of approaches. After all, behaviorists are concerned with how particular behaviors are learned and maintained and have traditionally avoided "mentalist" concepts about implicit beliefs and working models. It is important to remember though, that a great many things are happening in the course of development and different perspectives, while directing one's attention to different elements or phenomena, may, in fact, possess useful and interesting convergences and synergies. Thus, caretakers are (often without explicit intention) modeling behaviors and responding to some of their child's activities with approval, interest, and engagement. Other behaviors may go unnoticed or elicit disapproval or withdrawal of attention.

These processes of modeling and reward—the traditional domain of behavioral psychology—are not separate from the concurrent processes of an unfolding attachment to the caretaker and the construction of a working model of that attachment. Rather, the two domains overlap and include each other. The repeated, attuned exchanges between a caretaker and a child (traditionally a concern of attachment researchers) can certainly be viewed through a behavioral lens in terms of patterns of alternating mutual reinforcement in which both the child and the caretaker are learning how to regulate each other. Ultimately, the cumulative history of these repeated exchanges or reinforcements contribute to the creation of what attachment researchers have called an "internal working model of relationships" (Bowlby 1969, Bretherton, 2008)

The fundamental correspondence between these two ways of looking at development can be further demonstrated by the importance of the concept of contingency to both perspectives. Thus, from the most basic explanations of what makes an event reinforcing (Kazdin; 2001, for example) to the most sophisticated behavioral accounts of family processes (Reid et al., 2002) close attention is paid to the concept of contingency: the notion that one event (a behavior, for example) is connected to the occurrence of another event (sometimes a behavior by the other). It is a basic truth of learning theory that contingency between a behavior and an event in the environment is an essential condition for that event to be an effective reinforcer. Similarly, attachment researchers and theorists have focused on the critical role of "contingent communication" in the development of a secure attachment (Siegel, 1999) and have observed that infants are extremely interested in detecting contingent relationships between their own physical acts and emotional expressions, on the one hand, and the response which comes back to them from both the physical and interpersonal environment on the other. Detection of these contingencies is thought to play a role in the differentiation of the self and in the development of early representations of the social world (Fonagy, Gergely, Jurist, and Target, 2002). In a similar vein, Schore (2003a) speaks of "contingent responsivity" as a key ingredient in the development of a secure attachment. In a recent volume summarizing a social learning approach to understanding and intervening on conduct problems in children, Patterson (2002), in a chapter on the development of coercive family processes, notes, "The attachment and the social interactional theorists are in surprising agreement about the centrality of contingencies in the socialization process. The two groups even use the same language to discuss the nature of contingent interactions." (p. 26).

The continuity between theoretical perspectives is emphasized because it is precisely at this convergence that programs can find effective interventions to assist the very challenging and vulnerable children who are the focus of this book. The approach described here involves an intentional weaving together of these perspectives and their methods into a coherent intervention strategy in which each way of thinking supports and enriches the other. Thus, from a relationship or attachment perspective, it is necessary to understand and describe the client's attachment history and how that history has contributed to the development of a working model of relationships. This in turn permits the worker to better understand the client's invitation to reenact important, often traumatic scenarios from his interpersonal history. (Please note that this "worker" may be a clinician, a community support counselor, a teacher, a foster parent, a residential counselor, or any individual who is part of an intentional treatment intervention.) Once these invitations have been deciphered, it may become clear what sorts of stances will actively disconfirm the child's implicit negative beliefs about himself and the interpersonal world. At the very same time, the treatment team can be working from a behavioral perspective to discover the antecedents, settings, and consequences that are associated with the client's problematic behaviors. Armed with this understanding, they can then develop strategies for interrupting the forces that maintain these behaviors. Inevitably, doing this successfully requires careful attention to the teaching of alternative skills and capacities that can serve similar functions for the child. Thus, she may learn more successful ways of securing and sustaining safe, supportive engagement with adults and learn to regulate the inevitable emotional challenges that have so disrupted these relationships in the past. When one is attentive to learning histories in this way, the danger of falling into yet another repetition of the highly practiced, negative scenarios which have derailed so many of the child's relationships in the past is greatly reduced. Remaining focused on the teaching of new behaviors and skills provides protection from the "gravitational pull" exerted by the child's negative behavior. It is this pull to engage with and confirm the child's working model of relationships that has so often led to the emotional and behavioral crises that are reliably, and tragically, associated with placement failure in vulnerable populations.

Many of these high-risk, very vulnerable children have been the objects of multiple intervention efforts. For some, the very first intervention may occur at birth, when a toxicology screen detects the presence of one or more illicit substances in the newborn. Others may first receive treatment in nursery school when, after being found too challenging and disorganized for family day care or Head Start programs, they are referred to a therapeutic preschool program. Still others will enter treatment through the child protection door and receive outpatient psychotherapy and some form of in-home support while in foster care. Finally, some children may not receive treatment until they are a year or two into primary school and behavior problems and academic challenges bring them into the special education system. After their first contact with a treating professional, a child protection agency, or school-based program, the journeys of these children may vary greatly. As has already been noted, their challenging, provocative behavior too often results in a series of failed interventions and failed school and home placements. The approach to treatment presented here is intended to be useful to clinicians, child-care workers, foster parents, and agency administrators who encounter these children at any point in this journey. Thus, an integration of concepts from attachment theory and behavioral intervention is useful to the clinician working as an out patient therapist seeing a child in foster care and providing support to the foster parents. It is useful to a clinician working in a community-based "wrap-around" program that supports parents and children being reunified after out-of-home placement. It is useful to a therapist providing family and individual therapy in a day treatment program for youngsters who have failed a series of school-based interventions. It is useful for a program director of a therapeutic preschool attempting to formulate interventions and guide staff who are working with severely traumatized toddlers. It is useful to a team of counselors doing milieu treatment with high-risk, physically and sexually abused girls who have failed multiple foster and group home placements.

It should go without saying that the operational expression of this treatment approach will look very different in the various intervention modalities and programs just described. Consider the following examples:

A clinician is working in a community-based wrap around program and supporting a relative foster placement of a 15-year-old boy with his adult sister and her husband. The client has been in out-of-home care since the age of 7 and during those years has been in multiple group homes and foster homes and has had two brief psychiatric hospitalizations. The clinician has a team of three support counselors who can work with the client at school, in the community after school, and in the home with the foster parents. The team identifies the boy's school placement as a key risk factor in the success of the placement. They advocate for a more suitable placement and then function as supports/consultants to the classroom teacher and aide. This involves assisting with a functional assessment of key disruptive behaviors and developing, with the teacher, a plan for rewarding more adaptive replacement behaviors. At the same time the clinician assists the classroom staff in understanding the client's history and the meaning and functions of some of his provocative, disruptive behavior. Together, they articulate an interpersonal stance that most effectively responds to the boy's efforts to elicit retaliation and rejection. In the home, the team collaborates with the foster parents to establish a program of rewards and consequences that will provide a reasonable structure for the foster parents to encourage positive participation in the family.

A therapist in a school-based day treatment program is working with a 12-year-old client who resides with his mother and two younger siblings. The client has a long history of belligerence, physical intimidation of adults and peers, and academic failure. He is infamous in his school district for the resources he has consumed since kindergarten and is viewed as being well on his way along a fixed trajectory toward delinquency and eventual transition to the juvenile justice system. At home, the three siblings are in fairly constant conflict, struggling for attention and fighting over space, toys, and time with mother. The client also has significant trauma history, having witnessed as a toddler the physical battery of his mother on several occasions. In this case the worker will need to slowly and carefully build an alliance with the mother, whose experience has taught her that she is likely to feel judged and blamed as yet another intervention is attempted with her son. She is surprised then when the clinician is prepared to meet with her at home and is anxious to hear about what concerns she has about her children but also what her experience has been with earlier interventions, what hopes she has for her son's progress and development, and what supports might be found in her extended family and community. As an alliance is gradually built with the mother, the clinician is also able to function as a clinical informant to the school treatment team and make the client's behavior and its functions more intelligible. Through careful observation the team comes to see that some of their interventions are actually maintaining negative behaviors and that by shifting their focus to thoughtfully chosen replacement behaviors they can begin to teach new skills that will serve the client more successfully.

In a residential setting the treatment team is confronted with a 9-year-old girl who was regularly sexually abused by her stepfather and cousin from the age of 4 to 7. She is disorganized, her behavior is highly sexualized, and she needs a very high level of supervision to be maintained even in a very structured milieu program. The team comes to see that unsupervised contact with her mother contributes greatly to her level of disorganization and moves, with the support of the county child welfare worker, to keep the visits briefer and fully supervised. The team constructs a list of the client's various sexualized behaviors and develops a relational stance that provides all staff with ways to respond to each of them, and working within the program's behavioral system, they begin to systematically reward nonsexualized, age-appropriate play with her peers.

In each of these examples the clinician or the treatment team has different resources available and may be working in very different program models. Nonetheless, their work in these varied settings can be usefully informed by an approach that integrates behavioral and relational and thinking and methods. In some settings, such as milieu programs, the team may have elaborate behavioral systems available to implement the treatment plan as well as regular opportunities for communication and problem solving about the clients and their families. In outpatient settings the clinician may be functioning as the sole intervener and must become an active consultant to caretakers, classroom staff, and extended family members. The influence and effectiveness of an outpatient clinician are enormously enhanced when he or she is able to offer concrete behavioral methods for responding to problematic behavior in addition to providing the more familiar developmental guidance and collateral treatment.

While the conceptual base of the approach described here arises from behavioral and attachment theories, it is also informed by a third stream, that can be referred to as the "ecological stream". In this domain attention is directed at the environmental context in which the child and the family are operating. Inclusion of this stream as a fundamental "third leg" of the stool arises from the simple recognition that even the most sophisticated and well-planned interventions can fail when they do not acknowledge the realities of people's lives. The sources of this third stream are multiple and varied. They include work on risk and resiliency, elements of "wrap-around" practice currently utilized in social welfare, and values derived from an interest in and a commitment to social justice.

The chapters that follow are organized according to the following scheme: Chapter 1 introduces the key concepts of relationship and engagement as they are encountered in intensive work with vulnerable children and their families. These concepts are linked to an approach to treatment based on "unconditional care" or a no-fail policy in which clients are never discharged from programs for showing the behavior that led to their placement. Chapter 2 provides a detailed description of the population of children and families who are the focus of this book and the multiple risk factors or areas of vulnerability that are often encountered in work with them. Chapter 3 is a discussion of key concepts from attachment theory and focuses particular attention on the importance of the "internal working model of relationships." This useful concept will become a centerpiece of assessment and intervention.

Chapter 4 addresses issues of assessment and case formulation from a general clinical perspective, proposing some guidelines for a collaborative, relationship-based approach to assessment. Chapter 5 examines some current challenges in the field involving diagnosis and assessment and proposes an attachment-based approach to case formulation and intervention. This approach is based on understanding the child through the lens of the internal working model and details a way of thinking about "relationship-based intervention."

Chapter 6 reviews basic concepts in positive behavioral intervention, emphasizing the importance of initial behavioral definitions and developing a strong understanding of the function of problematic behaviors.

Chapter 7 includes a more detailed methodological map that describes how the more general and abstract concepts of behaviorism and attachment theory are applied in a systematic way in real programs. In Chapter 8 two case illustrations are provided, which describe both relational and behavioral interventions with children who are fairly typical of the population of traumatized vulnerable clients. In the appendices that follow, worksheets and forms are provided that are useful in organizing a team's efforts in assessing clients and planning interventions that are directly linked to the results of those assessments. These forms are a guide for day-to-day practice and also convey a sense of how the various "pieces of the puzzle" are assembled by a treatment team that is confronted with real clients and their families.

Throughout this book, as the processes of assessment and intervention are described, the people making these assessments and interventions will often be referred to in the plural form as "staff" or "the treatment team." This occurs for a simple reason. While it is the case that lone clinicians sometimes encounter these children in outpatient office settings, such as private practice and community clinics, they are very often seen in the context of more intensive treatment settings such as day treatment programs, residential settings, school-based mental health programs, and treatment foster care agencies or other community-based interventions such as "wrap around" programs. As a result, the reader may also encounter references to wider organizational processes and values, such as training, supervision, and collaboration. The reader who is one of the "lone clinicians" described above should, nevertheless, find the approach to treatment described here to be a useful one.

Finally, a note on pronouns; rather than rely on the cumbersome "he or she" and "himself or herself" at every turn, an effort has been made to use gender pronouns interchangeably throughout the book.

Chapter One

Relationship and Engagement
as Treatment

While there are numerous elements that contribute to treatment in programs that serve very vulnerable children, the fundamental, underlying
ingredients are the twin concepts of relationship and engagement. The great value
attached to these concepts, the intensity of interest in how they play out in the lives
of children and their families, and the single-minded attention that is given to
using them in treatment should be regularly evident in even minor interactions
and exchanges. This attention may be focused on interactions and exchanges that
occur in many places: between the client and program staff, between the parents
and the client, and even between members of the treatment team. *The most
important expression of an organization's beliefs about relationship and engagement
may be found in efforts to establish and sustain a policy of unconditional care.*
Unconditional care is defined, most simply, as a commitment to never discharge
clients for showing the behavior that originally led to their referral for treatment or
placement. In other words, it is an intention to remain connected to the client and
the client's family in the face of their most provocative, difficult behavior and their
most disturbing ideas.

It is important to keep in mind, though, that unconditional care is not simply a
policy or an expression of an abstract philosophical position. It can also be thought
of as a method or an intervention. Unlike other methods which are applied in
response to particular behaviors or in particular situations, unconditional care is
an intervention that is always operating in the background. Thus, it may not be
referred to explicitly in discussions of a client and it is not listed in a child's
treatment plan as one of the methods used to help him accomplish goals and
objectives. Nevertheless, when it is present, it becomes a key ingredient in the
progress of all children and families.

How can an intervention be implicit? Unconditional care functions as treatment
by giving all interactions between staff and clients a particular feeling tone that is
different from what clients have experienced before and different from what they
have come to expect as they move forward in their lives. Specific, explicit interventions
may come into play in response to the appearance of behaviors or beliefs of the

1

client, but the staff's persistent, fundamental commitment to remaining in relationship with the client is always present and always operating in the background.

It is worthwhile to briefly consider the issues that arise in a program that is not organized around this implicit intervention of unconditional care. Children who have had repeated experiences of placement failure have come to expect that they will inevitably be rejected in each new setting in which they arrive. For many of them, this belief about themselves leads to an active effort to provoke rejection. If they sense that there is a set of behaviors that has reliably led to their premature discharge from many settings, then it is very difficult for them to resist testing a new environment for the same reaction. This equation can also be stated as, "I will cause you to reject me and then I am at least the author of my own story. You didn't do this to me; I caused you to do it to me." In the same way that unconditional care is an implicit, nonspecific intervention, discharge is an implicit, nonspecific intervention for those programs in which unconditional care is not practiced. That is, the possibility or the threat of discharge or loss of relationship is always present. For many of the most traumatized and vulnerable children in various systems of care, this possibility is terribly compelling. Having been placed repeatedly (Baker and Curtis, 2006) in the position of passively experiencing ejection from homes, programs, and classrooms, they actively scan the environment for cues that they may, once again, be forced to pack up and leave. This vigilance is often too sensitive, too exquisitely tuned to the possibility of rejection; and as they perceive the possibility of these feared outcomes, they often shift into an active, counterphobic mode in which they may escalate their current behavior until they provoke the response they are expecting.

Understanding the importance of relationship and engagement begins with an understanding of the life experiences of children and families who have repeatedly experienced loss of placement or other forms of treatment disruption. Chapter 2 will provide a more detailed description of the important challenges and risk factors which they have typically confronted in their journeys through various systems of care. What follows here is a more general account of their experiences that is aimed at illuminating the critical role played by unconditional care and a relationship-based approach to intervention.

These children and families do not move, as we might wish for them, from more intensive interventions to less intensive ones that ultimately make it possible for them to exit "the system" successfully. Instead, their trajectory is in the opposite direction. They seem to proceed inexorably from their first contacts with child protection, mental health, and special education systems to more and more intensive programs and interventions. Their experience of treatment is increasingly one of failure and exclusion. Less intensive programs, with fewer resources, are overwhelmed by their behavioral challenges; and they are moved along, by fits and starts, to increasingly intensive settings. These moves seem to take on a tragic inevitability, and overstressed systems of care find themselves directing more and more resources at these challenging consumers.

It is important to note that this story of exclusion and failure does not typically begin in the life of the child but in the lives of grandparents and parents. When parents reveal the circumstances of their own lives, it is usually found that as children they also encountered very difficult challenges. They, too, may have grown up in foster care or group homes. They, too, may have experienced disruptions in their relationships with caretakers. They, too, may have struggled to be successful in school. And finally, at the very critical point in their lives when they became parents, they very likely were without the resources and support that might have enabled them to be successful with their own children.

It is also important to note that the experiences of failure and exclusion encountered by vulnerable children are often repeated over and over (Baker and Curtis, 2006). Many of these young people have regularly encountered these reactions from caretakers, teachers, and other professionals. It has become part of their story. It is woven into their images of themselves and their images of how the world works, and it has become what they anticipate.

A treatment stance that has a policy of unconditional care as its underpinning is an immediate and powerful response to this story. It is of great importance to provide an experience to the youth and their families that is very different from what has happened before. In some cases, these children or teens are well aware that they have overwhelmed the resources of many agencies that have tried to serve them. Occasionally, they ask explicitly, "What do I have to do to get kicked out of *this* place?" When such a question is asked, there is the opportunity to engage the child's story in a direct, verbal exchange. Other children ask this question implicitly or through their behavior. That is, they quickly begin to enact the story of failure and exclusion behaviorally by engaging in the provocative, high-risk activities that led to earlier placement failures. In these cases, the direct verbal exchange is not sufficient and staff must disconfirm, through their own behavior, the children's negative beliefs about themselves and the world. Thus, children's dangerous, provocative behavior must be met with neutral, nonretaliatory limits that always convey the expectation that they will continue to participate in the program.

All children and youth are actively construing their worlds (Piaget, 1954; Bruner, 1996). Children who have experienced multiple placement failures are no exception. They are, without any conscious awareness of the process, struggling to organize their experience (most significantly, their experience in relationships with caretakers and other important adults) into a set of operational hypotheses or a "working model" which represents the world. This working model is made up of beliefs and attitudes about the behavior of others, as well as images of the self. The shape and content of this working model can be inferred from a variety of sources: from what is known of their histories, from their behavior, from their verbal accounts of their lives, from their predictions of their own futures, and, perhaps most importantly, from their responses to offers of relationship. While a working model may be represented, in part, by conscious attitudes and beliefs, it is primarily implicit. A youngster who enters a treatment program may be able to tell many stories about his or her experience with others, but much will have to be inferred about the working model from how the child makes use of relationships with staff and peers. (The working model will be discussed in more detail in Chapter 4.)

In the simplest terms, treatment consists of providing a setting that will allow and encourage the modification of clients' working models. Issues of inclusion and exclusion are often the first arenas in which there is an opportunity to engage the child's working model of relationships. Also, their experiences have led them to believe that entering a new setting may place them at risk for being revictimized. It is almost a certainty that their experiences will also lead them to expect adults they are encountering for the first time to find them too "hyper," too crazy, too sexual, or too dangerous to be kept around for very long. Thus, a commitment to unconditional care drives the first encounter with the child around these issues. This commitment is expressed in many ways in the first months of a child's treatment. The key expression, though, is the simple fact that the child is not discharged. This important shift from their experience in earlier placements begins the process of disconfirming or modifying their stories about themselves and their models of relationships.

As the work with a child or teen unfolds, she presents staff with new opportunities in other domains to help revise or repair her picture of the self and the world.

OPPORTUNITIES FOR ENGAGEMENT

Consider some examples of these opportunities to engage the child around the behavior that is often an important expression of his working model of relationships.

> *A neglected child may have little experience of being adequately and safely supervised and may engage in risky physical behavior during play. This represents an opportunity for staff to actively intervene to keep him safe. Over time, these regularly repeated experiences of a vigilant adult who is attentive to the child's safety are internalized and become part of how the child sees himself (as worthy of being kept safe) and the environment (as peopled by concerned, attentive figures).*
>
> *A sexually exploited girl may present with behavior that is sexually provocative or even actively seductive. Sometimes this behavior will be startlingly direct, and at other times it will be very subtle, evoking only vague feelings of discomfort and uneasiness. In such a case, staff will have opportunities to address these aspects of the child's beliefs about herself through many, many interactions. These may include guiding her away from provocative dress, confronting sexualized behavior, closely supervising all play with peers, and encouraging age-appropriate play. Again, over time, these varied interactions, only some of which will explicitly refer to sexuality, will contribute to a revision of the child's beliefs about herself and the possibility of safe, authentically gratifying*

relationships with adults and peers. She will become more genuinely childlike, more playful, and less preoccupied with appearance and the effect of her physical being on others.

In a more complex example, involving work with a parent, one can see how these opportunities may take place over several years and may involve many small interactions embedded in a general approach which stresses inclusion and engagement. In a community-based intervention, a mother who has had all of her eight children removed by Child Protective Services maintains a stance of silent, angry resistance. At the busy, chaotic family visits in which the children are assembled from their various placements, she avoids any eye contact with support counselors and social workers. She has significant cognitive limitations and has refused to acknowledge the sexual molestation of which the older daughters accuse their father. While staff are doubtful that there is any likelihood of reunification (or even unsupervised contact), they feel strongly that they must stay engaged with her and help her to have the best possible relationship with the children. Initially, and for many months as the work unfolds, one of the workers pursues engagement with a daily telephone call to the mother. The worker often speaks only to voice mail but notifies the mother of meetings and developments in the children's placements, confirms visit schedules, and makes himself available to answer questions. Gradually, he fosters a spirit of collegial competition on the team to see who will be the first to get eye contact from the mother, to have a friendly smile returned, or to achieve some real connection with her. During the holidays, the support counselors have a series of professional photographs taken of the children and present the mother with an album. A successful collaboration with the mother's caseworker from the Regional Center is developed. When the oldest son plays drums at a revival at the mother's church, two staff members attend. They actively participate in the service and discover that the mother has a beautiful singing voice. In the next collaborative meeting, they invite her to close the meeting with a song. She responds by suggesting that they close with a prayer. The family support worker offers a prayer which acknowledges the mother's pain and struggles and speaks to the growing collaboration between them. This relationship grows very slowly over several years and provides the mother with a new experience of being recognized, included, and listened to. There are several bumps in this road when difficult decisions need to be made regarding the children's placements, but care is taken to always remain attentive and available to the mother. Ultimately, one of the older daughters, for whom a satisfactory placement had never been found, returns to living with her mother. The two oldest siblings, who live on their own, also have regular contact with her.

These examples are intended to convey the treatment possibilities that are always available in staff interactions with children, teens, and parents in treatment programs. Thoughtfully exploiting these possibilities can involve using behavioral interventions, simple verbal prompts, systematic efforts to teach new behaviors and skills, psychotherapeutic exploration, and various group interventions. It can involve manipulating the child's environment to minimize risk factors, supporting strengths in the family to empower parents, and making alliances with other professionals in the child's community. The key factor that remains invariant behind this array of supports and interventions, though, is the relationship between the child and family and the treatment team. By embedding efforts in relationships with clients, one is always positioned to respond to their gains and retreats with thoughtfulness and compassion. Connections made over time with clients provide the most powerful opportunities to revise their stories of who they are and who they might become. A key ingredient in how these "treatment moments" contribute to shifts in the child's working model is the cumulative effect of many such interactions over time with the same clinicians, counselors, and support staff. This is possible only when there is a consistent focus on relationship. The final example shows, among other things, that time is often a key ingredient in the success of such an approach. Just as it has taken many years for clients to develop a particular working model of relationships and a particular story of who they are, so too it can require a long, sustained engagement to assist clients in modifying those models and arriving at a new story of who they are.

Engagement may be seen as the moment-to-moment expression of a focus on relationship. What then are the key ingredients of engagement as it applies to treatment in intensive programs?

Engagement is active. It means that adults working in settings that serve these children are not waiting for behavior to occur so that they can react to it. Instead, engagement conveys a sense of actively working to create a milieu in which new learning can occur and new kinds of relationships can be made. Engagement means workers are committed to connecting themselves to the behavior of the child. When it is said that engagement is active, this means that the staff–client relationship is used to promote self-regulation of emotion and behavior. This is in contrast to an essentially custodial or reactive orientation, in which staff members are trained to use a largely consequence-based approach where behaviors occur and are then responded to.

Engagement may be thought of as participating in a conversation in which the child or teen is asking questions or seeking information from staff. Sometimes these questions are verbal and explicit, but often they are implicit and are "asked" by the behavior the child directs at adults. Among the most important questions traumatized and vulnerable children will ask are the following:

- *Will you keep me safe? Can you protect me?*
- *Will you be sexual with me like other caretakers in my past?*
- *Can I provoke you to reject me? Abuse me?*

Engagement means always knowing where a child is, both physically and emotionally. At any given moment staff are engaged in an active accounting of the physical location and activity of the client as well as a recognition of his or her emotional state. This includes regularly revising (and communicating about) an assessment of his or her strengths, vulnerabilities, and behaviors. Thus, a staff member regularly working with a child should be able to answer questions like the following:

- *What are the capacities I am drawing on and trying to develop in the child?*
- *What are the ingredients that have been associated with this child's success in other programs and his or her current placement?*

- *What resources does this child have that have not yet been fully recognized and that can be assisted in developing?*
- *What do I need to know of my client's culture to understand how he sees me and experiences my efforts? Am I paying attention to how my own culture and life circumstances influence my experience of him?*
- *What are the conditions or settings that have most enabled this child to create relationships with staff?*
- *What are the risk factors in the life of this child that have been related to placement failure?*
- *What are the values, dreams, and hopes for the future of this child and family?*
- *What antecedents or settings are related to dangerous behavior on the part of this child?*
- *What are the interventions that have been reliably found to be successful with this child?*
- *Who are the key people in the life of this child who have important relationships with him or her and how can they be included?*

It is an absolute responsibility that team members be capable of answering these questions with regard to every child.

Engagement also means that one is thoughtful about the sources and meanings of a client's troubling behaviors. This requires developing knowledge of the client's (and family's) history. The team must always strive to make connections among life experiences, emotional states, and behavior. An understanding of these connections will always be part of the interventions which will then be utilized in moment-to-moment interaction with the child.

Engagement means being attentive to and thoughtful about boundaries in work with children and families. This adherence to thoughtful and culturally and clinically appropriate boundaries is a key ingredient in creating engagement with clients. Many clients have endured repeated traumatic violations of their personal boundaries or need support in creating new, more effective boundaries in their lives. While some interventions, such as working with clients in their homes and communities, require flexibility of roles, one must always remain alert to the risks involved in these approaches and hold each other and oneself accountable to an absolute respect for boundaries of safety and personal integrity.

Engagement means that team members are always working to be aware of their own emotional states in relation to the children and their families. It means that attending to the states induced in workers (and sometimes between workers on the same team) by the child or teen will yield important clues to their experiences.

Engagement means being attentive to moments of exception, in which one's interactions with the child or family are different from the pattern of difficulties that has dominated their experiences in the past. When these moments are noticed, workers can try to identify the ingredients that created the conditions for this exception to occur.

Engagement means working to contain the inevitable drift toward judgment which can arise in work with troubled children and their families. Judgment (and its twin, blame) is almost always a barrier to engagement. Its arrival can mean that staff have ceased to reflect on the other, her experience, and her mental states and instead have begun to see the client as no more than her behavior.

Chapter Two

Strengths and Risk Factors of Children with Intensive Needs

C hildren and families who have experienced repeated placement failure or treatment disruptions have often experienced a particular set of challenges and stresses. Before the problems of actual program design and intervention methods are addressed, it is important to describe some of these challenges. An organization's beliefs about what constitutes key ingredients of treatment programs arise, in part, from how the resources, needs, and difficulties of this client population are understood.

RISK FACTORS AND VULNERABILITIES

What follows is an attempt to describe some of the key challenges in the lives of families who have experienced treatment failure. The elements considered here may also be thought of as categories of risk factors or categories of experiences in their lives and the lives of their children that are regularly associated with referral for treatment and treatment failure. These risk factors are inevitably expressed in the actual circumstances of children's lives in a variety of ways and may be experienced internally with equal variation. It certainly can be said, though, that the presence of these risk factors in a child's life is regularly associated with placement failure. It must also be acknowledged that not all families present all of these risk factors. Some may show very few or even none, most will have some, and some will present with all of them. Sometimes the pervasiveness and severity of a child's or a family's problems can dominate early efforts to engage with them. *Therefore, it should always be remembered that a thorough, thoughtful assessment is a collaborative inquiry into both risk factors and strengths.* This discussion of risk factors is followed by a consideration of strengths and protective factors in the lives of vulnerable and traumatized children.

Problems with Concrete Resources and Other Risk Factors Present in the External World Surrounding the Family

A great many of the families of traumatized and vulnerable children are struggling with inadequate resources in areas such as housing, employment, income, education and educational opportunity, and access to health care. These challenges are historically complex and associated with the long-term effects of inequalities arising from race, class, and gender. Thus, the heading "Problems with Concrete Resources" covers a broad domain that could be renamed, with some justification, "Poverty and Its Effects" and should be seen as something of a catch-all category of multiple, more specific risk factors that include those already listed as well as exposure to violent communities and substance abuse and exposure to environmental hazards such as lead poisoning and deficits in nutrition (see, for example, Brooks-Gunn and Duncan, 1997; Bolger, Patterson, Thompson, and Kupersmidt, 1995; Berger, 2004, 2005). It is important to be aware of these difficulties because they are present for a large proportion of the families of the most vulnerable children and because they almost always interact with and amplify other risk factors which have overcome the family. Because these resource problems are so common in this population, it is easy to become habituated to their presence and to underestimate or deny their effects. Consider these examples:

A family with an infant or toddler who is not developing normally may recognize the problem in a timely way if one parent is employed and possesses health insurance. Regular well-baby visits with a pediatrician can be an opportunity to share observations and discuss concerns. In the absence of this basic resource, however, a mother may try to ignore her worries and uneasily hope that things will just work out. Treatment may then be delayed, and the family's difficulties may gradually escalate until much more complex and expensive interventions are needed.

The treatment of a young adolescent boy with a long history of exposure to domestic violence and seen in an outpatient clinic for anxiety and depression will unfold very differently if there is a high level of youth gang activity in his immediate neighborhood. The ready availability of a peer group in which concerns about safety and vulnerability can be dramatically enacted is likely to amplify, in potentially very dangerous ways, the meaning and effects of the client's initial symptoms.

An older adolescent who has spent many years in the child welfare and mental health systems is approaching the age of emancipation. Her original removal from her family at the age of 8 involved severe physical abuse and repeated exposure to domestic violence. After years of multiple placements in various settings around the state, her extended family members have lost track of her and she has become disconnected from siblings, aunts and uncles, and one surviving grandparent. As her team begin to prepare for his move to transition-age housing, they encounter the stark reality of her disconnection from family and community. The young woman is without any reliable, emotionally vital relationships with family members or other concerned and committed adults.

A number of efforts (see, for example, Miles and Franz, 2006) have been made to describe key domains in which families may be confronted with these various external challenges. Such discussions are efforts to direct the attention of assessors and interveners to key features of the environment in which the family is struggling to support the development of their children. Often, they include issues such as:

- Neighborhood and housing challenges: adequacy, safety, affordability
- Networks of support: extended family, neighborhood and community social support systems, friendships and other supportive social connections
- Legal resources: particularly when a child in the family is in the juvenile justice system or adult family members have contact with criminal justice system or immigration authorities
- Medical care: its proximity, ease, and timeliness of access and responsiveness to the family's concerns and needs
- Employment/economic resources: the economic health of the immediate community, job opportunities and stability, challenges with credit and predatory lending
- Spiritual supports: proximity to and participation in a community of faith
- Safety: can relate to problems in many of the other domains and may include problems with community violence, youth gangs, inadequate local policing, and unsafe schools
- Transportation: viability of private automobiles, access to public transportation

Clinicians and larger treatment teams who intervene to support vulnerable, multirisk children often work in programs that are implicitly or explicitly designed to address only those issues that are immediate to the child himself or, at best, the family itself. The behavioral and relational streams of intervention described earlier are, in fact, largely concerned with addressing the child's problematic behavior (and, by implication, his immediate learning environments), attachment experiences, and caretaking relationships. Awareness of the multiple external risk factors confronted by these families highlights the need for a third tier of evaluation and intervention that first recognizes and assesses, in a structured way, these problems of context or environment and then includes some effort to mitigate their effects on the life and functioning of the family. Attention to these issues provides an additional lens for assessment and then directs intervention and support efforts to additional life domains.

Referral documents of vulnerable or traumatized children who present for services almost never encompass or even make note of these various external risk factors that may be of critical importance as a cause or amplifier of symptoms or problem behaviors. Instead, they are often known and acknowledged in a cursory or passing way and no formal effort is made to recognize their effects or anticipate ways in which they may disrupt or impede treatment. It is also the case that the efforts of workers and programs serving a child are regularly derailed or undermined because of these very real challenges present in the environment in which the family is trying to function. These treatment obstacles or disruptions may include very specific logistical problems, such as the lack of a telephone or a family's frequent moves, but may also include more general and pervasive effects, such as those related to unsafe, violent neighborhoods. Clinicians and programs that fail to recognize these factors and that fail to undertake some effort to address them inevitably encounter them as obstacles to a more narrowly defined treatment that recognizes only symptoms and problem behaviors.

The multiple specific challenges that families face in this category of risk constitute an authentic third stream in assessment and intervention, which underlies and is often fundamental to the effectiveness of the behavioral and relational streams described earlier. This third domain of assessment and intervention was referred to as the "ecological stream" in that it represents an effort to always be aware of the broader environmental and systemic factors which may be playing a role in the child's and the family's struggles. The ecological stream is centrally concerned with problems of the broader community context in which the family is operating and in which various helpers are working to understand their struggles and assist them.

It is also the case that many of the issues which arise when programs engage with ecological risk factors are matters of public policy, and for this reason, it is of real importance that organizations engaged in supporting these families make efforts to influence the planning of systems of care. Experience in work with families who face multiple challenges yields an understanding of what they need and what are likely to be more effective service-delivery models. This understanding can then be made available to policy makers and public agencies working to develop programs and to access funding streams in the most effective ways. This form of advocacy can yield relief for families and create conditions that make intervention easier and more effective. For example, as more flexible ways to serve youth who are returning to the community from out-of-home care are found, organizations need to provide their funding sources with alternative models of community-based services that more effectively meet the needs of families who are facing the challenges of reunification.

An understanding of risk factors related to problems of concrete resources also bestows a responsibility on the clinician or staff person to be alert to differences in life circumstances between clients and her or himself. It is important to be conscious of these differences and to be capable of recognizing the effects of one's own background (whatever they might be) on expectations for clients and on one's own beliefs about how the world works.

Risk Factors "Internal" to the Child and the Family

The group of risk factors described in this section consists of those challenges that are found within the family and the child's experience. They are internal to the child and the family in that they can operate and have effects independently from those contextual factors that have just been discussed. Thus, they may be found in families that have relatively few struggles with the environmental stressors associated with poverty and its effects. Again, though, in many cases families are struggling with complex combinations of both internal and external risk factors.

Multigenerational patterns of difficulties

A review of the family histories of this population of children often shows that their difficult life circumstances—their disturbing behaviors, the challenges they face in learning, the traumas they have suffered—are also found in the lives of their parents and grandparents (Hurst, Sawatzky, and Pare, 1996). This recurring quality of family difficulties is sometimes strikingly specific: For example, a child's mother has been the victim of the same pattern of abuse or exploitation by a person of the same relation to her as the abuser is to her child. Sometimes parallels are more general, such as a child's struggles with academic performance and behavior at school echoing the struggles of the father. In some cases, there is a great deal of information available when work with a child begins and the team must simply sift through various reports and evaluations to develop an initial picture of the difficulties encountered by prior generations. In other cases, there may be no information about these patterns as work with a family begins, and instead, the team's understanding of them develops during the intake process or very slowly in the course of working together. In either case, it is not difficult to see that problems in the lives of parents, grandparents, and even earlier generations are likely to present significant challenges to families struggling to nurture and guide their own children. It is also striking how little support these families have received as they have made the transition to parenthood. Even relatively modest interventions, such as assistance with concrete resources, case management, developmental guidance, and brief infant–parent therapy, might have made a significant difference in the lives of these families if they had been delivered as the transition to parenthood occurred (Mayers and Siegler, 2004).

The particular difficulties that have overtaken earlier generations of clients' families are varied. They include struggles with medical issues, problems of substance abuse and addiction, sexual and physical abuse, and repeated experiences of disrupted relationships. A review of the histories of just a few children in intensive programs will yield an understanding of how varied these difficulties may be. A useful way of presenting these historical data is a "table of critical life events," examples of which are shown in Tables 2.1–2.3.[1] These tables summarize in a systematic, chronological form the key events in the life of the child and his or her family. The narratives summarized in these tables may also reveal long histories of failed, inadequate, or poorly coordinated interventions. Such interventions may have involved contact with special education services, the mental health system, child protective agencies, and the criminal justice system.

Why is it important to be aware of these challenges in the lives of families? First, an awareness of the real difficulties faced by some families allows interventions to develop that are more likely to fully address their needs and problems. Second, some of these challenges represent important obstacles to the supportive, attuned parenting which is associated with good outcomes for children. By knowing of these challenges, the fullest possible picture of all the factors that have contributed to the client's current functioning can be developed. Third, it is now well understood that the effects of trauma and abuse are felt well beyond the lives of the immediate victims (Fraiberg, Adelson, and Shapiro 1980; Fonagy, 1998). Injuries of these kinds are regularly repeated in the lives of succeeding generations, with sometimes very direct effects and sometimes more subtle ones. Knowledge of past traumas prompts workers to look for and anticipate these effects.

Unfortunately, it is often the case that the parents and grandparents of these clients have received little in the way of useful support or effective psychological treatment for the traumas or difficult life circumstances which they have endured. Addressing both the absence of adequate support and treatment resources and the continuing psychological effects of unintegrated traumatic events is important in work with families. Parents who receive assistance to more fully recognize and integrate their own traumatic life circumstances are much more able to accurately see and understand the role of trauma in the lives of their children. The reverse, sadly, is also true: Parents who have not had the support and resources to recognize and then begin to integrate the traumatic events in their own lives may have a great deal of difficulty recognizing the effects of trauma in the lives of their children (Hesse, 1999; Lieberman, 1997, 1999). This may lead the parents to minimize their child's own history of trauma or to feel threatened by the child's treatment.

When these important events in the lives of parents are not known, there is the risk that their reverberations may intrude on work with the child and the family in ways that can be sudden, mystifying, and frustrating. A posture of respectful interest and curiosity can offer direct support to a parent who has been afforded no real opportunity to speak about or reflect on the meanings of his own life experiences. This opportunity, which must always be offered, may be a parent's first real opportunity to reflect on and integrate his own traumatic experiences and thereby become better able to support the child in doing so.

It is useful to consider a brief example of the sorts of challenges that parents and grandparents of these children have faced. An excerpt from a table of life events of one such child is shown in Table 2.1. Here, only that portion of the table that refers to the histories of the parents prior to the birth of the client is shown. In all the tables shown details have been altered to protect confidentiality.

This vignette captures a number of the hurtful influences and struggles present in the lives of parents. Between them, mother and father have had contact with the mental health system, the juvenile justice system, and various child protection

Table 2.1 Table of Life Events: Michael V., Events in Parents' Lives Prior to Michael's Birth

Ages/ Dates		Events
1956	B	Birth of father, Ed V., in Fremont, CA—later was known in the family as "Evil Ed."
1		Father's parents separate, and he is raised by his mother.
12		During Ed's teenage years he was shuttled between parents and juvenile hall. He was unable to write.
17	A	Father arrested for auto theft at age 18 and then rearrested two times for violating parole, by carrying firearms. He had serious learning disabilities and at one point was diagnosed as "bipolar."
1958	B	Birth of mother, Margaret V., in Redding, CA, fifth of 10 children. Her mother was from Oklahoma and father was a military man stationed at Fort Bragg.
1	A	Margaret's father tried to set her mother on fire. Parents separated when she was 6 months old, and her mother locked her in the trunk of a car to die. Her mother was then institutionalized for 3 years in the state of Washington after attempting suicide. Describes her mother as alcoholic who was gone 3–4 days at a time.
5	A	At age 5 Margaret found her infant half-sister dead in a crib with a heating pad over her face.
7	A	At age 7 her stepfather beat Margaret and impregnated her 13-year-old sister. He and the sister left together.
12	A	At age 12 Margaret left her home, went to authorities, and turned herself in for placement. She was in first foster home for 3 years. Felt her foster mother was crazy. There were four children in home aged 1–4, and she had to babysit.
15	A	Margaret returned to her natural mother for 3 months at age 15. She then spent 4 months in juvenile hall and went to other foster homes.
18	S	Margaret attended 1 year of college at San Francisco State.
	S	Before starting family, Margaret had jobs in department stores and as a nurse's aide.
1975		Parents meet and date for 9 months before getting married—mother is 19, father is 26.
1977	B	Birth of client, Michael V.
1979		Death of maternal grandmother (Margaret's mother)
1979	A	Margaret separates from Tom for first of several times because he was physically abusive to her and Michael.
1979	B	Birth of sister, Susan Smith

(Continued)

Table 2.1 (Continued)

Ages/ Dates		Events
5		Repeated kindergarten.
10	A	At age 10 he was forcing his sister, Susan, to perform fellatio on him when everyone else was asleep.

Key: A, evidence of abuse, trauma, or other hurtful influences; B, birth; S, evidence of strengths, resources, or other exceptions to the history of problems; R, important relationship; m, medical; e, evaluations; P, problems. Ages are shown in years-months. For example, 3-6 indicates an age of 3 years, 6 months.

agencies. It is striking to see how little treatment or support was available to their families. In the case of the mother, at the age of 12 she approached the child protection authorities herself and asked for placement out of the home. The remainder of her development seems to have been an effort to navigate her way through a series of foster homes and attempted reunifications with her mother. The violence that was present in the earliest years of her life reappeared when her own children were in the earliest years of their lives. Traumatic experiences of violence by caretakers (and to caretakers when the child is very young) are now understood to be risk factors for both becoming violent and becoming a habitual victim of violence (van der Kolk, 1989; Zeanah and Scheeringa, 1998). As Margaret and other mothers with similar histories are engaged, the team will be at a great disadvantage if nothing is known of these histories of family struggles. If some of this information can emerge, then a new picture of their vulnerabilities and their strengths can be constructed. It is also true that in engaging a parent it is important to know not only the factual details but also the meaning of these details to the parent. Does she minimize and dismiss adverse events from her own development? Is she preoccupied with her history and persistently caught up in the emotional turmoil associated with it? Or is there some measure of resolution and a capacity to reflect on these struggles and a foundation that can be supported and built on?

Early instability of attachments
This risk factor refers to disruptions in the child's earliest relationships with caretakers. As can be seen in the discussion of the role of multigenerational family patterns, there are many elements that may disrupt a child's critical early relationships with parents and other caretakers. Some of these disruptive factors may be present even before birth, such as poor prenatal care, exposure to substances in utero, and domestic violence. Another example of a very early challenge to the formation of a secure attachment to a caretaker is premature birth (Plunkett, Meisels, Stiefel, Pasick, and Roloff, 1986; Zelenko, Lock, Kraemer, and Steiner, 2000). Babies born prematurely often require lengthy hospitalizations and then

may be slow to engage with the environment and respond to caretakers. There is also a growing body of research that shows very clearly that parents' own attachment histories can greatly influence the way in which they develop attachments with their own children (Hesse, Main, Abrams, and Rifkin, 2003; Hesse, 2008).

The events and circumstances that overtake or intrude into these critical early relationships are many and varied. In some cases, difficulties arise in the caretaking relationship itself: A child may possess a particularly difficult temperament which is a poor "fit" with the parents' capacities as caretakers (Thomas and Chess, 1977). These problems of temperamental fit are sometimes associated with difficulties in establishing and sustaining a vital, attuned connection with the infant. These difficulties are, in turn, related to problems in arriving at an effective rhythm of co-regulation between the infant and caretaker. In other cases external forces intrude to disrupt the development of a secure connection between parent and child. These may include difficulties in the lives of the parents that overwhelm their capacity to be emotionally or physically available to their children, actual physical separations that result from medical hospitalization or incarceration (Bowlby, 1977, 1980), and the effects of other problems in the family such as domestic violence (Lieberman and Van Horn, 1998). In some cases a mother who has been a victim of domestic violence has difficulty accurately viewing her own child's capacity for aggressive behavior. She may feel that she sees characteristics of her batterer in the child, which can influence the child's behavior and his ideas about himself (Lieberman, 1997, 1999).

In Chapter 3, the ways in which children actively construct and revise their "working models" of relationships based on their experiences with caretakers will be discussed. This process begins well before children are first seen for treatment or enter an intensive treatment program and, in fact, occurs during the very earliest exchanges with caretakers. Therefore, disruptions or distortions in early attachments have important consequences for each child's capacity to create a secure base from which he or she can venture into the world and learn new skills, form gratifying new relationships, and learn to flexibly regulate his or her own behavior. Most of these children and youth have difficulties in regulating their emotional states in ways that allow them to meet the demands of the environment and manage their reactions to disappointments, frustrations, and injuries to their self-esteem. For this reason, it is critical to develop a picture of a client's history of relationships with caretakers that attends to any disruptions, losses, or distortions which may have occurred. This risk factor also folds back into multigenerational patterns of difficulties. As a picture of the challenges faced by parents and other caretakers is developed, their own attachment histories should also be attended to.

Table 2.2 presents a portion of a table of life events of a former client that illustrates some of these issues. Some explanatory comments follow.

This case illustration shows the presence of a number of familiar elements related to the risk factor that is referred to as "early instability of attachments." First, the lack of data concerning the mother's own attachment history suggests

Table 2.2 Table of Life Events: Jimmy P., Including Events in Parents' Lives Prior to Jimmy's Birth

Ages/ Dates		Events
?	B	Birth of maternal grandmother, Sarah K. As of 6/1997 lived near mother in Mountain Creek.
1961	B	Birth of father, Samuel P. History of relationship with Jimmy's mother not known
1961	B	Birth of mother, Jane P. Her own parents divorced when she was 7. One brother had epilepsy.
	R	Jane's father was not sympathetic toward her. At times he was physically and emotionally abusive toward her. Described as very obsessive.
	R	Jane's mother was described as critical and unsupportive, and their relationship was hostile.
1982	R	At age 21 Jane became pregnant, the father not involved. She had a premature baby boy, who died some weeks after labor. During this time Jane's mother was not available to give any support.
5/1986	B	Birth of client, Jimmy P.: weight 7 lb, 3 oz. Apgars 8 and 10.
	R	Pregnancy normal but mother used alcohol heavily during first month before she knew she was pregnant—stopped as soon as she knew. There were parental difficulties prior to pregnancy—not described.
	R	Was active, cried a lot, could not be comforted, and needed feedings every 2 hours. Mother felt this sleep deprivation led to her postpartum depression. Mother had no backup or support during this time. Apparently, Jimmy's father was not available.
0–6 months	R	Mother experiences severe postpartum depression and anxiety with an inability to think clearly at times and a feeling that she called "paranoid." The combination of Jimmy's irritability and his mother's vulnerability at this time created a very difficult period with little chance for engagement.
	R	Mother nursed Jimmy until 18 months because "it was the closest I could get to him." Mother says Jimmy "didn't bond." While nursing he was "stiff, with legs moving."
	A	Mother later reported that during Jimmy's first year of life he would start crying uncontrollably. Mother would find herself grabbing him and screaming at him. He would begin shaking, stop crying, and then become very quiet and withdrawn.
1–6		Mother has second pregnancy. No records.
1–9	B	Miscarriage of second pregnancy in second month.

(Continued)

Table 2.2 (Continued)

	R	Mother relieved since she knew she couldn't handle another
	P	child with Jimmy. Notes that Jimmy already had destructive and perseverative play.
2	m	Mother puts Jimmy on a special diet—felt there was a reduction in his activity level.
3		Seen at Children's Hospital—no records.
	e	Diagnosed with attention-deficit/hyperactivity disorder and put in a clinic. Mother didn't feel this helped much.
3–7		Began therapy at a special nursery school in Berkeley, CA.
	P	Had been asked to leave normal nursery school because of sudden violent eruptions toward other children and disruptions of class activities.
	P	In this setting he exhibited sudden bouts of throwing, hitting, or crying and had difficulty following directions in structured activities. These outbursts seemed related to anxious feelings, which he could not name.
	R	During this month staff learned that parents were planning a separation. Actual dates of separations, etc., are almost impossible to discern in the record.
4–0		By one report, parents divorced at this point.
	R	Mother had new boyfriend, Ben, who lived in home for about 3 years—no other information. Treatment Summary—Early Intervention Agency—Elaine M., LCSW
	P	Exhibited primarily parallel and very simple social play with peers and this infrequently. Usually engaged in isolated play of fantasy type.
	P	When there were unexpected occurrences like a fall or loud noise, this resulted in intense fear reactions, for which Jimmy could not readily tolerate comfort from adults. He told his favorite teacher, "I don't like to be near people when I get hurt." Ms. M. states, "One senses that this child rarely shows a positive or hopeful view of the world and acts as if he sees danger at every turn. He exerts great effort to avoid anything that might have a disorganizing effect on him. As a result, he often is unable to benefit from the attempts of adults to soothe or comfort him."
	P	Jimmy seems oblivious to issues of mastery and takes no obvious pride in activities.

Key: A, evidence of abuse, trauma, or other hurtful influences; B, birth; S, evidence of strengths, resources, or other exceptions to the history of problems; R, important relationship; m, medical; e, evaluations; P, problems. Ages are shown in years-months. For example, 3-6 indicates an age of 3 years, 6 months.

that her relationships with caretakers were less than optimal. The mother's account yields a picture of parents who were, at best, unavailable and dismissive of emotional needs and, at worst, actively abusive. Against this background, she then experienced the death of her first baby. In her report of this time in her life, she makes note of her own mother's absence in what can reasonably assumed was a very painful period during which she was receiving no help or emotional support from her partner. Some years later, when Jimmy was born, difficulties immediately arose in the mother's earliest efforts to feed, soothe, and regulate her new baby. Very rapidly the mother became sleep-deprived, depressed, and overwhelmed. In spite of her difficulties with her own attachment figures, she persisted in trying to connect with her baby, nursing him for 18 months. Sadly, though, some important emotional component was not present and she came to feel that the baby was not bonding with her. She was later able to recall that she was so distressed and helpless in the face of Jimmy's affective states that she found herself screaming back at him when she could not soothe him. Rather than relieving his distress in a way that he might internalize, she would overwhelm him with her own frustration and helplessness. All of these elements soon found expression in Jimmy's behavior and adjustment to the world. Lacking the experience of a regulating external figure, he was unable to develop an internal capacity to regulate himself. As a toddler, he was subject to emotional and behavioral storms and could not make use of proximity or comfort from adults when he was in distress. Thus, the cumulative effect of these many disruptions of the relationships between the child and his caretakers was an inability to reliably use others to proceed through important developmental tasks. Some years later, when Jimmy was a client in an intensive residential program, he could explicitly state that he did not wish others to be close to him when he was experiencing pain or distress. Workers who accompanied Jimmy on visits to his mother's home described these outings as consisting of little more than the mother and son being briefly in the same physical space while no real engagement occurred.

Trauma, maltreatment, and neglect

This risk factor is most often found in the lives of vulnerable children and youth who come to treatment via a referral from child protection agencies. The presence of child protective services in the lives of these children and their families is, not surprisingly, an indicator that there has at the very least been some sign or report of abuse, maltreatment, or neglect. Some clients who gain access to intensive services through other routes, such as a school district or mental health referral, may also have significant experiences of trauma in their lives. What is trauma? *Trauma* is exposure to events involving actual or threatened death, serious injury, or destruction of the self. The individual may experience the events as a direct victim or as a witness (American Psychiatric Association, 1994). Many factors may then affect how disruptive the experience is to development, relationships, and functioning

(Perry, Pollard, Blakley, Baker, and Vigilante, 1995; Van der Kolk, MacFarlane, and Weisaeth, 1996).

The actual traumatic life experiences of such clients are extremely varied, and the particular events that have led to child protection involvement with the family may not be the most important. Many of these children have been in the child welfare system for several years before they find their way to a level of service in which their needs could be effectively met. In the course of these years new information is sometimes disclosed, allowing a fuller picture of the child's experience to gradually develop. It is important to keep in mind that not all of the traumatic experiences suffered by these clients are directed, intentional child abuse. Children and teens may witness violence or exploitation of others (often, their caretakers), and they may witness violence or other life-threatening events in their communities. Several factors seem to be important in determining the degree to which abuse, neglect, or other forms of traumatic experience are hurtful to a child's functioning and development. These include level or intensity of exposure, the relationship to the child of the person who inflicts the traumatic experience on the child, concurrent effects on (or danger to) caretakers, the age at which the experience occurs, and the support provided by adults in the child's environment in the aftermath of the traumatic events. This brief list of factors once again reveals the importance of relationships in these clients' lives. For example, when a child experiences traumatic abuse by a caretaker, he or she is left with an especially profound dilemma: The person to whom the child should instinctively turn for safety and support is now experienced as a source of danger (Main and Hesse, 1990). This extraordinarily difficult predicament has enormous negative consequences for the child's development of a positive sense of self and for basic psychological functioning. A fuller discussion of these issues follows in Chapter 3.

Why is it important to know about trauma in the lives of children and their families? As has been just noted, traumatic experience has the capacity to disrupt the functioning and development of affected children and youth, and it often recurs in the lives of victims. For example, children who have been sexually abused are at high risk to place themselves in situations in which they may be abused again. Other victimized children may repeat their abuse by becoming perpetrators themselves. Whatever the circumstances might be, it is now well known that repetition of traumatic experience in some form is regularly seen in the lives of abused or traumatized children. Sometimes these repetitions are subtle and difficult to discern in the child's relationships or internal life, while in other cases such repetitions are startling in their clarity, taking the form of reenactments in play, fantasy, or actual relationships. Elements of the trauma, particularly emotional states, may be evoked in others who have a relationship with the child. And finally, aspects of the trauma may be embodied by the child or reexperienced in a variety of physical sensations, distortions, or symptoms.

It is always the case that awareness of the facts and details of trauma in the life of the child or in the lives of the parents prepares the worker or treatment team to understand a variety of behaviors that might otherwise seem perplexing and very disturbing. This knowledge can then be built into treatment plans and interventions. Instead of reacting with anger, rejection, and essentially arbitrary interventions, the goal of providing reassuring containment and safety can inform intervention. Most importantly, it must be a response that sustains relationships and avoids disengagement.

Table 2.3 illustrates some of the issues discussed here.

Table 2.3 Table of Life Events: Thomas S., Including Events in Parents' Lives Prior to Thomas' Birth

Ages/ Dates		Events
7/1962	B	Date of stepfather's birth (David S.). Biological father (Cal C.) has never contributed to support.
4/1963	B	Date of mother's birth (Darlene S.), in Miami, OK.
3	A	She reports being sexually molested by father at age 3. There was also history of physical abuse in the home.
	A	Older sister Betty molested at age 13. Father sent to jail.
1977		Mother becomes pregnant at age 15 by Cal C. (friend of Mr. S.— all three attended high school in Miami).
11/1977	B	Birth of Thomas S. (aka F.).
0–3	A	Thomas primarily cared for by maternal grandmother, Sally F., in
	R	Miami while mother finished high school. There were reports that the grandmother physically abused another grandchild placed in her home.
2–8		David S. joins military service.
3		Mother and David S. married in Miami, OK.
	R	Mr. S. sent to San Diego, CA, and mother moved with him.
3–1		Thomas is moved from grandmother to mother. Mother has grandmother send Thomas to live with her and Mr. S.—this was first time she had care of him.
3–5	B	Half-brother, David S., Jr., born.
3–8	e	Psychological evaluation by Dr. Jay S. in San Diego, CA, gives diagnosis as reactive attachment disorder, residual type. States he was a victim of intermittent severe physical abuse.
	S	Saw Thomas as having superior cognitive development and motor skills.
4	A	Thomas made dependent of court in San Diego on petition alleging his feet were burned while he was under mother's supervision—that his mother put his feet under scalding water. Later, his Uncle Sid F. took a knife and peeled off the skin from his feet.
4–3		Mr. S. transferred to naval station in Oakland and entire family was moved from San Diego.

(Continued)

Table 2.3 (Continued)

	A	Anonymous report to Alameda police that mother is beating Thomas and David Jr. Physical exam at Oak Knoll Naval Hospital revealed radiator burns on David's forearms. Children are returned to parents.
	B	Date of half-sister's birth (Carmen S.)
4–5		Neighbor reports abuse.
	A	Investigation discovers loop scars over Thomas' entire body, scratches on his face, and a black eye. Case transferred to Protective Services. Thomas in the home, and worker meets with mother over next couple of months.
4–7		Thomas' report of abuse.
	A	Said stepfather stuck his finger down his throat to make him vomit and then put his head in toilet and flushed it.
	A	Mother signed note asking that Thomas be removed from home so he will not be hurt anymore. Thomas stated that his mother bit his thumb.
4–7		Placed in Mary D. emergency foster home.
	P	Enuretic night and day—provocative with other foster children. Eats voraciously.
	P	Thomas urinates on floor—as often as once every hour. Foster parents tried putting diapers on him.
		Thomas made dependent of court in Alameda County.
4–?		Placed in home of Jason and Kathy M.
5–8	P	Removed because of difficulty adjusting to school, hyperactive, oppositional, unable to stay seated, and assaultive to teachers. Same problems at home exacerbated by problems with peers.
5–11		Case transferred to Permanent Placement Program, Alameda County.

Key: A, evidence of abuse, trauma, or other hurtful influences; B, birth; S, evidence of strengths, resources, or other exceptions to the history of problems; R, important relationship; m, medical; e, evaluations; P, problems. Ages are shown in years-months. For example, 3-6 indicates an age of 3 years, 6 months.

The problems of this family also illustrate the risk factors discussed earlier. Earlier generations struggled with a variety of problems that included physical and sexual abuse as well as early pregnancy. There is also a possibility of attachment disruption when, at the age of 3, Thomas left the care of his maternal grandmother and went with his mother and stepfather when the latter was transferred to San Diego. The evidence of maltreatment arose after this move, when the child was found to have burns on his feet. As the months passed, more evidence appeared, and Thomas was ultimately removed from the home. It is worth noting that this case may also be seen as illustrating the special dilemma of the child whose attachment figures are also a source of danger and maltreatment. In this situation, the figures to whom the child would instinctively turn for protection and the restoration of a sense of safety are the source of threat to the child. This situation is particularly disruptive to development.

Multiple placement failures

This final important risk factor in the lives of children and teens comes into play once the child protection system (or the special education system or the mental health system) has identified the child or family as in need of services. Often, the interventions that many clients receive fail to fully address their needs in a timely way. Thus, in reviewing the histories of many of these families, it appears that their difficulties might have been successfully resolved if more resources had been more thoughtfully deployed at an earlier point in the child's life. In the case of many children in the child protection system, it seems that greater support for the family while the children were very young, availability of infant–parent interventions, and ongoing family-based services might well have prevented the need for much more expensive and more drastic interventions later on. These sorts of early interventions are not purely matters of applying resources more generously; they also require the development of a collaborative relationship with the family that works to amplify strengths and resources while addressing difficulties and challenges.

Returning to the case of Jimmy, the little boy whose early relationship with his mother was so challenged, perhaps a supportive, comprehensive infant–parent program might have prevented his ultimate need for expensive residential treatment. An infant–parent program with regular in-home services for mother and child and personal psychotherapy for the mother would also have been very costly, but in the long run it would have been a more cost-effective and humane intervention. Sadly, human service-delivery systems are still rarely organized with prevention in mind. Instead, vulnerable clients have often been the recipients of interventions which may be just barely enough to address the immediate situation or interrupt the immediate crisis but fail to adequately engage the underlying problems and issues faced by the child's family. The unintended result of this pattern of inadequate interventions is often a long series of failed efforts in which placements collapse and the child is left with the sense that he has failed and is, perhaps, untreatable. In the most extreme cases, some children or youth entering intensive residential programs have experienced more than 20 placements prior to their arrival. More typically, children have lived in six to ten placements. Baker and Curtis (2006) report average numbers of prior placements as between five and six for their large sample of children and youth in residential placements and treatment foster care. The highest number of placements was 16. It should be remembered, though, that in the most intensive programs, which placing agencies reserve for their most difficult-to-serve adolescents, clients with numbers of placements higher than this are regularly seen. When the programs serve older teens, some of whom have been in the child welfare system since the age of 3 or 4, these very high numbers of placements are even more common. Multiple placements are not an experience that any child is able to understand and then dismiss as a problem with how social services are organized in the United States. Instead, the history of placement failure is inevitably merged with the history of failure in the family, failure in school, failure in foster homes, and failure in mainstream classrooms, becoming part of the child's story about who he is. It is the history of multiple placements experienced by so many children in the child protection system that makes the policy of unconditional care such a critical ingredient in serving them successfully. As has been already noted, a history of failure and exclusion often drives the first phase of work with a child. It is critical to meet the child's inevitable expectation of failure with an even stronger commitment to sustaining a relationship with him.

It is probably not necessary to include a table of life events to illustrate a child's journey through mental health, special education, child protection, and juvenile justice systems. In any group of the most troubled children and families, it is inevitable that many will have had these long and sometimes grim trajectories before arriving in a program that has adequate resources to address their needs. This is partly a financial issue. Programs that are relatively rich in staffing and treatment services are very expensive, obliging county or school district "gate-keepers" to first try lower levels of service. Unfortunately, these financial considerations are not always linked to a thoughtful assessment of the actual needs of the family and child. Too often this approach turns out to be short-sighted and simply forces the child and family to fail many times before they can actually receive an intervention that has a chance of being successful. One of the most destructive experiences that can occur for these children and youth is the further loss, trauma, and victimization to which multiple placements may expose them. Many children who were victims of abuse or neglect in their families then go through a series of placements in which they are again hurt, exploited, or harshly punished. This repeated retraumatization has terrible consequences for the child's capacity to trust and forge relationships with new caretakers.

As noted at the beginning of this discussion, not all children and their families show all these risk factors. Some may have only one or two. It is generally the case that when more risk factors are present in the life of a child or family, difficulties are likely to be longer-standing and to require more thoughtful and more intensive intervention.

STRENGTHS, PROTECTIVE FACTORS, AND EXCEPTIONS

Adequately serving children and families begins with a respectful, collaborative inquiry that recognizes their strengths and resources as well as the challenges and risk factors with which they are confronted. While, of course, it is the case that the families and children arrive for help with a variety of problems and vulnerabilities, it is also true that they always possess strengths and capabilities. At the outset, it is important to expand the notion of strengths to include all the compensatory or protective factors that work to preserve or activate good functioning and to safeguard development from adverse circumstances, trauma, and other familiar stressors (Cicchetti and Toth, 1987; Werner, 1995). Such protective factors may be found in the child, the family, the community, and the various intervening agencies arrayed against the child's difficulties. Strengths and protective factors do not fall into easily described categories. They can be attributes of the child or the parents, such as abilities or personality traits (Masten and Powell, 2003). They may also be capacities present in the family, such as a clear recognition on the part of the parents of the child's difficulties and a readiness to collaborate with helpers or resources in the community that can support the family's efforts. Very often, key protective factors are relationships with important figures who have been associated with safety or emotional support (Masten, Best, and Garmezy, 1991) or who have in some way encouraged the child's learning and mastery of new, adaptive skills.

Why is it important to pursue strengths and protective factors as part of an initial assessment? Again, attention to strengths is one part of an interest in and curiosity about clients and how they make their way in the world. Perhaps more importantly, though, workers' efforts to amplify the presence of these protective factors are a key part of any intervention effort. These factors are likely to be associated with placement stability, higher functioning, and greater self-management. They are an antidote to the stories of failure and exclusion that children and families may carry with them. From the perspective of behavioral intervention, attention to strengths and positive behaviors will often reveal behaviors in a child's repertoire that are incompatible with the problem behaviors that are driving services. As these adaptive behaviors are responded to in a positive way and as they in turn increase in frequency, there is less "behavioral space" for the problem behaviors which led to the child's history of placement failure. This behavioral shift then allows or drives changes in the child's story about him- or herself.

Another way to think about, or discover, strengths and resources in the life of the child, the family, and the community is to consider exceptions (Berg, 1994; Madsen, 2007). In looking at the lives of some of the families of vulnerable children, there appears to be a great deal of chaos, dysfunction, and pathology. However, when one sits with these families with a posture of respectful interest and curiosity, there are almost always pockets of exception in which family members have had success confronting their problems, interacting with their environments, and supporting each other. If these patterns of exception are attended to, important data will emerge that relate to those factors that have been associated with that child's or family's success. Such factors may include important attachment figures, settings in which the child had success, or situations that activated other strengths present in the family. In the field of clinical work with children, there has been a tradition of applying a narrowly medical approach to mental health problems, which pursues understanding primarily through reviewing symptoms or by giving the child a diagnostic classification. While arriving at a psychiatric diagnosis may be one important element in a comprehensive assessment, failing to fully explore protective factors and strengths misses a key opportunity to adequately utilize the rich data present in those situations in which the family has been successful.

An interest in these protective factors, and collaborating with families to build on them, is a key ingredient in a relationship-based approach to intervention. Many parents have come to expect that their encounters with social workers, therapists, and other helpers will involve a painful review of their failings and faults (Collins and Collins, 1990). When one pursues family successes and strengths with diligence equal to the interest shown in their struggles, the relationship begins with the family on a very different note and is more likely to create conditions that will make authentic engagement much more likely.

A FINAL NOTE ON ASSESSMENT, TREATMENT PLANNING, AND INTERVENTION

The preceding brief consideration of risk and protective factors inevitably anticipates some discussions of assessment, treatment planning, and intervention that are to come. These later discussions require a review of fundamental concepts from behavioral intervention and attachment theory. As these discussions unfold, it will be useful for the reader to keep in mind that attention to risk and protective factors is one of several lenses that can be usefully applied to the assessment, planning, and intervention. Thus, clinicians will at times utilize a behavioral lens and attend to the antecedents and settings that elicit behavior, the consequences that seem to maintain it, and the meanings it has for the child. At other times the team may attend to the child's attachment history and work to describe key disruptions in relationships with caretakers. It should also be clear, however, that somewhat separate from these two more clinical streams is an additional lens in which the team looks for risk factors, striving to diminish their power and influence in the life of the child and the family, and simultaneously looks for strengths, values, and protective factors that can be elicited, amplified, and built on.

Chapter Three

Attachment

A ttention to relationships in the lives of vulnerable clients is critical to an understanding of their struggles and successes. Further, relationships are a key ingredient in any intervention that will be of real assistance to them. It becomes important then that the meaning of "relationship-based" be clarified. What follows is an effort to elaborate the role of relationships in development, psychopathology, and treatment beginning with four brief samples of work with children that illustrate some "treatment moments" of a type which regularly occur in intensive-milieu and community-based interventions with children.

SOME EXAMPLES OF RELATIONSHIP IN PRACTICE

An 11-year-old boy in a group home regularly has difficulty at bedtime. Throughout the evening he becomes increasingly active, silly, and disorganized. Once he is in bed he makes frequent requests to get up and use the bathroom and calls out to staff with questions about who is coming in to work the overnight shift and who will be on duty to help with wake-ups. As the evening progresses, he becomes more of a challenge and soon calls out to peers with silly provocations and has to be moved to a couch in the living room so he won't wake up or escalate the other residents. The treatment team devises a bedtime plan that establishes a reliable routine of a staff member reading him a story, remaining in his room for 5 minutes after finishing the story, and then sitting in the hallway outside his room until he has fallen asleep. The plan is put into place, and the staff quickly learn that the 5 minutes in the room doesn't help; it's too interesting to the client to have someone right there who he can talk to. This part of the plan is removed, and instead, the staff member simply moves to the hallway after finishing the story. Over several weeks, bedtimes gradually improve and the boy is soon reliably falling asleep within 10–20 minutes of finishing his story.

A 9-year-old boy in a residential program is reunified with his mother after several years of being separated from her by a series of out-of-home placements. He moves into an apartment with the mother, her new partner, and an adult sister who has a small child of her own. He is attending a day treatment program for educational services and receives some hours of in-home support. His original removal from his mother's care was the result of neglect and mild physical abuse. The mother had struggled for many years with alcohol and substance abuse. She has been clean and sober for 14 months and attends meetings regularly. Her partner is very quiet and seems to want to stay in the background but has a calming presence in the household. After the boy has been at home for some months, his mother discovers some pieces of partly burned paper around the house. When she confronts her son, he confesses that he has been setting small fires in wastebaskets. He can offer no explanation for this behavior. The child and family-planning team decides that the mother should continue to speak to him about the danger of this behavior, install smoke detectors in the apartment, and involve the boy in putting them up. In individual therapy, he discusses some of his concerns about the safety of living with his mother and some of the frightening things that happened when she was using drugs. The play with fire stops, and the placement continues to be stable.

A 6-year-old boy, newly placed in a group home, is aggressive toward other children in the house at every opportunity. Without provocation and without any apparent connection to what is occurring in the milieu, he will reach out and strike any child who comes within his range. When asked about the hitting, he simply says that he doesn't like the other kids or insists that they somehow provoke him. The behavior regularly earns him time-outs and extended periods of time away from the group. Typically, these interventions require that a single staff member supervise him. Repeated interventions of this kind have no impact on the behavior. Each time he is returned to the milieu he strikes another child within minutes. The treatment team decides that the boy has learned that aggression toward peers will lead to the reassuring proximity of an adult. They decide to simply provide this proximity consistently and unconditionally instead of making it a consequence of negative behavior. A schedule of one-to-one supervision is devised so that during all transitions and less structured times in the milieu the boy is either holding the hand of his one-to-one or is within arm's reach. The hitting ceases almost immediately, and after some weeks the one-to-one is gradually phased out. The hitting does not return, and the boy begins to make some initial efforts at cooperative play with his peers.

A boy in a day treatment classroom regularly gets into a state in which he is disorganized, overactive, and silly. If he is not removed from the setting promptly when he enters this state, he tends to escalate into giddy, desperate anxiety. The team meets and reasserts their commitment to intervening quickly with time-outs. They feel strongly that they have been waiting too long to intervene. They have success in identifying some antecedents and begin to intervene more quickly, but the basic pattern seems to continue with no real change. Worse still, a number of staff report that time-outs seem to activate him even more and inevitably lead to removal from the classroom. One day, a staff member happens to be standing directly behind the boy's desk when he begins to giggle and whisper provocations to the child next to him. She promptly asks him to take a time-out, and since she knows this will lead to his needing to leave the room, she moves to the time-out spot with him and actually places a hand on his back. To her surprise, the boy glances up at her, makes brief eye contact, and takes his time-out without escalating. He then returns to his seat and resumes participation in class. This fortuitous event is discussed at some length in a team meeting. The curious staff reexamine their data, and many note that the success of a time-out with this boy is a function of physical distance. If they are across the room (and perhaps engaged in a task or are with another child) any time-out is doomed to failure—it reliably provokes escalation. If they are in immediate proximity to the child, though, their intervention is much more likely to succeed. Excited by this new way of thinking about the boy, they write a plan in which all time-outs will be given within arm's-length distance and will be accompanied by the placement of a neutral hand on the back or shoulder. The plan meets with quick success. Gradually, key staff who work regularly with the boy are able to experiment with varying proximity, and they find that he is able to respond with more flexibility.

COMMONALITIES OF THE CASE EXAMPLES

All of these problems and the interventions that the various teams devised in the examples above are typical of the sort of work that can occur in settings in which very vulnerable, behavior-disordered children are served. But what do these various approaches to assisting clients have in common? What informs these interventions? Couldn't the team have concluded that the boy in the first example needed medication to help him sleep? Or decided that the boy in the second example would be unable to remain living with his mother? Or insisted that the third boy would ultimately respond to continued use of a time-out strategy? Or concluded that the boy in the final example suffered from a biologically based attention or mood disorder?

All of these examples involve thinking about problems and interventions with attention to the following issues:

- The client's sense of safety
- The role of proximity to caregivers in creating a sense of safety
- The importance, for the client, of having an experience in which caregivers reliably know where he is (physically and emotionally) and what he needs
- The feeling of being known and contained by caregivers that arises when the child sees that she is held in their minds

- Creating a sense in the child that the adults around him apprehend his states and adjust their behavior to amplify his positive states or to downregulate his negative states
- How one makes the shift from being a person on the outside who helps the child regulate herself to being a figure within the child who helps her regulate herself even when one is physically absent
- The development of an implicit working model of relationships that influences how children view and interact with people in their lives

Attention to these issues can ultimately contribute to a conceptual scheme that can enable workers and teams of workers to be helpful to clients who have great struggles in making stable, satisfying relationships with others and in controlling their own feelings, thoughts, and actions.

ATTACHMENT PRINCIPLES OF ASSESSMENT AND INTERVENTION

The approach described so far has already been generally elaborated as arising from both experience with and conviction about the importance of relationship and engagement in work with children and families. In what follows, a more detailed description is provided of the background of these ideas as well as some fundamental principles of assessment and intervention.

This discussion of human connections can begin with some simple questions that focus attention on the child's first relationship with a caregiver:

- What does a mother (caregiver) do?
- What sorts of exchanges and interactions occur between a caregiver and a child that are important to the child's development and later functioning?
- What constitutes good or good enough caregiving?
- Where can (does) caregiving go awry?
- How do the answers to these questions inform what "relationship-based" work with children and teens should look like?

Some of these questions may seem odd. When one thinks of the fundamental activities of caretaking performed by a mother, most will seem familiar or obvious. There are a great number of verbs to describe these activities: "nurture," "sustain," "raise," "love." But these words don't always have real explanatory power; instead, they simply emphasize or describe different parts of what caregivers do. Finally, the ordinary observer of these activities is likely to see little that is surprising or new. Work done in the last 50–60 years, though, suggests that this pleasing tableau of a mother and her child actually has great complexity and great importance for the future development of the child (Cassidy, 2008).

Attachment Theory

This discussion of attachment starts with a few things about babies. It is now understood that all babies (all baby mammals, actually) are born with a hardwired need and a capacity for relatedness with others. This need is a primary motivator (Bowlby, 1969; Cassidy, 2008). That is, it does not follow on the heels of, nor is it behaviorally linked to, some other biologically determined drive, such as hunger. This very simple idea actually runs counter to fundamental premises of both behaviorism and psychoanalysis, which argue that the child's pursuit of proximity with a caretaker is a by-product of, or secondary to, more fundamental survival motivations such as hunger.

In fact, well-nourished infants who are deprived of human contact will physically decline and can even die. This phenomenon was very clearly described in the 1940s with observations of institutionalized infants who were not handled, played with, or held (Spitz, 1946; Robertson, 1953; discussions in Karen, 1994). In some cases this absence of social contact was intentional. It reflected the latest thinking about the risks of infection from "unnecessary" contact. It was shown that even though their physical needs were met, these infants rarely thrived. Instead, nearly all had little or no physical resilience, many were highly vulnerable to infection, and a great many simply died. It is now understood that these well-intentioned efforts to protect infants and toddlers from infection could not have been more wrongheaded: The absence of emotionally available caretakers resulted in the decline of the children's immune systems and vastly greater physical and developmental vulnerability. These tragic outcomes starkly illustrated the critical psychobiological interdependence of infants and young children with their caretakers.

This raised a simple but very important question: Why should certain forms of social relatedness be as important to survival as physical nourishment? John Bowlby, a British psychoanalyst who worked to place the relationship between infants and mothers in an evolutionary context, provided a simple answer to this question. His work, and that of subsequent researchers and clinicians working from similar perspectives, is now placed under the general heading of "attachment theory." (It is worth noting that this work is now well beyond the theory phase and the implications of Bowlby's ideas have been well established in a variety of areas—see, for example, the collections of Cassidy and Shaver, 2008; Greenberg, Cicchetti, and Cummings, 1990; and Oppenheim and Goldsmith, 2007).

Bowlby (1969) argued that babies arrive in the world with an innate attachment behavioral system that drives them to seek proximity and engagement with their caregivers. In terms of immediate, moment-to-moment emotional experience, this means that proximity to a responsive caretaker is associated with feelings of pleasure, safety, and equilibrium. Conversely, separation from the caretaker places the child in a state of anxiety and increasing distress. The adaptive value of having such a hardwired system in the brain is not difficult to see: It involves the protection, safety, and survival advantage of being near the caretaker. The benefits of such a system of behavior include feeding, learning about the environment, and protection from predators. When the caregiver is optimally available to the infant and optimally attuned to the infant's emotional states, the attachment gradually contributes to the creation of a sense of being securely attached or an internal sense of having a "secure base" (Bowlby, 1988). When the attachment behaviors of the child—chiefly vocal, postural, and physical efforts to establish proximity with the caregiver—are ignored, rebuffed, or met with humiliation, the creation of a secure base and a felt sense of security is impeded. This has negative consequences for development in other domains (DeKlyen and Greenberg, 2008).

Attachment and the Development of Relationships

Many other critical developmental processes flow from the creation of this attachment between child and caregiver:

- The child's attachment to the caregiver, in addition to creating real safety and protection, works on a psychological level to reduce distress and to lower the intensity of arousal to manageable levels.
- When the attachment behavioral system has successfully established reassuring proximity to the caregiver, in the absence of overtly frightening conditions in the environment, a complementary behavioral system of exploration can be activated. This behavioral system has as its goal knowledge and mastery of the environment. Thus, the child who "knows" he can rely on the parent or caregiver's protection and thoughtful attention is then free to pursue important developmental tasks such as exploration, play, relationships with peers, and other forms of learning about the environment (Bowlby, 1969).
- The relationship between child and caregiver not only confers survival and safety advantages on the child but also establishes a relationship in which the undeveloped, unregulated brain of the child can make use of the developed, regulated brain of the adult. Over time, this results in the child gradually achieving self-regulation of emotion and increasing organization of all internal states (Siegel, 1999; Schore, 1994).
- The accumulation of experience in this relationship, occurring in many interactions, contributes to the child's development of a sense of self. The child sees herself and comes to know herself, in part, from the reflections that she sees in the behavior and emotional tone of the caretaker (Bowlby, 1969; Bretherton and Munholland, 2008).
- The experience accumulated in the course of this relationship is organized into an internal working model of relationships that will influence the child's later approach to, view of, and behavior in relationships with others. Thus, the working model that arises from

repeated experience with caretakers is manifest in personality traits and a more or less stable orientation to others.

- Departures from optimal caregiver availability and emotional attunement result in predictable departures from felt security and optimal attachment status in the child (Bowlby 1969, 1973, 1980).

Initially, Bowlby was chiefly concerned with explaining the effects of very significant disruptions and losses in the attachment relationship between children and their caretakers, as well as articulating a comprehensive theory of the development of relatedness. As the field has continued to progress, though, attention has turned to more subtle distortions in attachment relationships, styles of attachment, the effects of trauma on attachment, the effects of the caregiver's pattern of attachment on his or her children, and the neurobiology of attachment (see, for example, the work of Schore, 1994, 2003a, 2003b, and the indispensable collection of Cassidy and Shaver, 2008, as well as that of Solomon and Siegel, 2003).

Attachment and Treatment

When basic program structures and intervention methods are developed for traumatized, vulnerable children, they can be connected to an understanding of the development of secure attachments between children and caretakers in a number of ways:

- *Unconditional care.* Most important of all, it must be understood that children will be unable to benefit from any intervention without a sense of relative security regarding their placement and their relationships with staff and other caretakers. After repeated experience with unsuccessful treatments and the failures of earlier placements, many clients have internalized these experiences and come to engage the world from a stance of "I have always been rejected, I am confident that you will reject me and, in fact, I am fairly certain that I can provoke you to reject me."
- *Emotional availability.* In focusing on relationship as a key ingredient in treatment, there must be a commitment to be emotionally available to the children and youth in care. Being *emotionally available* means attending to the emotional states that underlie behavior and being prepared to acknowledge and engage with these states. It also refers to working, when appropriate, in a particular range of emotional expression that consists of a combination of joy and interest. This particular emotional "posture" has been found in infant research to produce attachment (Schore, 1994, p. 97).
- *Attunement.* It is vital not only to be aware of the emotional state of the client but also to resonate with it in much the same way a parent does

with a child. This involves reading the child's emotional state accurately and coordinating one's own expression of emotion with that of the child. This sort of contingent engagement in which the two participants mutually regulate each other enables the parent to help the child downregulate states of distress and amplify states of pleasure, delight, and joy (Schore, 2003a, p. 280).

- *Responsiveness.* The value of providing children (or parents) with success (an available, engaged adult) when they initiate attachment behaviors should be emphasized. That is, proximity seeking and other actions intended to pursue relationship or engagement should be met with physical and emotional availability, respectful interest, and contingent responses (Siegel and Hartzell, 2003).
- *Predictability and consistency.* Again, trying to replicate the efforts of good parents and caretakers, clients must be provided with a stable interpersonal environment in which the individuals who work with them (e.g., care for them in the group homes, teach them in the classrooms, support them in the community) do not come and go unpredictably or interchangeably but are reliably present and available. *Predictability* and *consistency* also mean that the contingencies that children and youth encounter in intervention settings are stable and reliable.

The Internal Working Model

A useful idea that Bowlby proposed was that of the "internal working model" (Bowlby, 1973; Bretherton and Munholland, 2008). This model or representation is constructed by the child in the course of repeated interactions with important caregivers or attachment figures. An internal working model contains images of the self and of the attachment figure in a way that reflects their actual history together. It follows that this representation of the self and the important other will have a particular emotional tone that is directly tied to the quality of their relationship. These images of the self and of caregivers come to govern the child's attachment-related behavior in subsequent experiences with new others—with adults, with peers, and ultimately with partners in adulthood. Thus, the internal working model becomes something like a map or a set of implicit rules that influence and guide the child's social behavior as he continues to develop. This map, in that it is a representation of past experience with attachment figures, influences expectations and can therefore influence how the behavior of the other is actually experienced. For example, a child who has been neglected or whose proximity seeking has been frequently rejected will, in the absence of any other benign, countervailing experience, possess an internal working model in which the self is represented as bad or undeserving of care and attention. This image or set of beliefs then becomes part of the child's expectations for how she will be treated in new relationships and may in all likelihood make it very difficult for the child to see that proximity or responsive support might now be available or is deserved.

In the earliest months of life, internal working models are already being elaborated from repeated exchanges with caretakers in which states of distress such as hunger and fatigue are relieved and physical caretaking and handling are occurring. Prior to the development of language, it is likely that these early models are made up entirely of clusters of visual images, sensations, emotional states, and motor experiences. Schore (1994) has described these earliest representations as "olfactory–tactile–thermal models" and hypothesizes that toward the end of the first year they evolve into "kinesthetic-dominant representations" (p. 312). In the course of development and with attainment of language and ongoing cognitive development, working models can become more complex and differentiated and will involve anticipation of the behavior of caretakers and increasingly complex schemas that represent repeated exchanges and relationship scenarios.

While the term "internal working model" is Bowlby's, the concept of stored representations of relationships with key caretakers and of the self in relation to caretakers is found in a variety of different approaches to both infant and child development and clinical work with adults and children. Thus, Sullivan (1953) in his efforts to place psychiatry squarely in the interpersonal domain, spoke of "me–you patterns." Within infant research, Stern has described what he calls RIGS, or "representations of interactions that have been generalized" (1985) and "schemas-of-being-with" (1994). Young (1990) and Young, Klosko, and Weishaar (2003) have developed a psychotherapeutic approach to work with adults that emphasizes efforts to address "maladaptive early schemas." The psychoanalytic literature uses several terms interchangeably for these internal models. Greenberg and Mitchell (1983), in their discussion of the object relations approach and writing from the point of view of psychoanalytic work with adult patients, observe the existence of these mental representations of others and note,

> Such images go under various names in the psychoanalytic literature. In different theoretical systems they are called variously, "internal objects," "illusory others," "introjects," "personifications," and the constituents of the "representational world." Their functions within the psychic economy are likewise a matter of debate. They may be understood as serving as a kind of loose anticipatory image of what is to be expected of people in the real world; as persecutors, fulfilling the function of a kind of internal fifth column; or as a source of internal resource and security, invoked in times of stress and isolation. (p. 11)

It was Bowlby's view that a key adaptive value of these internal models is that they enable the child to anticipate how exchanges with caretakers will go, how he can most easily achieve proximity with attachment figures, and how he may need to modify or shape his behavior to secure this proximity. Or, in the vocabulary of Greenberg and Mitchell (1983), they are "anticipatory images." It follows, then, that working models come to include or elaborate expectancies about how caretakers and other adults behave with and respond to the child. In their discussion of the influence of infant research on psychoanalytic psychotherapy with adults, Beebe and Lachmann (2002) explicitly equate representations with "patterns of expectancies" (p. 14). Sroufe, Carlson, Levy, and Egeland (1999) observe, "Children inevitably extract from their experience expectations regarding likely behaviors of others and themselves in relationships. Humans cannot keep themselves from doing this" (p. 5).

Related to the element of expectations is that of associated patterns of interpersonal behavior. Crittenden (1990), for example, has observed that working models come to have particular behavioral strategies associated with them. She writes, "Behavioral strategies reflect internal representational models in that they are selected by individuals on the basis of expectations of themselves and their attachment figures in the specific context at hand" (p. 269). Such behavioral strategies, just like the internal models they emerge from, are reflections of the child's actual experience with caretakers. This idea, while strikingly simple, is of great importance in understanding the ways in which early interpersonal experience influences later behavior and ultimately contributes to the development of the various problematic behaviors that generally go under the heading of "psychopathology." As Sroufe et al. (1999) note, "Early experience, therefore, has special significance because it frames the child's subsequent transactions with the environment. The child not only interprets experience, the child creates experience" (p. 5).

One additional and important feature of these behavioral strategies that evolve in coordination with working models is the way in which they typically evoke behavior from others that is consistent with and tends to confirm the content of those models. Thus, the child who has had essentially benign, sensitive, and responsive caretaking is likely to expect similar behavior from others as she makes her way in the world during the years of development. Conversely, the child who has had rejecting, abusive, or coercive experience in relationships with caretakers is likely to anticipate the possibility of similar treatment from others. These differing sets of expectations will inevitably find expression in the characteristic behavioral patterns or strategies of each child. The first child may, all other factors being equal, approach others with a cooperative stance and with a certain openness and interest. In most environments such behavior is likely to evoke roughly complementary responses involving a similar benign affective tone and a readiness to engage. The second child, on the other hand, acting from decidedly more negative expectations, may approach others with guardedness, efforts to control or manage the other, and a generally distrustful resistance to engagement. In this way, each child's basic behavioral stance is likely to evoke reactions that tend to confirm the underlying internal model.

The capacity of internal models to elicit reactions from others that confirm the implicit beliefs that are the content of the model is a concept that can also be found outside attachment theory. Thus, cognitive behavior therapists use the term "schema" (Beck, 1976) to describe a concept quite similar to the internal working model. Persons (2008), in her description of a systematic cognitive behavior approach to case formulation and to the treatment of depression (see also Persons, Davidson, and Tompkins, 2001), emphasizes the importance of the concepts of schema and schema change. In discussing how schemas function she notes that, "schema-driven behavior can produce evidence that confirms the schemas" (Persons, 2008, p. 29). While this certainly occurs as a function of the ways in which schemas create interpretive biases and accordingly filter or skew incoming data about the behavior of both self and others, it also occurs at the level of actual behavior by eliciting reactions from others or constraining their responses in ways that validate the pathogenic convictions that make up the schema.

With children who have experienced trauma and maltreatment, this issue of behavioral provocation of responses that confirm the content of the working model is especially salient. In the case of these clients, additional trauma-related processes further increase the likelihood that they will engage in behaviors that evoke complementary responses that will strongly confirm their implicit beliefs about themselves and the interpersonal world. In this regard, it is worth noting that the formal diagnostic criteria for posttraumatic stress disorder (American Psychiatric Association, 1994) make special note of the possibility of "trauma-specific reenactments" (p. 428) as one form of reexperiencing in child patients. These trauma-specific reenactments can take many forms and were first described by Freud (1955) and then placed in the context of modern trauma studies by van der Kolk (1989). In their most mild form such reenactments may occur in symbolic play. Here, the child recreates, often with dolls or similar materials, some or most elements of the traumatic experience. In its most concerning form this revisiting of traumatic experience involves repeated full-blown reenactments of complex interpersonal scenarios in which the traumatized individual is at great risk for revictimization. In some cases the child's (and eventually the adult's) aggression is turned outward, away from the self; and in these scenarios the child or young person is likely to victimize others.

This discussion of the behavioral strategies that accompany particular working models and their effects on the interpersonal field in which the child is operating is an effort to emphasize the transactional nature of attachment phenomena in the course of development. For children whose caretaking has been essentially benign and sensitive, this transactional quality is correspondingly positive in its effects. The child's beliefs that others are likely to have good intentions and that he or she is deserving of the kindness and interest of others is repeatedly confirmed by the responses of new figures encountered by the child. For children whose caretaking has included significant elements of rejection, neglect, or abuse, the effects of these feedback loops are entirely pernicious. In their encounters with the interpersonal world many of these children are likely to lead with distrust and efforts to negate and control. These behavioral strategies inevitably elicit confirming responses from new figures encountered by the child; distrust and resistance to engagement will provoke withdrawal and negation, and control will provoke retaliation and countercontrol. The final result of these oft-repeated transactions is the confirmation and strengthening of the child's belief in the unreliability and dangers of the interpersonal world and in his own essential badness and unworthiness.

It is, of course, the case that most children do not experience unrelenting maltreatment or neglect. In almost all cases, these adverse experiences are interspersed with moments of availability and some level of attunement and support (Lieberman, Padron, Van Horn, and Harris, 2005). Even highly abusive caretakers show affection and provide some proximity and protection. Many maltreated children have also had some caretakers or important figures in their lives whose presence was largely benign. Thus, very few children present with evidence of wholly negative internal working models or interpersonal behavioral strategies that are unremittingly provocative, although in intensive residential treatment programs and juvenile justice facilities one is certainly more likely to encounter young people who approach such an extreme. Bowlby himself (1973) noted that any particular child's internal working model can be complex and contain contradictory elements which reflect the enormous diversity of interpersonal experience encountered in the course of development. Thus, many vulnerable and traumatized children show evidence of a hopeful readiness to engage with others and to make enduring connections. Nevertheless, these more positive elements of the internal working model are extremely vulnerable to disruption by relationship ruptures such as losses and separations or even relatively momentary failures of availability or attunement. It is also the case that young victims of trauma are likely to have particular triggers related to their specific traumatic experiences. At the same time, many of these children also show, as will soon be discussed, significant deficits of self-regulation. The behavioral difficulties that are the expression of self-regulatory problems increase the probability that the child will greatly challenge the resources of whatever setting he is in and place him, again, at risk for loss of placement.

Finally, it is important to note that internal working models are not readily or easily revised. They function outside of conscious awareness (Crittenden, 1990), and their organizing principles or rules are not stored in semantic memory in such a way that the individual is able to simply summon them up for discussion (Bretherton and Munholland, 2008). It is also the familiar clinical experience of therapists and other interveners that the working models of traumatized children are strikingly resistant to change. This is probably due in part to a simple additive effect of cumulative experience. The more pervasively negative experiences the child encounters in attachment relationships, the more fixed are her beliefs about herself and the interpersonal world. When the systemic failure of repeated placement changes is then layered on top of these multiple earlier adverse attachment experiences, the contents of the working model are likely to harden into an even more rigid and inflexible narrative. The behavioral strategies that evolve in concert with this process are then working overtime to provoke congruently negative responses from others.

When a clinician reflects on the data that have emerged from initial contacts with a child and family or when treatment teams meet to discuss and plan work with a client, they are, in part, attempting to develop a description of the client's working model of relationships. This description will be gradually constructed from multiple sources: historical accounts of the lives of the child and family, from the child's own stories about how he came to treatment, from his response to the offer of relationship that is present in the program, and from the thoughts and feelings evoked in staff who engage with him.

Following are some of the questions that should be asked to begin constructing this description. Please note that these are not questions that must necessarily be explicitly asked of staff in a team meeting. Instead, they are the organizing questions that are "in the room" as data emerge.

- What does the child seem to expect in interactions with adults?

  For example, the child in a residential program who asks, with a combination of fear and excitement, if a staff arriving for the evening shift has a gun in his shoulder bag has revealed something about his expectations regarding safety. Similarly, a child who regularly accuses the overnight staff of having sex with each other is showing something about how she views the capacity of adults to delay gratification and attend to the needs of children.

- How does the child make use of the adults in the program or in his or her life?

  For example, the child who doesn't look to staff for support or first aid when he hurts himself during play is telling something about his \ experience with and expectations for care and support. Or a mother who, with some pride, describes her 4-year-old as "independent" after she wanders out of the family home and into the yard of a neighbor down the street is providing important information regarding the child's tie to her.

- What are the themes that come to organize the child's relationships with the adults in a treatment program?

  For example, the child or teen who regularly employs intimidation and threat in interactions with adults may be revealing something about how he has seen important adults in his life achieve control and obtain gratification in exchanges with others. He might also be giving information about how dangerous he believes it is to show any sort of vulnerability. Similarly, a girl who sexualizes all her interactions with adult males may be providing information about her experience with men, her history of victimization, and her culturally supported beliefs about the role of women.

- What are the emotional states that are evoked in staff who work with the client?

  For example, when the members of a treatment team find themselves feeling irritated, impatient, and negative after repeated interactions with a child, there is a good chance that these reactions are reflections of ideas and beliefs that the child has about himself.

- How are the patterns of relatedness seen in the child present in earlier generations of the family?

    Here, emphasis is placed on the importance of an interest in multigenerational patterns of problems and solutions in work with children and families: It is important to be curious about more than a child's history of symptoms and syndromes. It is important to embed an understanding of these problems in an understanding of relationships in the family as a whole as they are found across generations and in current attachments. In this particular area of inquiry, the interest lies in knowing more about those forces that have supported attachments between parents and children and those that have challenged attachment.

When team members approach work with children and families with such questions in mind, the answers that emerge do not, in and of themselves, lead to any particular or absolute construction of the child's difficulties. Instead, these answers are considered in the light of other sources of data, such as historical narratives, descriptions from other observers, and results of more formal evaluations. As the information gained from these sources is integrated with experience with the child and the family, a set of hypotheses is developed that guides thinking and interventions. As new information is gained, hypotheses are revised accordingly.

Behavioral Systems: Attachment and Exploration

In describing attachment behaviors seen in the developing child, Bowlby (1969) proposed that they are organized in what he called "an attachment behavioral system." With this term he wished to call attention to the way in which the variety of attachment behaviors—crying, calling out, seeking and approaching, gesturing, etc.—arise from a common drive, that of seeking proximity with caretakers when in danger or distress. The particular behaviors that the child shows will occur as a function of his experience with caretakers and what he has learned about the particular setting or situation he is in at that moment. The regular, successful operation of this behavioral system would mean that the child reliably finds a responsive caretaker who more or less appropriately provides safety, reassurance, and comfort. These behaviors constitute a system in that they are activated when the child detects danger or feels distress and have as their goal a common result, achieving proximity with the caretaker.

Bowlby (1969, 1988) and Ainsworth (1979) further proposed that such experience would, over time, result in the development of what was termed a "secure base," or a reliable conviction on the part of the child about the availability of protection and comfort. This sense of safety and of having reliable protective figures to return to supports the development of a complementary behavioral system in concert with the attachment system. Bowlby (1969) designated this additional set of behaviors and activities the "exploratory behavioral system." These behaviors include all pursuits that might reasonably go under the heading of "exploration": locomoting away from the attachment figure to investigate objects, play, manipulating the environment, and even more formal kinds of learning. It is worth noting that, as with the attachment behavioral system, the exploratory system was thought to have evolutionary benefits for a species. Hence, just as a hardwired drive (and an accompanying behavioral system) that led young organisms to seek the protection of their elders confers certain survival value, so too does an exploratory drive that leads to exploration and understanding of the larger environment.

Thus, the sense of security and safety needed to investigate the world, to initiate all manner of adventures, to play freely and without apprehension, and to learn new skills and capacities arises from repeated transactions with attachment figures in which they function as protectors and sources of comfort. In that these two behavioral systems develop in concert and operate in balance with each other, it becomes important to understand the consequences for exploration, curiosity, and the development of a comfortable and safe but open and interested relation to the environment beyond the immediate range of the caretaker's attention. Lieberman and Pawl (1990) have described distortions of secure-base behavior in the second year of life, a period of development when exploring the world while maintaining a connection with attachment figures is of special significance (Bowlby, 1969). In the context of a clinical intervention with high-risk mother–toddler dyads, they observed several patterns of problematic secure-base behavior. In one group of cases, exploration seemed to overtake proximity seeking, resulting in counterphobic recklessness. In a second group, exploration seemed to be inhibited or suppressed; and a third group showed what the authors describe as "precocious competence," in which the child does not rely on the mother for protection but, instead, seems to try to care for her. In each of these patterns the behavior of the child was related to the behavior of the mother in a meaningful way. Thus, for example, the counterphobic, reckless toddlers had mothers who were generally unavailable and failed to "anticipate danger and modulate the child's exposure to it" (p. 382). Lieberman and Pawl observe,

Recurrent experiences of feeling unprotected have a profound influence on the process of internalizing the role of the attachment figure as protector. When the working model of attachment incorporates salient features of unprotectiveness (including abuse and neglect), the child's ability to develop reliable mechanisms for self-protection is in turn jeopardized. Distortions in self-protecting mechanisms may then be observed in many areas of the child's behavior, particularly those that involve the need to negotiate a balance between the attachment system and the child's involvement in exploration and learning. (p. 375)

Self-Regulation

Another useful idea or area of inquiry from attachment and infancy research has to do with self-regulation. What is striking about this work is the way in which it expands thinking about the activities of caregivers beyond concepts of safety and reassurance. It describes how attuned, contingent responding by the caregiver reflects back to the child her own emotional states and thereby assists her in learning to recognize and modulate them.

Children in the earliest months of life are relatively unregulated and depend on their caregivers for help in maintaining (and returning to) a comfortable range of emotional experience. Fundamentally, attachment theory is concerned with the ways in which relationships with caretakers support the regulation of emotional arousal in young children. During childhood there is a gradual shift toward greater self-regulation of emotion and decreasing dependence on the attachment figure for preserving or restoring emotional equilibrium. A great many children in the child protection, special education, and mental health systems are placed in intensive programs because their capacity for self-regulation is inadequately developed and they have a great deal of difficulty responding to the usual (and unusual) stresses, transitions, and disappointments of daily life. In the face of these challenges, their behavior may become disorganized, impulsive, or aggressive (or "dysregulated") and usually gets them into a good deal of trouble with those around them.

To briefly return to the internal working model concept, it should be noted that these models themselves provide an early form of self-regulation. As representations of caregivers, such models are available to very young children to assist them in modulating emotional states in the absence of the actual caretaker. Schore (1994) has marshaled considerable evidence that even the earliest representations—stored visual images of the caretaker's face—can provide this regulatory capability to the child when the caretaker is unavailable.

Developmental research with very young infants and children has also begun to provide additional descriptions of the complex exchanges and interactions that underlie the achievement of self-regulation (see, for example, Fonagy, Gergely, Jurist, and Target, 2002; Siegel, 1999; Schore, 1994). In that "pleasing tableau" of the mother caring for her child, the various natural language descriptions of these behaviors, such as "sustaining," "nurturing," and "raising," were noted. It is now understood that beneath the familiar surface of these processes, the mother is constantly regulating the child's behavior and physiological state through her own behavior and the quality of her presence. Some of this regulatory behavior is easily seen and involves some of those familiar functions that have already been noted, such as feeding and physical contact. More subtle processes of regulation are also occurring, involving body warmth, tactile and olfactory cues, and the reliable rhythms of activity, sleep, hunger, and satiation (Hofer, 2006). In addition, certain kinds of very simple, familiar interactions between caregivers and babies have powerful regulatory effects. During these exchanges the caretaker will mirror the emotional state transmitted by the child's behavior with gesture, facial expression, and voice tone (Schore, 1994; Fonagy et al., 2002). In other words, observation of mothers and babies has shown that in the earliest months of life caregivers coordinate or align their vocal and facial expressions of emotion with those of the infant. Babies as young as 3 months are capable of discriminating contingent expressions in the caregiver and will actively search to establish this sort of engagement with the other if they are deprived of it. As development progresses, the child's capacity to recognize emotion in the other becomes more complex. When, for example, a child as young as 1 year is in an ambiguous situation and is unsure about how to proceed, he will scan the face of the parent and choose a behavior based on the expression seen there (Sorce, Emde, Campos, and Klinnert, 1985). The development of these capacities occurs together with the emergence of other forms of communication in which the child will intentionally display his own emotional states and try to alter or manipulate the states of others by pointing and showing objects. There is also some evidence that children as young as 1 year are capable of early forms of voluntary control of emotional expression and that during the second year of life they begin to modulate the expression of emotion via control of the muscles of the face (Fonagy et al., 2002).

Other work in this area has focused on understanding how the interactions between very young children and their caregivers provide the child with the earliest representations of her own emotional states (Fonagy et al., 2002; Schore, 1994). These early representations constitute the first knowledge that the child will have of herself and are the first step in the process by which the child will come to regulate her own emotional experience and expression. Once again, this work shows how critical the familiar, instinctive interactions between caregivers and babies can be. Observations of mothers across many cultures find them interacting with their babies in this particular patterned way in which they mirror, with subtle modifications, the emotional expression of the child. The child then first sees his own emotional states reflected in the facial expressions, vocalizations, and physical postures of the caregiver. Such reflected representations become associated with the primary felt experience of the emotion and form the basis of the child's own representations of his emotional states. Through endless repetitions of these exchanges, the child comes to learn that he can, through the expression of his own internal states, exert some measure of interesting control over these reflected expressions coming back to him from the environment. It is in these back-and-forth emotional "conversations," in which child and caregiver exert mutual and gratifying influences on each other, that the development of self-regulation begins. One group of workers in this field (Fonagy et al., 2002) has suggested that biofeedback is a useful analog to illustrate how this process might work. In biofeedback procedures, patients can learn to exert control over various "unconscious" physical processes by viewing some external marker of the process. A common example might be a patient learning to control blood pressure by viewing a video display that represents her moment-to-moment blood pressure reading. Without knowing how she does it, the patient learns to control her internal state by making a marker on the screen go up and down. For an infant or a toddler, it is the face of the caregiver that is the external marker of his or her emotional states. As the child expresses an emotional state, he is able to observe shifts in that external marker ("A change is happening!"), he is afforded some sense of agency in his social environment ("Whenever I am in this state, I see that result. I must have made that change happen!"), he comes to know something about his internal state ("This state I am experiencing looks like that."), and ultimately he achieves some measure of control over those states ("How interesting! I can change my expression and when I do, I can make that face out there change too.") When these transactions are repeated endlessly in the course of many, many exchanges suffused with a variety of emotions, the young child gradually arrives at greater awareness and understanding of his own affective states and increasingly flexible, adaptive regulation of those states.

How are such concepts of emotional regulation present in work with clients? As has already been noted, a great many of the clients seen in intensive intervention programs come for treatment with a variety of problems of self-regulation. These difficulties are now well recognized in, for example, the proposed new diagnostic category of "developmental trauma disorder" (van der Kolk, 2005) and in recent discussions of "complex trauma" (Cook, Blaustein, Spinazzola, and van der Kolk, 2003). Offered as an addition to the current diagnostic classification of posttraumatic disorders, developmental trauma disorder describes the special experiences and distinct symptoms of children who have suffered chronic traumatic experience, often at the hands of caretakers or other trusted adults. Difficulties with self-regulation are among the primary categories of symptoms in discussions of both complex posttraumatic stress disorder and developmental trauma disorder.

In the simplest terms, it can be said that many high-risk, traumatized children and youth continue to need external assistance with regulating their emotional states as well as support in developing their own self-regulatory capacities. In assessing them, a detailed picture of their strengths and vulnerabilities in this area must be developed and an effort to understand how the key figures in their development assisted or disrupted their achievement of successful self-regulation should be made. At the level of intervention, ideas about self-regulation are used in several ways. First, it is very important that clients experience the adults who engage with them as capable of, interested in, and committed to containing their negative or unregulated emotional states. A number of writers, starting with Bion (1962), have used the term "containment" to describe the ways in which caretakers assist very young children in managing high levels of distress and dysregulation by containing or internally processing the emotional state and transmitting it back to the child in a manageable form.

Thus, those who work with children and youth who are highly vulnerable to intensely dysregulated states must be able to tolerate the emotional and behavioral expression of such states and must have curiosity about and a capacity for empathic understanding of the child's immediate experience and state of mind. Containment is a process that can take many forms. It is sometimes understood too concretely as physical containment in the form of restraint or seclusion. In fact, containment is a good way of thinking about many of the very simple, almost unconscious ways a worker intervenes in the course of a day. In some situations, it may simply mean that caretakers, clinicians, and team members demonstrate their capacity to bear very intense displays of unregulated emotion directed at them by clients. In other situations, it may mean that the worker makes an effort to respond to the client's emotional expression in a reflective way that communicates an understanding or curiosity about the mental states underlying her behavior. All of these transactions provide clients with an experience that their emotions are being taken in and processed in a way that renders them more tolerable. In other situations, particularly when the child's emotional disorganization or rage threatens injury to herself or others, it may be necessary to physically contain her in a neutral, nonretaliatory fashion. For some traumatized children, rage, aggression, and intensely disorganized states have been key ingredients in their long histories of placement failure. The inability of caretakers or treatment settings to tolerate, contain, and manage these states may produce in the child a profound feeling of danger and a complete absence of the sense of safety that is so vital to effective treatment. While physical management of aggression, against self or other, may be necessary, it also carries with it significant risks of retraumatization and should be undertaken only when adequate resources in the form of well-trained staff are available and all other methods have been exhausted.

Another interesting aspect of regulatory exchanges involves the inevitable failures of attunement and contingent communication between young children and their caregivers. Common sense would suggest that no parent or caregiver does a perfect job; there are regular moments of misattunement in the unfolding relationship with the child in which he enters or is pushed into a state of distress or negative arousal. Such disruptions are not of great importance in and of themselves. How a caregiver manages them and what happens after them, though, do seem to be of importance. Infant researchers (Gianino and Tronick, 1988; Tronick, 1989) have used the term "interactive repair" to describe the process of reattunement and reconnection which, under optimal conditions, follows these ruptures. This process of interactive repair is an important part of many exchanges with the children, teens, and parents with long experiences of failure in multiple systems of care. In many ways, their journeys through these systems constitute a series of disrupted relationships in which repair has been impossible and important or potentially important connections have been lost.

Thus, just as disruptions of attunement and engagement inevitably occur in the course of moment-to-moment interactions between mother and child, so too do such ruptures occur in the course of work with clients. These ruptures take many forms and can involve emotional confrontations arising from limit setting, simple failures to read the state of the client with "good enough" accuracy, or the loss of connection that occurs in busy treatment milieus in which staff have to respond to the needs and states of many clients. In the face of these breaks or pauses of connection and attunement, it is important that team members maintain a stance in which they are prepared to notice these breaks and then move as quickly as possible to repair them. These repairs take many forms, and some are very simple and direct, involving a brief acknowledgment of an interruption of relationship or a misreading of the client's state, while others are more formal and intentional. Pursuit of these opportunities for repair and reengagement is an important ingredient in providing a treatment experience that is a clear departure from what clients have experienced in prior settings. Not infrequently, their behavior has overwhelmed the resources of these settings and led to a permanent disruption of connection.

RELATIONSHIP, ATTACHMENT, AND THE DEVELOPMENT OF PSYCHOPATHOLOGY

Attachment theory provides an account of the unfolding capacity for relatedness that occurs in the course of development. This description is also extremely helpful in thinking about the behavioral difficulties that are regularly seen in children and youth who are referred to intensive treatment programs. Much of the early research on the development of the tie between a child and a primary caretaker involved both naturalistic observation of mothers and babies across cultures and observation of mothers and young children in laboratory settings (Schaffer and Emerson, 1964). In these latter settings, Mary Ainsworth, a collaborator of Bowlby's, devised, together with her colleagues, a simple procedure for observing interactions of mother–child pairs under standardized conditions (Ainsworth, Blehar, Waters, and Wall, 1978). One of the basic tenets of attachment theory states that the child seeks proximity with the attachment figure when experiencing fear or some other form of distress. Ainsworth felt that any assessment of the child's connection to the caretaker would have to involve some element of distress so that patterns of proximity seeking could be directly observed. She created what came to be called "the strange situation" as a way of directly observing how young children manage, both behaviorally and emotionally, separations and reunions with their primary caretakers.

It is important to understand that this work was guided by a conviction that interactions between caretakers and children involve highly complex exchanges in which each participant elicits and responds to behavior in the other. While attachment theory is certainly one aspect of developmental psychology, it is certainly not a psychology of the child alone. Instead, it is concerned with events in the interpersonal field between the caretaker and the child, and it seeks to understand how these events exert influence on the unfolding of the child's capacity for relatedness. To call attention to this profound, unfolding interdependence, Donald Winnicott, a British pediatrician and child analyst, noted, "There is no such thing as a baby, there is a baby and someone" (Winnicott, 1964, p. 88). Others may also be "present" in these exchanges; important caretakers bring to the task of parenting their own histories of attachment relationships and internal representations of their own attachment figures. These representations of the parents' caretakers then inevitably influence what the child's working model will look like. Selma Fraiberg, one of the earliest clinicians working in the field of infant mental health, called attention to this issue with the title of an influential paper, "Ghosts in the Nursery" (Fraiberg, Adelson, and Shapiro, 1980), noting that in some families the transition to parenthood revives a variety of traumatic events and relationship patterns from the childhood of the parents. These unintegrated experiences have the power to intrude into the life of the family by affecting how the parent views the child, how care is delivered, and which behaviors are responded to and which are not.

Ainsworth and her coworkers (1978) gave attachment theory the beginnings of an empirical foundation by directly observing interactions between infants and their caretakers. They were interested in individual differences in infants' responses to separations from and reunions with their caretakers and whether children showed stable, characteristic patterns of attachment-related behavior. At the same time there was curiosity about whether these differences could be shown to arise from differences in caretaker responsiveness, availability, and sensitivity. The laboratory procedure they developed, called "the strange situation," allowed Ainsworth's team to directly observe the following kinds of behavior: the child's "secure-base behavior," which refers to exploration with the caretaker present and available; the child's response to the presence of a stranger (a researcher in Ainsworth's group); the child's response to separation from the caretaker; and the child's response to reunion with the caretaker. Initially, they were able to reliably detect three patterns or styles of attachment in the samples of 1-year-olds observed: "secure," "avoidant," and "resistant/ambivalent." These styles represent stable individual patterns of behavior in each of the domains of behavior observed in the strange situation.

Ainsworth's team classified the attachments of the largest group of infants as "secure." This did not mean that these children showed no response to the moderately stressful conditions of the strange situation. When separated briefly from their caretakers, they showed some distress and their play with the toys in the room usually diminished. They tended to show some openness to the comforting of the benign stranger, but they very clearly demonstrated a preference for their primary caretakers. At reunion, they sought proximity with the caretaker and could be reassured or comforted relatively easily. Most secure babies resumed play. Some secure babies were less distressed by the brief separation of the strange situation, but they too reacted to reunion with the caretaker with an emotional display, such as a smile, or with some other effort to reengage with the caretaker.

Ainsworth's team then described two patterns of insecure attachment revealed by the strange situation. The first was designated as an "avoidant" attachment. These babies explored and played with the toys in the presence of the caretaker, but they showed less emotional engagement with her. At separation, they showed little distress and their responses to the stranger did not look very different from the engagement they had shown with their caretakers. At reunion, an avoidant baby looked avoidant. That is, he or she did not engage with the returning caretaker and, instead, looked away or seemed to actively ignore her. Efforts by the caretaker to reengage did not seem to be reciprocated by the child.

The third attachment style described by Ainsworth and colleagues was called "resistant" or "ambivalent." These babies had obvious difficulty exploring the toys in the presence of the caretaker and seemed anxiously preoccupied with her. They showed considerable distress at separation, and the stranger had little success in comforting them. At reunion, resistant babies sought contact with their caretakers but often the contact seemed to do little to reduce their distress. A subset of resistant babies was described as notably passive, continuing to show significant distress when the caretaker returned but doing nothing to actively pursue contact. The term "ambivalent" has sometimes been applied to this group because these children's pursuit of proximity or comfort sometimes contains an element of anger. For example, the child may greet the approaching caretaker with arms up, inviting the caretaker to pick her up. As the caretaker moves to respond to this gesture, the child may resist the approach and even arch away. Thus, the descriptor "ambivalent" is meant to capture this combination of proximity seeking with angry resistance.

These three patterns or styles of attachment first described by Ainsworth et al. (1978) seemed to capture the behavior of most of the children observed in the strange situation. Nevertheless, there remained some children whose behavior in the strange situation was difficult to classify. Notably, a number of researchers who were looking at attachment in samples of maltreated infants found it difficult to fit the behavior of these children into the three existing attachment categories (Main and Weston, 1981; Main and Solomon, 1990). Similarly, research with nonmal-treating, middle-class samples also found some infants who could not easily be classified as secure, avoidant, or resistant/ambivalent (Main and Weston, 1981; reviewed in Hesse and Main, 2000). At times, these children showed behavior that seemed to more or less fit one of the existing attachment patterns but also presented some behavior that fell outside the definition for that attachment style. A small number of children presented many of these hard-to-classify behaviors, and observers felt they could not place them in any of the then existing three categories. These behaviors seemed to lack a clear goal and often appeared contradictory or conflicted in their intent (Main and Weston, 1981). Many of the behaviors were very brief and difficult to even notice in the midst of other activity between the child and caretaker. Initially, it was felt that this group of infants did not have an organized strategy for seeking comfort and reassurance from a caretaker. Main and Solomon (1986,1990) studied videotapes of these hard-to-classify children and came to see them as a separate group. The behaviors observed in these hard-to-classify infant–parent dyads led Main and Solomon (1986) to view them as representing a fourth pattern of attachment, which they designated "disorganized/disoriented." The behaviors fell into the following groupings:

- Contradictory behavior patterns occurring sequentially, such as strong displays of proximity seeking immediately followed by avoidance
- Simultaneous displays of contradictory behavior patterns, such as moving toward the caretaker sideways or with head averted or down
- Undirected, misdirected, incomplete, and interrupted movements and expressions, such as becoming distressed and moving away from the parent or sudden crying after a long period of contented play
- Stereotypies, asymmetrical movements, mistimed movements, and anomalous postures, such as extended rocking and ear pulling or assuming a huddled, prone, or depressed posture
- Freezing, stilling, and slowed "underwater" movements and expressions
- Direct expressions of fearfulness in response to the caretaker, such as a vigilant, alert posture only in the presence of the parent
- Direct reflections of disorganization and disorientation, such as wandering, confused or dazed expressions, and multiple, rapid changes in emotional expression

It is interesting to note that infants classified as disorganized in the strange situation appear to shift during early childhood and their behavioral strategies in relation to caretakers take on an increasingly controlling quality (Main and Cassidy, 1988; Main and Hesse, 1990). At age 6 their reunion behavior after a brief separation from the parent is described as "insecure-controlling" or "disorganized-controlling" (Main and Cassidy, 1988). This description was used when the children "seem to actively control or direct the parent's attention and behavior and assume a role which is usually considered more appropriate for a parent with reference to a child" (Main and Cassidy, 1988, p. 418). Further, this "role-inverting" (Hesse and Main, 2000) behavior seemed to come in two different possible modes, punitive and caretaking. Hesse and Main (2000) describe them: "Some D-controlling children ordered the parent about in a punitive manner ('Sit down and shut up and keep your eyes closed! I said, keep them closed!'), while others were excessively and inappropriately solicitous (e.g., 'Are you tired, Mommy? Would you like to sit down and I'll bring you some [pretend] tea?')" (p. 1106). Lyons-Ruth, Bronfman, and Atwood (1999) comment on this developmental transition from disorganized infants to controlling preschoolers and school-age children:

> *... during the first two years of life, infants within the disorganized spectrum may combine disorganized behavior either with behavior that preserves the outlines of a*

secure attachment strategy or with behaviors characteristic of an insecure-avoidant or ambivalent strategy. With the increasing cognitive capabilities of the preschool or school-age child, the disorganized infant reorganizes attachment behavior toward the parent into a controlling attachment strategy, a strategy reoriented away from seeking comfort and protection around the child's own needs and toward maintaining engagement with the parent on the parent's own terms. (p. 34)

It is a fundamental assumption of attachment theory that differences in attachment-related behavior in children arise from differences in caregiver behavior (Bowlby, 1977). Thus, attuned, responsive, and available caretakers are seen, in the absence of other developmental insults, such as loss or trauma, as creating the conditions in which a child can become securely attached. The mothers of babies showing an avoidant attachment style were notably avoidant themselves and seemed uncomfortable with displays of emotion or dependency. Ainsworth (1979) describes these mothers as showing a "deep seated aversion" (p. 933) to close bodily contact. They tended to hold their babies as much as parents of securely attached babies did, but often this holding was not at the times that the baby was signaling a need or wish to be held. At times, they were mocking or sarcastic with their children, and this behavior was sometimes in response to proximity seeking on the part of the child.

Parents of children who showed a resistant or ambivalent style of attachment were often unpredictable and inconsistent in their responses to their children's attachment behaviors. They presented somewhat haphazard styles of engagement that sometimes worked and sometimes did not. They were frequently attentive to their children but did not seem to be attuned to their babies' specific states. In a word, these parents sometimes seemed insensitive to their babies' proximity needs and proximity-seeking signals. Ainsworth and colleagues (1978) noted that ambivalently attached babies seemed to lack confidence that their caretakers would respond, leaving them in a state of uneasy uncertainty. As a result of this interactional pattern, these babies then invested more energy in and attended more closely to the caretaker's behavior and emotional states. As a consequence, they had less energy and resources available for exploration of the environment and at school age presented as less assertive and more inhibited (Renken, Egeland, Marvinny, Mangelsdorf, and Sroufe, 1989). Renken and his colleagues note: "Because of inconsistent, chaotic, and haphazard care these infants have come to doubt the certainty of care. They have not given up on the possibility of nurturing adult care, but they doubt the effectiveness of their efforts to achieve it or to function autonomously without it. They remain adult-oriented and emotionally dependent. Their agency is compromised and they are inept with peers, resulting in the appearance of apathy and lack of social salience" (pp. 260–261).

Parents of securely attached babies were not necessarily any more available to their babies than other parents were, but they seemed to be available at the times that their babies most needed them to be available. They were also more tender and affectionate, and in the course of moment-to-moment physical caretaking they were rarely distressing to their babies. Secure attachment has emerged as an import contributor to resiliency, positive relationships with peers, and general social competence (Weinfeld, Sroufe, and Egeland, 2000).

The following question arises, then: What sort of parental behavior might be related to the development of disorganized attachments? Not long after the fourth pattern of attachment was first observed and described (Main and Solomon, 1986), the hypothesis was advanced that this disorganized proximity seeking was related to "frightened or frightening" behavior (Main and Hesse, 1990) on the part of the parent. This hypothesis was offered, in part, because of the particular difficulties attachment researchers had had in placing *maltreated* infants in any of the original three attachment classifications of Ainsworth et al. (1978). At the same time, this fourth pattern of attachment occurred significantly more often in high-risk samples of infant–parent dyads than in low-risk, middle-class, nonclinical samples. In other words, infants who were maltreated or whose mothers suffered from clinically significant depression were much more likely to present with disorganized patterns of attachment. This hypothesis also emerged from a consideration of some of the specific features of disorganized behavior itself. Some of the behavior categorized as disorganized involved direct expressions of fearfulness. As Main and Hesse (1990) noted, though, the disorganized attachment pattern often involves the initiation of an attachment behavior (approach, for example), followed or interrupted by an apparent expression or movement of apprehension (averting head, for example). This display of fearfulness then seems to inhibit or contradict the attachment behavior the child initially displayed. If the child's disorganized pattern of attachment seems to contain elements of apprehension or fearful retreat from proximity seeking, then it becomes important to look closely at the caregiver's actual behavior as well as the caregiver's internal experience of attachment relationships. The questions then become: What is the caretaker's current view and emotional posture (state of mind) with regard to attachment? Is there any evidence of behavior (arising from the caregiver's state of mind) that might induce fear in the child?

To pursue these questions, Main and Hesse (1990) went directly to their original data, examining videotapes of infant–parent dyads in the strange situation and investigating parent behavior in response to proximity seeking. The first observations of this kind were nonblind, retrospective reviews of videotapes of the strange situation dyads in which disorganized behavior on the part of the infant had been observed. These informal "re-observations" found a variety of parental behaviors that struck investigators as potentially frightening to a baby. They included extreme timidity in handling the infant, notable sensitivity to any sign of rejection (of the parent by the child), and threatening vocal patterns and postures. These behaviors were generally not observed in the interactions of parents with children who presented as secure, avoidant, or resistant.

Finally, though, among the most interesting work that placed disorganized attachment in a broader conceptual scheme were investigations of what came to be called "adult states of mind with respect to attachment" (Main, Kaplan, and Cassidy, 1985; Hesse, 1999, 2008). This work was not initially concerned with the actual behavior of parents in response to their children's attachment behaviors but, instead, sought to understand parental representations of their own histories of relationships with important caretakers. This mental content is accessed through a 1-hour semistructured interview (the Adult Attachment Interview, or AAI), in which the parent is asked to reflect on and describe her own early attachment relationships and any experiences of loss and attachment trauma. These responses are then coded according to a schema that does not consider the actual content of the parent's experience but rather evaluates the coherence of the parent's account. What emerges from this work is clear evidence that the parent's readiness or capacity to provide a coherent account of his own attachment experiences is highly predictive of how he will interact with his own children and of the attachment style that the children will then develop. Surprisingly, this capacity for providing a coherent narrative of one's own experience was significantly more predictive than the content of the experience itself. Thus, some parents who described extremely negative or traumatic early histories still raised securely attached children if they could describe those negative experiences in a coherent fashion. As responses to the interview were coded and sorted, they began to cluster into four groups: secure/autonomous, dismissing, preoccupied, and unresolved/disorganized. When these categories were related to the attachment style of the child in the dyad, the following striking correspondence emerged. This congruence between adult states of mind with respect to attachment and infant behavior in the strange situation is shown in Table 3.1.

The finding that the results of a parent's AAI can reliably predict the attachment status of his or her child has now been replicated many times. A variety of studies have established meaningful associations between AAI classification and other variables, such as actual caretaking behavior and clinical distress in the child (Van IJzendoorn, 1995). Thus, the effect of the caregiver's state of mind with respect to attachment on the attachment status of the child is, not surprisingly, mediated by actual behavior on the part of the caregiver. Mothers classified as unresolved-disorganized were found to be markedly more frightening, frightened, and dissociated in their interactions with their infants (Lyons-Ruth and Jacobvitz, 1999). Similarly, when the caregivers of clinically distressed infants and children are assessed for AAI classification, they are rarely found to be secure-autonomous. A diagnosis of conduct disorder in children is significantly more related to maternal unresolved-disorganized AAI status than to any other AAI classification.

To summarize, then, the genesis of disorganized attachments in infants and young children begins in certain states or vulnerabilities in the caretaker. These vulnerabilities are thought to arise from unresolved loss or trauma, which, when

Table 3.1 Adult Attachment Interview Classification and Corresponding Infant Attachment Style

"Adult State of Mind with Respect to Attachment" of the Caregiver	Infant Strange Situation Behavior of the Child
Secure autonomous: The individual provides a coherent narrative in a collaborative fashion. Descriptions and evaluations of early attachment relationships match. Shows a capacity to reflect on his/her/their own experiences and thoughts. Generally valuing of attachment experiences.	Secure: Explores room and toys with interest with caregiver present, shows signs of missing caregiver during separation, often cries during second separation. Greets parents actively, initiates physical contact, and maintains contact at second reunion, but then settles and returns to play.
Dismissing: Not coherent. Dismissing of attachment-related experiences and relationships. Accounts of early experience are often normalizing and quite general and then are either unsupported or contradicted by actual descriptions of events and exchanges. Interview responses are often very brief.	Avoidant: Fails to cry at separation from parent and actively ignores parent upon reunion (getting up, moving away, or leaning out of arms when picked up). Little or no proximity or contact-seeking and no distress or anger. Focuses on toys and or environment throughout the procedure.
Preoccupied: Not coherent, preoccupied with or by past attachment experiences, and seems angry, passive, and fearful. Sentences often long, grammatically entangled, or filled with vague usages. Interview responses are often excessively long.	Resistant: May be wary or distressed even prior to the separation and show little exploration. Preoccupied with parent throughout the procedure; may seem angry or passive. Fails to settle and take comfort from the parent on reunion, and usually continues to focus on the parent and cry. Fails to return to exploration after the reunion.
Unresolved/disorganized: During discussion of abuse or loss, individual shows striking lapse in the monitoring of reasoning or discourse. For example, individual may briefly indicate that a dead person is still alive in the physical sense or that the person was killed by a childhood thought. Individual may lapse into prolonged silence or suddenly shift into eulogistic speech from normal conversational style.	Disorganized/disoriented: The infant displays disorganized or disoriented behaviors in the parent's presence, suggesting a temporary collapse of a behavioral strategy. For example, the infant may freeze with a trance-like expression, hands in the air; may rise at parent's entrance, then fall prone and huddled on the floor; or may cling while crying hard and leaning away with gaze averted.

Table from Hesse (1999 reproduced with permission from Guilford Publications, Inc.)

activated by questions in the AAI related to attachment and loss, have the power to disrupt the coherence of thinking and discourse. It is not difficult to imagine that if affects and memories of these unresolved or unintegrated experiences can become disruptive to thinking in an interview with a neutral researcher, they are certainly likely to be mobilized and become disruptive in the emotionally charged, attachment-laden arena of a caregiving relationship with an infant or young child. When such activations occur in the course of interacting with a child, triggered perhaps by the child's fear and helplessness, the caretaker may manifest behaviors that are experienced by the child as "frightened and/or frightening" (Main and Hesse, 1990). At this point the child is catapulted into a very real predicament, aroused into a fearful, apprehensive state; she is hardwired to seek relief from the very figure who is the source of fear. Hence, no coherent attachment strategy is possible and disorganization results. Main and Hesse (1990) write as follows:

> In conclusion, it seems apparent that the frightening behavior on the part of the still-traumatized parent should lead to the disorganized/disoriented infant behavior, since the infant is presented with an irresolvable paradox wherein the haven of safety is at once the source of the alarm. Moreover, the conflict between opposing tendencies to approach and to flee from the attachment figure stems from the single external signal (threatening or fearful parent behaviors); is internal to the infant; is self-perpetuating; and is exacerbated by placement in a stressful situation. (p. 180)

Subsequent studies have confirmed the hypothesis that the caretakers of disorganized infants do display frightening behavior (see, for example, Abrams et al., 2006; Lyons-Ruth et al., 1999) and that this behavior is significantly related to disorganized attachment. Finally, as has been described, in the course of development the behavior of these infants in relation to their caretakers takes on a notably controlling quality.

What then is the relationship between children identified as having disorganized attachments and the traumatized, very vulnerable children and youth who come to be clients of intensive service programs? There is every reason to believe that the group of children researchers describe as having disorganized attachments is well represented in the population of children who experience repeated failure in multiple systems of care. It is also easy to see that this will particularly be the case among those children who have been involved in the child protection system. This large subgroup of children and youth receiving some form of intensive services is composed, after all, of those most likely to have experienced maltreatment or neglect, which is perhaps the clearest example of frightening parental behavior. Studies that have investigated the long-term outcomes for infants having disorganized attachments confirm this. Multiple investigations (see, for example, Carlson, 1998; Jacobvitz and Hazen, 1999; Lyons-Ruth and Jacobvitz, 2008) have found externalizing and internalizing behavior problems and dissociative behavior during later childhood and adolescence.

This body of work demonstrates quite clearly the ways in which distortions, disturbances, and disruptions in early attachment relationships are implicated in the development of many of the behavior disorders that lead to placement in a variety of intensive treatment settings. Secure attachments do not constitute any guarantee of psychological health or good functioning; instead, they should be seen as protective factors that confer on children a significant measure of resiliency (Thompson, 1999). This resiliency then is available to them in the course of development as they encounter the usual, and sometimes extraordinary, challenges, losses, and traumas that may arise. Conversely, attachment insecurity—most strikingly, attachment disorganization—and the early experience with caretakers which seems to cause it are not guarantees of significant mental health problems but may be seen as critical risk factors, increasing the child's vulnerability to the same challenges, losses, and traumas. The developmental and placement trajectory and the ultimate outcome for any particular child with multiple early adverse experiences are always complex. Some are favored with easygoing temperaments, while others are lucky to have found enough "angels in the nursery" (Lieberman et al., 2005) to internalize some sense of a benign protector.

FROM ATTACHMENT THEORY TO "RELATIONSHIP-BASED INTERVENTION"

What does it mean, in terms of concrete practice, to make use of the insights of attachment theory and research? How can these insights lead to something that might accurately be called "relationship-based treatment"? Answering this question has its challenges. Faced with difficult and provocative behavior, workers often wish for a very concrete and specific toolbox that will tell them what to do in every situation. Some of the methods that are employed in effective treatment programs do lend themselves to a stepwise approach to intervention. Learning theory, and its practical application in various forms of behavior modification, is one powerful approach that can be concretely specified. Unfortunately, there is no attachment theory version of a time-out and no relationship-based form of a schedule of reinforcement.

So, then, how is relationship present in successful treatment efforts? If there is no concrete procedure, no specific method analogous to a functional analysis or a time-out that can be deployed to address particular behavioral problems, then how is relationship part of an intervention? In Chapter 1, it was asserted that unconditional care should not be seen only as an article of faith or a philosophical position but also as a method. More specifically, it is an implicit method. That is, while it may not be explicitly referred to in the treatment plan, it should be actively present in all interactions between staff and clients. It gives these interactions a particular momentum and quality that convey to clients the conviction that they can succeed, grow, and experience a sense of agency in their lives.

To further develop this idea of implicit methods, some things must be stood about how all people carry on relationships with others and ab particular vulnerabilities and distortions that clients bring to their im social ties. Some organizing questions and responses that can summar... key ideas about internal working models and point the way toward an approach to intervention are listed below. Many of the premises of this discussion should be familiar from the earlier discussion of attachment research.

1. How do children process and organize their experience in the interpersonal world? Children are not passive registers or accumulators of interpersonal experience. Instead, they are actively construing their experience and working to construct images of what drives the behavior of others, of who they are in relation to others, and of what they can expect in the future. The adaptive value of having such a picture of the social world is obvious. These images have been described in many different ways. Thus, people working in the field from diverse theoretical orientations have spoken of internal working models, cognitive schemas, cognitive structures, beliefs, stories, and narratives. The common thread to all these terms is the notion of a gradually developed representation of others and of the self in relation to others. The function of this structure is to assist the child in organizing and making sense of the world and to help him anticipate future experience and to plan behavior in relation to attachment figures.

2. Do all children have a representation of the interpersonal world? Yes. These models, beliefs, or narratives are held by all children, not only children who will eventually become consumers of intensive treatment services. In a child whose caretaking has been essentially benign, the internal working model reflects this experience. Such a child is likely to anticipate good treatment from others and will approach others in a way that reflects these expectations. It can be said that she comes to believe that she deserves this treatment and that under most conditions it will be forthcoming. Conversely, a child who has suffered a pattern of sustained, hurtful early experiences such as loss, neglect, or abuse will have a way of representing the self and the world that is consistent with or reflects that experience. She may believe that she is bad, damaged, or in some way deserving of this treatment and will expect the treatment to continue. In other words, these representations come to control the evaluation and processing of attachment-related events in the interpersonal field and can distort or skew this information in important ways. It should be noted that this example represents this process in only the most general way. Interaction with a child over time allows a description of the relation between lived experience and the working model with greater detail and specificity. Such a description might, for example, also include an account of how threat and coercion, sexuality, dependency, and the image of the self and its capacities all play a role in the working model.

3. What happens to these models in the course of development? Do adults have them? Yes. In work with families there must be a constant awareness that parents and caretakers bring their own complex representations (working models, narratives) to the challenging tasks of parenting. As adults, they may have multiple competing models of themselves and how the world works, and these models can be elicited or activated by stress and other events in the environment.

4. Can the models change? Some of these models can be very persistent. Children (and children who grow up to become parents of these clients) who have relatively little benign experience with caretakers have very durable negative beliefs about themselves and similarly strong convictions about what they can expect from the world. These ideas are not easy to revise in the face of new experience and are especially resistant to alteration by language.

5. Where are these models, beliefs, narratives stored? Remember that these models are being organized from experience from the very beginning of life. This means that they are initially created before the development of language and are encoded in nonverbal or "implicit" or "procedural memory" (Lewis, Amini, and Lannon, 2000). This accounts, in part, for their relative resistance to change via language.

6. So, internal models affect how experience is processed and may inevitably skew that processing, but do they also affect behavior? Internal models, beliefs, or narratives are not just organizers and holders of information. They are also important controllers of behavior. How does this work? First, the child's belief about how he is likely to be treated affects how he interprets incoming information. Thus, even relatively neutral or benign approaches from others may often be experienced as threatening, false, or unreliable. The child is then unlikely to react to the actual interpersonal stimulus; instead, he responds to his model-driven construction of it. Second, behavior the child generates is generally consistent with the internal model and, as such, will often provoke complementary or confirming behavior from the environment. Thus, the child's internal working model, by creating expectations and by guiding behavior, makes some developmental trajectories more likely than others. Similarly, internal working models developed under the influence of traumatizing, neglectful, or significantly misattuned caretaking have greater momentum (persistence, rigidity, and constriction) than those developed in a context of benign, adequately attuned caretaking.

7. When a child becomes a client, how do these processes play out in treatment settings? For clients (and this includes parents and caretakers), the environment that is being provoked and in which these trajectories are now unfolding is the treatment program itself. Therefore, clients regularly, even relentlessly, direct invitations at staff to respond to them in ways that will confirm their internal working models. Some simple but familiar examples illustrate this process:

a. A child with a long history of physical abuse at the hands of caretakers engages in needling, provocative behavior that arouses anger, frustration, and possible physical retaliation from peers and adults.

b. A child who has been a victim of scapegoating, neglect, and psychological abuse presents with poor hygiene and peculiar personal habits that arouse disgust and disengagement.

8. Are these invitations easily "seen" by clinicians and other team members? These invitations and the responses they evoke are often subtle and can involve exchanges that go on "below the radar" of the regular interactions of managing behavior and dealing with crises. In fact, it is possible to feel pretty sure that one is doing all the "right" things in exchanges with a client while actually, through emotional tone and posture, confirming the child's negative internal working model. Additionally, even in the most structured of treatment programs staffed with the best-trained counselors, the cruelty and aggression of these invitations inevitably arouse defensiveness and urges to disengage, punish, and otherwise retaliate.

9. How can an understanding of this process inform treatment? Treatment becomes a matter of providing experiences to the child that result in the modification of the child's internal working model and in the gradual creation of a new working model. This requires that workers do the initial work of "decoding" the child's behavior so that the invitations the behavior is presenting can be understood and a stance that declines these invitations can be articulated and rehearsed. This may include very specific descriptions of how behavior will be contained, how bedtimes should be managed, how demands for medication will be responded to, and how requests for attention from specific staff will be dealt with. This posture may also be more general and involve working to stay within a particular emotional range with a child or working to avoid particular kinds of interactions. In this approach, relationship is mobilized as an agent of change, disconfirming the child's image of who she is and what she should expect from the interpersonal world. Staff members work to provide the child with experiences in relationships that are different from those encountered in past relationships and to support the child in very gradually constructing a new model of how these relationships might unfold. In the psychological literature concerned with treatment of severely disturbed patients, this approach has been described as providing the patient with a "corrective emotional experience" (Alexander and French, 1946) or a "representational mismatch" (Horowitz, 1987; Bleiberg, 2001). In other words, in the course of treatment one often has opportunities, as the primary representatives of the external world, to provide clients with experiences that disconfirm, contradict, or in some way throw into question their beliefs or expectations. This creates the possibility of altering those beliefs and, in turn, altering the behavior that flows from them. In this way, the relationship-based method supports other methods that work to replace old behaviors with new skills. This concept of corrective experience applies equally to work with parents and families.

10. If all this is happening through relationship, does that mean clinicians or other workers engaged with the child wouldn't use language and verbally process experience with the client? Not at all. It does mean that relying purely on language would not be likely to work in many cases. It is necessary for the clinician and the team to avoid confirming the client's implicit beliefs and for the client to have disconfirming *experience* with others. The client's memories, thoughts, emotional responses to experience, anticipations of future experience, and narrative of her or his own life are all content worthy of curiosity and verbal elaboration, review, and investigation. These activities, though, will be most useful and successful when they occur in a relational context that involves attention to safety, regulation of emotional states, and alertness to invitations from the client to repeat problematic, often pathogenic relationship scenarios. Finally, it can be said that words are more than just words. That is, they are a powerful means of communication that give meaning and emotional tone to any interpersonal exchange. As such, they will be an important element in giving a response its disconfirming potential.

11. A natural question at this point might be, "What is up with this? Why would anyone ever do anything that could possibly repeat the client's negative experiences in earlier relationships? We are good people and we wouldn't do something like that!" Well, it's not that simple or easy. A child entering a high-level residential or day treatment program can have had 15–20 earlier placements. All the people working in all of those facilities, schools, and foster homes are good people too; and most of them were doing their best to help the children they served. Yet, in many cases the child's ferocious commitment to his internal working model won out and the child had to be discharged. Those discharges can be framed in all sorts of ways ("We didn't have the resources to serve a child with such severe needs," etc.), but often they are anticipated by the child: The internal model includes an image of himself as too disturbing or too aggressive, and his behavior then "engineers" the discharge (recall the inevitable urges to retaliate noted in item 7). Another way to underscore this idea is to simply note that in the course of 15–20 placements the child has become expert at provoking relationships that recapitulate his or her early experiences. It is incumbent on clinicians and caretakers to be curious and thoughtful about how these stories have worked in their clients' lives and to respond in ways that prevent their repetition.

12. How does this idea connect to unconditional care? In this regard it is important to recall the assertion that unconditional care is more than a philosophical position and is, in fact, a method. For a great many clients and their families, the first and most important intervention will be to *not* discharge them. This is their first encounter with a representational mismatch. Very often, it is their expectation that they will exhaust program staff, that they will somehow be blamed for their problems or their children's problems, or that their needs will not be understood and staff will not hang in with them. Unconditional care is the first and perhaps most important disconfirming stance enacted by clinicians and

other team members. As a client regularly encounters this stance, she will begin to have some confidence (a very small beginning of a secure base) that she is not about to fail yet another placement and then may be able to move on and present therapists and workers with new invitations or challenges that arise from other elements of the internal working model.

13. "Wait though! Couldn't we just be good limit setters and teachers of new behaviors and not worry about all this working model stuff?" Well, this could happen, and some progress with some clients could be made; but one can never underestimate both the persistence of the child's working model and the subtlety of the inducements offered to others to provide confirming responses to those models. In other words, it's very easy to feel that good treatment is being done when actually a reenactment with the client or a parent is happening. Again, remember the inevitable urges to disengage and retaliate described earlier and recognize that these urges are not always consciously experienced as such but, instead, seep into staff discussions, meetings, and treatment planning.

14. "So, what is the connection between this relationship-based approach and any systems of behavior change and behavior management that can be key ingredients in successful work with clients?" Behavior management and behavior change methods (which will be discussed in greater depth later) are those procedures that involve setting limits and providing structure and containment. They also organize efforts to teach new behaviors and are the visible foreground of many good treatment programs (i.e., they are explicit). The relationship-based elements are those processes that support a thoughtful discernment of the child's (or parent's) working model of attachment, as well as the behaviors that invite a confirmation of that model. These processes are the less visible background of a treatment program (they are implicit). This language may be somewhat misleading. It is possible to be explicit about adopting a particular stance with a child with a particular working model. The enactment of that stance, though, is not articulated explicitly to the child in the same way that a behavioral intervention often is. Instead, the stance is woven into how team members and caretakers respond to the various behavioral expressions of that working model.

15. "Why are behavior change and behavior management the foreground of the program?" Because they create safety and are therefore an essential, fundamental precondition for the creation of relationship. Without the rules, expectations, consistent responses, and readiness to both interrupt escalating aggression and initiate neutral, nonretaliatory containment, treatment milieus and individual treatment relationships would certainly become psychologically and physically unsafe.

16. "Well, if this relationship-based approach is in the background, maybe we could do without it. Let's just focus on managing behavior and teaching new behavior, right?" While it is true that one can have a certain kind of containment

(but not true safety) without relationship, it is always in danger of sliding into an unreflective, coercive, essentially corrective mode of interaction. This will yield an approach that can be very specific and concrete about methods but not about children. Such a stance will show little curiosity about or recognition of the specific strengths and vulnerabilities of particular children. From another point of view, imagine a program staffed by highly skilled behavior specialists. In this hypothetical program, though, circumstances dictate that new behavior specialists cycle through the program each week. In such a setting, relationship is effectively subtracted as an element in the treatment mix and few significant gains would occur.

17. "Okay, I get the working model concept, but what methods and procedures will support its presence in the programs? How do we go about 'decoding' the child's behavior and understanding how it expresses some element of the working model? Where does someone 'articulate and rehearse a stance that declines these invitations' that arise from the child's story of who he or she is and how the world works?" A thoughtful, useful description of a child's internal working model requires time as well as collaboration among the team members. (Please note that the "team" may be a group of workers employed by one entity and collaborating in a more or less formal way. It may also be the collection of professionals, paraprofessionals, caretakers, and community contacts involved with the child who are collaborating but may be employed by multiple entities.) Some useful observational categories that can guide the process are presented in Chapter 5 in a discussion of a relational approach to assessment. It is of great importance that all organizational "layers" have opportunities to contribute and collaborate. Team leaders (who may go by various other titles, depending on the organization) must be skillful at eliciting data from staff members, external "treatment partners," and caretakers. This material is used to develop two kinds of information. First, responses from staff are described that are likely to confirm the child's internal working model by in some way repeating early relationship patterns. Second, a stance (with specific behaviors) is described that would be likely to disconfirm these beliefs and promote a representational mismatch.

Chapter Four

Assessment, Diagnosis, and Case Formulation

Before taking up a discussion of a specifically relational assessment and case formulation, it is important to consider some general issues with respect to assessment processes.

What are the goals of assessment? The day-to-day documentation requirements and deadlines felt by clinicians and staff members working in agencies, public clinics, and managed care settings can sometimes make it seem that assessments are completed simply to meet the requirements of regulatory bodies or funding streams. While these sorts of demands are real and must be met in a timely way, it would be a mistake to view the completion of a typical intake summary as representing a final or definitive assessment of the child and family. The sorts of documents that meet these requirements are often concerned primarily with amassing bits of factual material. Often, there is no space for generating new questions and hypotheses or making inferences from this factual material. A thoughtful assessment process should allow the team to do a great deal more than gather data. It should throw light on where intervention is most likely to be successful in helping the family and the child to maximize their strengths and minimize their vulnerabilities. One key goal of intervention is to enable clients to have greater access to their capacities and to be less easily overtaken by their histories and vulnerabilities. A thoughtfully conducted assessment should provide a starting point for this intervention process.

In thinking about assessment, diagnosis, and case formulation, it is important to recognize that these three interrelated processes are concerned with the collection, evaluation, and organization of data from a variety of domains. "Organization of data" means something more than merely classifying information into various piles or lists. It is an active process of assigning meaning to various pieces of information according to a conceptual scheme which is based on values, clinical experience, and convictions about what is likely to be most useful in explaining clients' troubled and troubling behavior. Ideally, those convictions are based in part on currently available empirical evidence. Not all the conceptual schemes that might be utilized to sift and organize data are created equal. Some are more powerful than others, and all reflect the assumptions and beliefs of their practitioners. It is certainly the case that clinicians regularly encounter documents or assessments completed at earlier placements that assign different meaning or importance to bits of data and emphasize different domains of information.

Two important beliefs that underlie the conceptual scheme presented here are stated in the following paragraphs. They flow directly from the understanding of attachment processes developed in the preceding chapter.

The challenging behaviors that are encountered in children in intensive treatment settings are complex and may involve multiple factors, but in almost all cases they arise, in large part, from problems in relationships. In the most general terms these problems may be distortions, disturbances, or disruptions in the caretaking relationship. Biological factors may be present in these difficulties, for example, problems of poor temperamental fit between child and caretaker. The fundamental sources of clients' challenges and struggles, however, are not primarily biological; instead, they are interpersonal. These sources of difficulty may be dramatic and easily identified, as can be seen in the lives of children who have sustained multiple losses and a complete absence of stability in their relationships. It is also true, though, that in some cases the sources of a child's difficulties may be more subtle and involve long-standing family vulnerabilities.

Trauma is often present as both an independent cause and a critical amplifier of these difficulties. In this context, the term "trauma" includes the familiar sense of overwhelming threats to life, safety, and the integrity of the self; the cumulative strain trauma of neglect and emotional deprivation; as well as the more subtle forms of relational trauma that can result in disorganized attachments.

A note on blame: It might be thought that, by locating the sources of clients' difficulties squarely in relationships with caretakers, blame is being assigned to these caretakers. On the contrary, the task is to simply understand those things that have gone awry in the lives of families and to support the family in finding the best ways to manage their particular situation. This approach to work with children and families proceeds from a default assumption that clients have been doing the best they can with the resources they have available. This is especially true for parents who bring their own challenging, disrupted, and traumatic histories to the task of raising children and who often have very little in the way of reliable support as they try to navigate the demands of this difficult challenge.   It is also important to acknowledge that these experiences of disrupted relationships and trauma occur in communities and in a larger society, in which there are continuing inequalities of income, employment, education, and access to resources. Problems of racism, sexism, and insufficient and inequitable funding of education and family support services all add to the challenges faced by families.

Several general ideas about the actual completion of an assessment are also worth stressing.

1. Assessment is a configural process. This means that it is never the case that single (or relatively few) pieces of data are determinative. Instead, a picture is constructed of a child, his or her family, and the community context in which they are operating, which considers any piece of information in terms of its relation to other pieces of data. The meaning of any bit of data then can shift as new data arrive. Carrying out an assessment in this way prevents any simplistic, but seemingly logical, path from observed signs and symptoms to the statement of a diagnosis. Thus, symptoms are evaluated in the context of other information about family history and functioning, the overall progress of the child's development, and the various stressors faced by the child and the family. It should also be noted that while workers are constrained by regulations or funding streams to state a diagnosis from the *Diagnostic and Statistical Manual of Mental Disorders,* fourth edition (DSM-IV), this is certainly not the primary goal of an assessment process. Instead, it is important to create a flexible picture of the child's and the family's strengths and capacities as well as of the risk factors that have overtaken them. Another way in which assessment should be configural involves the weighing and synthesizing of data from multiple observers interacting with the child and the family in multiple settings. Thus, while a clinician may conduct the formal intake or history-gathering interviews, the observations, experiences, and inferences of all team members are vital to a thorough, accurate assessment. No child behaves in precisely the same way in every setting. To develop a complete picture of her or his strengths and vulnerabilities, data must be woven together from the various adults who interact with her or him. This type of configural assessment requires that nonprofessional or paraprofessional direct care workers be trained and supported to be curious, thoughtful observers who understand that their input is invaluable.

2. Assessment is a process that is done best when it is done with the people being assessed rather than to them. Ideally, every effort should be made to engage families and children in an assessment process that is fundamentally collaborative. Highly structured interview methodologies aimed at completing documentation requirements or navigating a diagnostic decision tree may seem to yield a great deal of information. Sadly, they may also feel objectifying to clients. Rather than encouraging an active curiosity about life circumstances, these instruments may encourage passivity and disconnection. Such an approach risks establishing the assessor as an authority who will solve the clients' problems for him or her. The team's intention, in the course of gathering information, is to create the conditions that will allow people to tell their own stories in the way that is most comfortable for them. This may require patience and flexibility. It may be necessary to see families in their homes and to find ways to create engagement that are less formal and for which many therapists are not trained. The first authentic moment of connection with a parent may come in a parking lot while kneeling at the side of their car when they have come to pick up their child.

3. It is not useful to entirely distinguish assessment from treatment. Unconditional care and the values that sustain it should inform the way in which the team approaches clients. This stance or attitude of respectful interest and curiosity represents an implicit treatment medium that is always active in the background. This is certainly true for an initial period of engagement that may be primarily devoted to assessment. It is also the case, though, that an atmosphere with richer possibilities for change can be created simply through support for curiosity and inquiry. Clinicians need to have confidence in the value of exploration, a belief that experience is intelligible, and a sense that it is valuable to make connections between feelings, thoughts, and events in the world. It is also true that once the real work of engagement and treatment has begun, the clients' responses to these interventions represent new, additional assessment information. Thus, treatment occurs from the moment the team says "Hello" and assessment continues until the moment the team says "Goodbye."

Any discussion of assessment must begin by noting that children and families enter treatment in very different ways. In residential programs, workers are often provided with thick stacks of information that include prior evaluations, court reports, hospital discharge notes, and therapists' letters. The value of these opinions, accounts, and reports may vary greatly. Almost always, some of this information is misleading, some may be factually incorrect, and all of it must be evaluated with attention to when it was gathered. This is part of what is meant by the idea of *configural* assessment: Data about a child's functioning at a particular point in time must be evaluated in light of what else was occurring in the life of the child when the data were obtained and in light of guesses about the assumptions of the evaluators. Additionally, workers should evaluate and weigh each bit of data in relation to the other bits of data. Thus, for example, a psychological assessment completed during a child's first psychiatric hospitalization (and perhaps first separation from caretakers) may provide a restricted sample of that child's functioning. In spite of these problems, thoughtful sifting (informed by a conceptual scheme) through the variety of reports, documents, and letters that accompany the child usually yields a picture of many of his life experiences, vulnerabilities, and capacities. It allows an initial summary of his history and the development of some questions and hypotheses about where things have gone wrong for the family and in his development. As the team gets to know the child and the family, they are able to understand, add to, and revise these data in a new light. Some of the data will turn out to be enormously helpful, and some will be puzzling in how they differ from what is learned through experience with and observation of the child and the family.

In other settings, such as day treatment programs or school-based interventions, a child can arrive with little or no paperwork and workers need to rely almost exclusively on the data that are developed in the course of their own work the child and the family. Because of this, the approach to assessment described here is one that is not always accomplished early in the course of the child's treatment. Sometimes it takes months of building a relationship with the child and parents to fill in a reasonably complete picture of their history together and their strengths and vulnerabilities. In programs in which there is little information prior to the child's placement, it is important to not fall into the trap of diving into the work in a way that simply deals with the child's day-to-day behavioral difficulties without thinking more systematically about how these difficulties arise from the history and the challenges and vulnerabilities of the caretakers or community.

At the outset of work with a child and family, there is hardly enough time to gather all the information or ask all the questions that may eventually seem important. Sometimes the momentum of needing to start doing things and the pressure of other demands on clinicians and administrators can lead to an acceptance of a premature or incomplete understanding of the child and family. Thus, for example, a diagnosis made in a prior setting may seem to be at least descriptively accurate and useful as an initial, provisional basis for a treatment plan. Similarly, the immediate reality of needing to manage the child's behavior may overwhelm the possibility of considering other theories. The danger of this process is that this premature or incomplete—or received—idea of what is going on with the child and family becomes objectified and takes on a life of its own. One implication of this process is that clinicians in programs in which there is very little information provided at the time of intake have a greater responsibility to undertake an information-gathering process after the child has actually been admitted and to make every effort to engage parents, treatment partners, and other informants and caretakers in a collaborative inquiry into the history, meanings, and sources of the child's behavior.

In programs such as school-based services, there may be little in the way of a real intake process in which a decision to serve or not serve the child is made. That decision may be made in an individualized educational plan meeting, and the child's first day in the program may occur at the same time that intake information, such as that from educational and psychological assessments, is received. In these situations it is important that parents be engaged very quickly in a collaborative assessment of the child's strengths and problematic behaviors. This inquiry should resemble more traditional intake interviews in which the family and the clinician work together to develop information that might illuminate the child's difficulties and behavior. In addition to the simple accumulation of useful data, this process should have a goal of engaging the family's curiosity, providing them with a sense of power and agency in dealing with the school and the program, and helping them feel connected to the goals of the intervention. Parents may view placement in a school-based day treatment classroom as no different from the child's earlier educational placements and have little understanding of the ways in which their involvement can be crucial to the success of the intervention.

Regardless of how a child's treatment or placement begins or what sorts of documentary information are provided at intake, there are domains of information that the team needs to fill in with data. What follows is a discussion of some general areas for curiosity. The ideas found here should resonate with the earlier discussion of attachment theory. Some of these ideas will be revisited when a more specific approach to working model assessment is discussed.

HISTORY OF THE CHILD AND THE PARENTS' ATTACHMENTS

Here, the goal is to begin to construct a chronological narrative of family and caretaker relationships. When a child has been placed out of the home, this narrative should include relatives, foster homes, and residential placements. This is a task that makes use of several different methods of data collection and different kinds of information. Thus, if documents such as court reports and psychological assessments are provided, a chronological account of the child's life can be constructed that should begin with the birth of the parents. At the very least, this will assist in constructing a broad-stroke account that includes important events in the family's history such as births, deaths, divorces, separations, losses, transitions, and placement changes. Using documents alone, it may be difficult to discern much about the qualitative aspects of relationships between family members; but patterns will often emerge which allow inferences about the quality of caretaking, the resources available to the family, and the risk factors that were regularly associated with placement failure.

In parallel with reviewing these documents, the clinician will seek the involvement of parents and surrogate caretakers and solicit their stories, theories, and opinions. It is, of course, very valuable to provide them with an opportunity to share an account of their own families and development. In these conversations attention is paid to what they reveal about how they experienced *their* caretakers, what sorts of struggles they faced in growing up, and who were important supports for them when they were young. Finally, it is crucial to pay careful attention to the quality of their narrative: Can they speak of their own development with coherence, or are they still very much at the mercy of traumatic events or unresolved feelings of fear, resentment, or disappointment?

CURRENT RELATIONSHIPS AS THEY EMERGE IN PROGRAM

An additional source of information about the child's and the family's relational style and capacity is found in their response to the offer of relationship that is part of whatever program is serving the child. In this domain two quite different sources of information are used: the current behavior of the client and the family and the experience of the staff who encounter them. In all programs there is what could be called a "default offer of relationship." It is characterized by respectful interest and warmth and should be expressed in intake procedures and in the routine stance of the treatment team and support staff toward the client and family. This general quality of availability and respect should be ongoing and can include pursuit of parent participation and a readiness to adjust services to most effectively meet the needs of families. Thus, a therapeutic preschool can have a regular family advisory and support group in which parents and caretakers are invited to help plan events, address problems, and share coffee and snacks. Support staff can help with child care and transportation. For children and youth served in intensive programs, this readiness to engage can be thought of as a generic disconfirming stance, to which additional specific elements are added based on assessments of individual clients. The client's response to this stance is an important reflection of his or her expectations, attitudes, and implicit beliefs about the interpersonal world. Thus, some children respond with a desperate, voracious effort to consume every resource and moment of contact offered to them. When the supply is interrupted or delayed, they may collapse into miserable, disorganized panic. Other children may view this readiness on the part of staff to engage as a sign of weakness and as an opportunity to exploit them. Others may seem to barely notice it and present a picture of indifference and self-containment.

This way of using interactions with clients as an important source of information about how they function in the world is not one that is limited to therapists but should be utilized by everyone who works with the child and parents. The task is to not simply ask what it feels like to be engaged with the child but how the child makes use of the entire program and what sorts of relationships he strives to create with the adults working with him. For a child, the key behaviors that will inform the team about his working model of relationships are many of those that have interested attachment researchers. Thus, it is important to see how the child seeks proximity with adults when she is in distress, afraid, or hurt and how she manages disruptions in relationships such as separations or misunderstandings. Also, the team must be alert for the emergence of themes in the child's relationships with adults and caretakers and take note of how selective she is in the relationships made with adults in the program. Is every adult seen as a potential gratifier of her needs, or is she connecting with particular adults in particular ways based on a sense of who she is and what sort of experience she has had with adults? Parents, too, will have their own unique and informative way of making use of a treatment program. Some will be reserved and slow to make connections with helpers while others will be anxious for assistance. Having workers attend to their own thoughts and feelings as they arise while engaged with the client or the family can also yield useful information. In monitoring their own emotional responses clinicians and workers are not operating in the more familiar, professional information-gathering mode but instead are attending to their own internal experience as it arises in the course of contacts with clients.

TRAUMATIC EVENTS

Trauma—in the form of intentional, directly experienced victimization, as well as other more general forms of traumatic experience—has already been described as a risk factor in the lives of many children and their parents. The facts and the personal meanings of traumatic events are revealed in several ways. Once again, a useful starting point may be the initial documents provided at the time of intake. Such documents are most likely to be available in those cases in which there is active involvement of child protection agencies. Typically, such documents will provide a narrative scaffold that must then be filled in with historical detail and emotional meaning. The actual facts of a child's history of victimization can be expanded and elaborated in many ways. Thus, the team must try to know as much as possible about the "who, what, when, and where" of the trauma and how the traumatic events were embedded in the life of the child and the family. As important as these factual details are the more subtle issues of the degree to which the trauma was seen or recognized by caretakers and other adults, how disclosure occurred, and what sort of support was present for that disclosure. In some cases an attachment figure was either the source of the trauma or was in a position to protect the child and did not. When this has occurred, the worker will want to know if and how the caretakers are able to understand and acknowledge their role in events. Once again, in pursuing these issues with children or parents, clinicians must pay attention to more than the factual content; they must also pay attention to the emotional tone and coherence of the narrative. This applies equally to the parents' accounts of any traumatic events in their own history. Such narratives will sometimes unfold with clarity and appropriate emotion; at other times they will barely emerge at all and then will quickly be dismissed as something that "happened a long time ago and I'm done with it," and in some cases the telling will happen in a confusing sequence that is disrupted by strong feelings. Each of these presentations is meaningful and can assist the clinician in discerning the degree to which the traumatic events have not been integrated and continue to be a significant ingredient in the caretaker's difficulties.

STRENGTHS OF THE CHILD AND THE FAMILY

Learning as much as possible about strengths and protective factors in the life of the family is an important piece of any assessment. Information about them may be gained by direct questions of parents and children but may also emerge in the course of a review of the family's history or will simply become apparent from observing their interactions and listening to their stories as they emerge. Often, some families have very little sense of the many things that they are doing well in raising their children. By the time they reach an intensive program, they have probably heard a great deal about the many things they are doing wrong. An interviewer's direct interest in and attention to exceptions, strengths, and resources may represent an important shift in their experience of a helping relationship and in their own sense of agency (Madsen, 2007). A sincere curiosity about their successful efforts can help parents to feel more connected to their children's behavior and lead them to greater engagement and activity with their children. Directing a caretaker's attention to moments of successful engagement with their children can be a prospective as well as a retrospective process. Often, investigation of these successes can yield important information about what is working and what might work in the future.

ADAPTIVE CAPACITIES

In this domain the central issue is the child's development of important capacities that are unfolding throughout childhood. Data about these capacities can be obtained from earlier reports and evaluations, the descriptions of caretakers, and to some degree a child's own account of his or her behavior. The very best source of information, however, is observation across time and across varied behavior samples from different settings. Some important capacities are listed here. It will be clear that these important behavioral functions are not perfectly discrete but overlap and support each other in critical ways.

- *Emotional regulation:* This domain includes the ability to more or less flexibly modulate emotional experience so that cognitive functioning is not overwhelmed, relationships are not damaged, and a continuous sense of personal identity is preserved. This capacity can be assessed (again, configurally) by observing, for example, the intensity of emotional expression, the range of affects expressed, the predominant emotional tone, the capacity to recover emotional equilibrium following more intense affective experience, and the sensitivity to external emotional stimulation.
- *Cognitive functioning:* This domain includes the degree to which the client's intellectual capacities are intact and more or less insulated from disruptive intrusions of emotion; the degree to which they are able to assist the client in meeting age-appropriate demands from the environment (also known as "learning from experience"), and the degree to which they enable the client to represent the external world in a flexible, accurate way. School staff and other professionals may assess these capacities through, for example, observations and formal assessments of intellectual ability and academic skills, as well as by direct interaction over time. It is worth remembering here that

attachments create the secure base needed for a child to feel sufficiently safe to explore his or her environment. Intellectual curiosity, learning of new skills, and openness to being "captured" by an interest are all forms of exploration that are easily observed in a therapeutic milieu.

- *Organizational capacities*: In this domain, which overlaps with emotional regulation, the focus is on the child's ability to put together increasingly complex sequences of behavior and sustain those sequences in the face of frustration, intruding feelings, and impulses and distractions from the environment. This domain of functioning is also related to what has been called "delay of gratification" and "impulse control." Information about organizational capacities is also gathered by observing the level and kind of supervision which the child or teen requires to sustain productive participation in the program. A disorganized child seems to be driven by momentary urges and needs, to be at the mercy of stimulation from the environment, to be easily overwhelmed by emotional states, to have difficulty putting together more complex chains of behavior in pursuit of more temporally distant goals, and to often need very high levels of adult proximity and supervision to stay engaged with peers in a play situation. Transitions of almost any kind are likely to be very difficult for the pervasively disorganized child.

- *Sense of self*: This important adaptive function is always working to integrate experience, attitudes, meanings, and emotions into a more or less coherent self which has some level of continuity over time. The sense of self is not something that develops in isolation; it is a profoundly social construction that arises from experience in relationships (Sroufe, 1995). Thus, a child's working model of relationships is in fact not simply a model of how others may act but also a model of myself-with-others. In the course of the assessment process, it is essentially impossible to make observations of a child' relatedness with others without also finding much useful information about her sense of self. Conversely, a description of the child's sense of self can illuminate her beliefs and expectations about the possibility of safe, gratifying connections with others. How does one know about another's sense of self, and how can it be described in a useful way? Older children may be in the process of constructing an explicit "story" of who they are, which will emerge in interaction with them. They may have a collection of statements such as "I'm a good student..." or "I'm just like my father..." or "I like to party..." or "It takes five staff to restrain me..." or "I'm going to the University of San Quentin...." Attending to such statements will often allow description of at least this one part-self that is active in certain settings or associated with certain feelings. In some adolescents these bit of data will be relatively consistent and on their way to becoming organized into a coherent identity; in others they will be varied and disparate and seem to be "rattling around" inside the teen as though competing for ascendancy. Other information can be developed from a child's important identifications, the peers she seeks to associate with and compare himself to, her position in the peer group, and direct inquiries about interests, abilities, and beliefs. It should be kept in mind that a child or a teen will very often not have a single coherent picture of who she is, what she is good at, what sorts of people she might want to have relationships with, and what sort of life experience she deserves or expects (Harter, Bresnick, Bouchey, and Whitsell, 1997). Instead, the sense of self is usually a complex structure that has public and private components, is under revision throughout development, and may change as a function of different social roles inhabited in the course of a single day (Siegel, 1999). Nonetheless, it is very helpful to consider questions about a child's story of who she is and who she is like, where she came from, beliefs about her own strengths and abilities, and the emotional tone that is associated with all these ideas. Certainly, extreme or very striking presentations of self-experience are important to note. These may include dissociative symptoms (representing a collapse of the integrative functions of the self) or strikingly inaccurate or defensive self-presentations such as an inflated, grandiose persona which protects the child from feelings of helplessness and vulnerability.

OTHER OBSERVATIONAL CATEGORIES

The domains which follow represent separate categories but also, inevitably, overlap with and relate to those discussed in the previous section. In a certain sense they represent slightly different windows on the same important functions and capacities.

- *Physical, somatic, and medical issues.* This category is important because working models of relationships and experiences of trauma often have a physical component (van der Kolk, 1994; Ogden and Minton, 2000). That is, they are embodied or find expression in physical symptoms, peculiar sensations, habitual posture, and the general way that the child inhabits the physical world. The concerns which are pursued here may include recurring medical complaints; development and intactness of age-appropriate fine and gross motor skills; observations of general physical functioning and activity level; diet, appetite, and relation to food; sleep and arousal; and physical sensitivities and response to touch.
- *Self-care and activities of daily living.* This category is concerned with the child's capacity to manage him- or herself and his or her immediate environment at an age-appropriate level, such as his or her hygiene, dressing, and care of personal space and possessions.

- *Play.* Observation of children engaged in play yields much valuable information regarding their important relationships and adaptive skills. Play activities that deserve attention may include cooperative play with peers, fantasy play, and play in formal games. Preferences for particular kinds of play or games, notable skills or competencies seen in play, the capacity to adhere to the rules and boundaries of play, and a description of any intrusive preoccupations or themes in fantasy play are of interest. If the child is being seen in individual psychotherapy, the clinician will have ongoing opportunities to observe themes in play, play inhibitions and disruptions, and the sorts of preoccupations just mentioned.
- *Functioning in the community.* If the child currently resides in the community, what is known of his or her capacity for independent functioning in that setting? Are there notable strengths or vulnerabilities present? Are there important risk factors present in the community to which the child is regularly exposed?

Finally, in carrying out any initial assessment clinicians and workers should keep the following ideas in mind:

1. *Salience.* Not all of these categories of data will be equally salient in every case. For one family, problems of hierarchy and effective parental authority will very quickly emerge as the most critical factor in the case and much of the data will relate to this issue. In another case, themes related to trauma and loss may "jump out" of the data, and the clinician's sense of the importance of this issue will then inform subsequent observations. Thus, while beliefs and experience indicate that certain domains of data are extremely helpful, this does not mean that work should be done in a purely linear fashion. Instead, certain problems, strengths, and themes are usually salient at the outset of work with a new client and must guide the pursuit of additional data.

2. *At the time of intake, never automatically accept a diagnosis or case formulation found in existing paperwork, prior evaluations, and reports or communications with past treating professionals.* Children and youth come to very intensive programs because they are failing in other settings. Given this fact, it is quite possible that ways of understanding the child and the family that were previously utilized may be incorrect or incomplete. The ways in which a client was viewed in prior settings is always of interest and worthy of consideration but should, as a matter of course, be re-evaluated.

3. *Beware of the pressures that may work to force a premature or incomplete initial evaluation.* These include requirements to develop plans and interventions very quickly (often prior to completion of an initial assessment) and the "noise" of other problems and crises. Falling into this trap results in generic treatment, that is, treatment that fails to recognize the details or specificity of the particular case.

While it may often be necessary to adopt a treatment plan which is in some sense provisional and based on initial review of presenting problems and behaviors, it is still a provisional plan and should be revised as new information is developed.

4. *Data developed from intake documents, initial interviews, and staff observations of behavior should be organized into a table of life events.* The first draft of the table should be completed by the time the treatment team first meets to share information and observations. This document is a chronological account of the child's life that should begin with the births of key caretakers and other adult figures in the life of the child. It should include important family events such as births, deaths, separations, moves, and transitions. Ideally, it will include a picture of the child's early caretaking environment, the resources and strengths present in that environment, as well as the risk factors and challenges that have been active. It should provide an initial sense of what factors have been associated with placement success and developmental progress and which factors have been associated with placement failure and delays or distortions of development. The table of life events is not simply an extra summary of historical data but, rather, a document that can be revised and added to as new data are obtained and new understanding is developed. It is an enormously valuable communication tool and, as such, should always be present at any meetings about a child, to keep workers focused on the real-life circumstances of the child and the family. During crises or other times when there is struggle about how to proceed, it is very useful to begin with a review of the table of life events.[1] This reconnects workers to the historical context in which the family began to encounter difficulties or the child began to present symptoms or other behavioral challenges. A genogram (McGoldrick and Gerson, 1985) can also be very helpful as a graphical representation of family relationships and history that conveys a great deal of information very efficiently. It should also be noted that as the team moves from assessment processes to discussion and planning, the table of critical life events and a genogram are enormously helpful tools for sharing information and ensuring that all team members are in possession of basic assessment information.

5. *A clinician undertaking an initial assessment must guard against the excessive influence of seemingly grave symptoms and high-risk behaviors.* Dramatic histories, replete with trauma and loss, and high-risk or very unusual behavior sometimes create a sense of urgency that becomes a barrier to authentic curiosity. While remaining alert to real danger the clinician must avoid rushing to do things simply for the sake of doing *something.*

6. *In interviewing parents and children, it is important to listen not only to what is told but also to how it is told.* The coherence of a client's narrative, the emotional tone of verbal expression, and the capacity to take the perspective of the listener are some of the qualitative factors that yield very useful assessment information. Thus, for example, when a parent talks about his own early relationships, he may

speak of painful events in a manner that is consistent and coherent. Another parent may speak of similar life circumstances in a way that is minimizing, vague, or very brief. These two different presentations may speak to very different responses to similar situations and point to different sorts of interventions. They may provide an alert to each parent's different vulnerabilities in creating a secure attachment for their own children.

Chapter Five

Relational Assessment and Intervention

Before an approach to assessment is articulated here, it is worth taking a moment to discuss some current trends in evaluation and diagnosis. In the course of carrying out an initial assessment of a high-risk, multi-problem child, a clinician or a treatment team is likely to receive a thick stack of documents that have been generated at each stop in the child's journey through multiple systems of care. This sometimes intimidating paper trail may include court reports, psychological assessments, educational assessments, individualized educational plans, letters from prior therapists, and discharge summaries from psychiatric hospitalizations. This material often contains enormously important data that can contribute significantly to assessment and treatment planning. It is of great importance, however, to read this material with a critical eye and to evaluate prior diagnoses and formulations with great care and thoughtfulness. This review should include a comparison of earlier views of the child's difficulties with his or her current presentation and response to staff and program structures in the new setting. To some degree, this process rests on the dictum "Consider the source." In other words, it is possible that accounts or descriptions of a child and his or her difficulties that come from settings in which he or she has failed may well be incomplete or fundamentally mistaken. The assessment process as a whole will be discussed in greater detail in this chapter.

It must also be acknowledged that in recent years the widespread use of pharmacological treatments for behavior disorders and the rise of managed care have led to what might best be described as a "medicalization" of assessment processes, a shift which has the result of focusing attention on immediately visible signs and symptoms and away from social context, family and developmental history and strengths, and protective factors. Many forces at work in contemporary culture have contributed to this shift, and a full review of their sources and interplay is beyond the scope of this book. Nevertheless, it is worth noting that, for many young clients with complex histories that involve the interaction of many of the risk factors discussed earlier, this sort of evaluation has not always been particularly helpful. Such evaluations are most often the final outcome of a psychiatric hospitalization and may carry great authority and weight in the young person's subsequent placement and treatment.

Stanton (unpublished manuscript, 2007) has written a critical comparison of the assumptions and practices of what he calls "relational" and "biomedical" assessment that captures many of the important issues that attend these developments in the field. His description of a relational model of diagnosis and assessment is similar to the approach described here. He has organized his review in tabular form for a point-by-point comparison. The comparative table follows his brief introduction.

UNDERLYING ASSUMPTIONS IN TWO DIAGNOSTIC MODELS

Table 5.1 describes two models. The column labeled "Relational" describes what is a useful way of understanding the children who come into intensive intervention programs. Workers in the field, however, reading assessments of such children regularly encounter the one labeled "biomedical." Both in and out of the medical establishment, this latter model enjoys great popularity.

The label "biomedical" is placed in quotation marks for a very important reason. It is to indicate that what is being described is a distortion of what one might term an authentic medical model. This "authentic" model utilizes all available information to create as complete a picture as possible of a patient's difficulties—whether it is a specific disease or a set of inexplicable symptoms. In addition to physical examinations and laboratory results, it includes a history of the symptoms *in the context* of environmental and relational factors in a patient's life. An example of such an "authentic" model is described in Dean Ornish's book *Love and Survival* (Ornish, 1998). He marshals many scientific studies that affirm the overwhelming importance of intimacy and relationship to heart disease. Most people remain ignorant of this information since the larger culture is primed to report the latest research on biological factors.

Undoubtedly, many psychiatrists and other mental health professionals would complain that the "biomedical" approach described here is a caricature and that ethical practitioners would never adhere to the narrow point of view described. They would say that their evaluations are "bio-psycho-social," indicating that they fully appreciate the social contexts of people's lives. Unfortunately, the description of the "biomedical" model accurately captures important assumptions and goals of many evaluations that are completed on highly vulnerable children. In fact, this model underlies the belief systems that "drive" many of the decisions that are currently made in the mental health field, particularly when schools, parents, and agencies are faced with children suffering from serious behavioral difficulties. As described in Table 5.1, these evaluations are predominantly focused on symptoms as clues to underlying genetically driven biochemical disorders. Once the child is diagnosed, proper treatment with psychotropic medication can be instituted to alleviate the suffering caused by the disorder.

This process is particularly salient in situations in which a system of care is feeling stressed and the behavior or thinking of the child is experienced as "out of control." At that point the assumptions described in Table 5.1 often become

Table 5.1 Assumptions in the Process of Evaluation: Two Diagnostic Models

Relational Model	Biomedical Model
Interpersonal processes in evaluation	
Evaluation involves active engagement with the child and the child's caretakers. This engagement clarifies patterns of relatedness. It is also the beginning of treatment.	Engagement is not stressed as part of a biomedical evaluation. Evaluations in offices can take place within 15–30 minutes and are focused on signs and symptoms.
In evaluating responses to treatment, all social and relational factors in the child's life are taken into consideration.	In evaluating responses to treatment, medication is seen as the primary factor creating change, superceding social and relational factors in the child's life.
Countertransference—the feeling reactions of the clinician to the child and family—are considered extremely valuable.	Countertransference is rarely utilized as a useful part of evaluation.
Role of symptoms	
Symptoms are driven by psychological forces. They have meaning in the context of the child's current and past relationships.	Symptoms help to identify specific brain disorders and possible genetic determinations.
Symptoms that appear early in life often reflect distorted relationships. The earlier the distortions, the more profound their impact on later functioning.	Symptoms that appear early in life are precursors of serious biological mental illness and need to be treated biologically. ADHD can progress to bipolar disorder.
Symptoms are expressions of "working models" of relationships.	Symptoms originate independently of relationships.
Evaluation of symptoms includes an assessment of current risks and strengths in relationships. It assumes that the character of current and past relationships is the pivotal factor in the child's functioning.	Checklists of symptoms are useful in that they give objective quantification of the child's behavior.

(Continued)

Table 5.1 (Continued)

Relational Model	Biomedical Model
Role of history	
History of context of symptoms is critical including, above all, interpersonal factors.	History of symptoms and their severity is important. Context is secondary.
History leads to a story.	The story is biological.
History of child's actual development and attachments is felt to be critical.	History of diagnoses within immediate and extended family is important to discover genetic patterns for the client's problem.
Distortion in earliest relationships is correlated with more serious difficulties later on. Attachment is critical.	Earlier relationships are often not explored or considered important. The concept of attachment is often unknown.
Actual life experiences are considered of great significance—particularly those that involved relationship and competency in the larger social world.	Most case histories written in the biomedical literature focus on how symptoms are present due to a hypothetical underlying disorder.
Goals of treatment	
Discovery of meaning of symptoms—symptoms seen as clues.	Control or "suppression" of child's symptoms—relief of suffering.
Greater awareness of feeling states and their contexts.	Reduction of feeling in order to minimize symptoms.
Enhancement of child's and family's curiosity concerning their own life experiences.	Since symptoms are a reflection of an underlying disease, curiosity about life circumstances is unnecessary.
Creation of safety in living circumstances.	Issues of safety are often not explored.
Change of life circumstances if necessary.	Help child to fit into current life situations (often unknown) with fewer symptoms.
Empowerment of child and family.	Control aberrant brain function. Locus of control is outside the child and family.
Discovery of unique capacities that heighten self-worth.	Concept of self-worth is not stressed.
Relatedness to people—engagement with caretakers and the larger community.	Relatedness to substances—medication compliance has overriding importance.

ADHD, attention-deficit/hyperactivity disorder.
From T. Stanton, MD, unpublished manuscript, 2007.

paramount. They are, however, usually not acknowledged. There is no need for such acknowledgment since they are ubiquitous in most professional circles and have been repeated over and over in mainstream journals. These assumptions have also become endemic to the culture. They are now the most widely accepted explanation for children's behavioral difficulties.

A relational model is based on different assumptions: By identifying historical patterns of relatedness and the stability of current placements (including relationships with caretakers), the treatment team will discover the most useful information regarding a child's strengths and vulnerabilities. Such a model is also consistent with the experience of many clinicians, in many settings over many years, that current relationships, not medications, create the most powerful forces for change in a child's life.

ASSESSMENT AND DESCRIPTION OF THE INTERNAL WORKING MODEL

For the purposes of treatment planning it is of particular importance to arrive at a description of the child's internal working model of relationships. As with arriving at a diagnosis or completing a functional analysis of problem behaviors, developing this description of the child's habitual interpersonal stance is not equal to completing a thorough initial evaluation. Rather, it is one of several critical elements in that initial evaluation.

First, though, an organizational note: How is such an assessment carried out, and who is responsible for completing it? For the purposes of this discussion, it is assumed that the assessment process is led by a clinician who, in addition to delivering direct service, is functioning as a clinical informant to the team that is working the child and family. The clinician is assumed to have two important domains of firsthand data: observations from direct interactions with the child, and observations from direct interactions with the family. The clinician is also assumed to be responsible for organizing what can be a very large body of secondhand data: the historical record of the child's interpersonal behavior found in documentation of prior placements, interventions, and evaluations. The direct care staff is responsible for providing firsthand observations from their own interactions with the child and family.

Clinicians working in outpatient or community- based settings may not have the advantage of a team of direct care workers who can provide rich data from their day- to- day interactions with the client and the family. Instead, they are in the position of needing to cultivate a less formal collaborative team of informants made up of key figures from the life of the child. These may include teachers, probation officers, members of the client's extended family, coaches, and any other adults who are in regular contact with the child. Consent for contact with these informants is, of course, required; and the clinician must keep in mind that each of these adults may view the child from a particular perspective based on his or her own culture, life experience, personality, and role in the life of the child. Ultimately, the clinician will need to weave together these data with his or her own views and experience with the child and the family.

What does a description of the child's internal working model yield? What sorts of information should it provide to the team as they begin to plan intervention? A thoughtful account of the child's interpersonal stance should provide answers to questions of this sort:

- What question or questions could the child's behavior be seen as asking of adults?
- What themes are present in the child's interactions with adults?
- What does the child seem to anticipate in the way of treatment from adults?
- Does the child seem to have consistent responses to adult caretaking?
- Does the child's behavior seem to invite any particular response(s) from the adults?
- Does the child show any consistent "interpretive bias" in his or her view of the behavior of others?

While these questions have typically been addressed directly or indirectly in the course of any good evaluation process, they take on special importance in settings where there is an explicit effort to attend to and make use of relationship as a key ingredient in intervention. It is important to regularly recall that clients (and this includes adults and children) may be directing a variety of invitations at those who work to engage them, and which, if accepted, would likely repeat and confirm the effects of important adverse or hurtful experiences in earlier relationships. Relationship-based treatment is about finding effective ways to decline these invitations and to disconfirm the implicit beliefs that they reflect.

Prior to developing useful strategies for arriving at a description of a client's working model, the following observations can be made about working models and interpersonal behavior and what constitutes useful information about them:

- Working models arise from real experience in relationships with caretakers. Therefore, as one comes to know a client, it is likely that continuities between the working model and his or her history should emerge in a more or less comprehensible fashion. It is sometimes the case, however, that important information about a child's early caretaking is not known and only slowly comes to light. It is also the case, as discussed later, that a client's working model can be a complex and layered construction that may not be understood fully for some time. For these reasons, continuities between actual experience and the working model may not emerge immediately.

- Working models are also working models of the self (Bowlby, 1980, p. 203). Recall that a working model represents relationships and, as such, also represents the self in those relationships. If experience in relationships has been largely benign and gratifying, then it is likely that the working model will represent the self in a positive way and as deserving of good treatment. If there has been significant deprivation or maltreatment, then it is likely that this experience will be represented in the working model and the self will be seen as somehow damaged, bad, and undeserving of kindness and gratification.

- Generally, individuals do not present with a single, pervasive interpersonal stance that is easily and immediately seen in all interactions. (Such a presentation would, in fact, likely be a reflection of a highly pathological sort of rigidity.) Instead, there may be a more or less dominant orientation toward others that observers will generally agree on but which demonstrates some degree of variability.

- This means that it is also useful to try to track how a client's interpersonal behavior shifts and varies as a function of the situation, interaction, or behavior of the other. This is very much akin to the concept of the functional analysis in behavior modification. In other words, the settings and conditions (generally people or interactions of particular content or emotional tone) that elicit or trigger particular kinds of interpersonal behavior from the client are of particular interest.

- Thus, working models are not always simple, unitary representations of experience, but sometimes layered, complex constructions that may include elements that can serve protective functions for the child by shielding him from painful emotions. Some individuals seem to have an "excluded" working model, which is activated under particular conditions. Thus, children who have been victimized by their parents but then must live in a family in which this abuse is persistently denied, often need to desperately maintain an image of their parents as good. Some of these children seem to have a working model based on the implicit belief that, "Nothing happened, everything is fine." Bowlby (1980, p. 64) describes this process as "defensive exclusion" and notes that it is related to a variety of later difficulties.

In striving to arrive at a description of the child's internal working model, the clinician utilizes two broad domains of data. The first involves the child's actual experience with her caretakers and the second involves the current interpersonal behavior that one can observe in the setting in which service is being provided. Attention to the child's actual experience with caretakers is critical because it is assumed that the internal working model, which is now guiding interpersonal behavior, is a fairly direct representation of the child's real experience of caretaker availability and attunement. As Bowlby (1973,) notes, ". . . the varied expectations of the accessibility and responsiveness of attachment figures that individuals develop during the years of immaturity are tolerably accurate reflections of the experiences those individuals actually had" (p. 202). Despite this fundamental assumption of attachment theory, it is certainly the case that, in actual practice, clinicians are sometimes in the interesting position of receiving a packet of intake information that includes some compelling and detailed descriptions of the child's experience with caretakers, which would lead them to expect a child whose interpersonal behavior will be concentrated in a very particular range. The child who ultimately arrives, however, presents behavior in a very different range. Inevitably, this turns out to be a problem with the data contained in the documents and not with theory. That is, new data will eventually emerge that show the intake material is inadequate, skewed, or too general. Over time, the continuity between early experience with caretakers and current working models is almost always confirmed.

In some cases, clinicians will be working with children who are currently still in the care of parents or other long-term caretakers. In other cases, the clinician may begin treatment at the point when the child is newly placed in a residential facility, in a foster home, or with a relative. Some of these clients may not have been in the care of their parents for many years. In either case, the focus of inquiry can be thought of as the child's history of caretaking relationships. Thus, the team is hoping to develop information about key dimensions of caretaking as they played out in the earliest years of development as well as in current relationships with parents or substitute caretakers.

The second broad domain of data, the child's current interpersonal behavior observed in the treatment setting or treatment relationship, and referred to as "the child's response to the default offer of relationship," is directly observed by all team members working with the client. In this domain, themes or recurring interpersonal scenarios are observed from which implicit beliefs, expectancies, and other elements in the working model can be inferred. Following is a description of useful dimensions or observational categories to be employed by staff in making these observations.

Within the assessment process, what is the relationship between data derived from these two domains? Sometimes data from one domain come well before data from the other. Clinicians working in residential settings, for example, often receive volumes of data on the child's actual caretaking experiences before even beginning to observe his or her actual interpersonal exchanges in the program. Conversely, in day treatment services or other out-patient interventions, little historical material may be provided and clinicians may need to work for months to secure the active participation of the parents in the treatment process. In this situation there are many opportunities to develop a very clear picture of regularities in a child's interpersonal behavior long before there is any opportunity to learn much detail of his actual experience with caretakers. In any case, though, there is a moving back and forth between the two sources of data as hypotheses are developed about the child's working model of relationships. "Moving back and forth" means, for example, that the presence of a particular trend in the historical data, concerning the regular experience of harsh, abusive physical discipline, may lead the clinician to look for certain kinds of traumatic repetitions in the behavior of the child. Regularly finding physical intimidation and assaultiveness in the interpersonal behavior of the child could similarly be an alert to the possibility of persistent exposure to physical abuse or domestic violence in the child's encounters with caretakers. This description of the synthetic interplay between the two domains of data is entirely consistent with the earlier assertion that assessment processes must be *configural.* To restate that concept briefly, bits of data in the assessment process are never determinative in and of themselves, but derive their meaning from their position in relation to other bits of data from other sources and modes of observation.

THE CHILD'S EXPERIENCE WITH CARETAKERS

Knowledge of the child's experiences with caretakers is gained from the following sources:

- Direct observation of interactions between child and caretaker
- Statements by the caretaker
- Statements by the child
- Documents from various sources (courts, other agencies or treating professionals), which may include descriptions of interactions or patterns of interaction between the child and the caretaker
- A sense of the "adult state of mind with respect to attachment" (Hesse, 2008) presented by the parent during interviews

There are a great many possible "presentations" that may emerge in this initial data- gathering process. These data may suggest many important areas of interest, all of which would be helpful to us in generating hypotheses about the child's internal working model. The data, however, do not automatically yield these initial guesses about the child's view of important relationships and the inter-personal world but, instead, must be evaluated in terms of several key dimensions of caretaking capacity. While these qualities of the caregiving relationship are expressed in vocabulary that is found in attachment theory and research, they are generally consistent with concepts from work in developmental psychology and family therapy and research. These dimensions are as follows:

- Availability
- Attunement or contingent responsiveness
- Engagement

- Regulatory functions
- Tolerance of and support for exploration/autonomy
- Reflective functions
- Traumatic factors
- Projective processes directed at the child by the parent
- Boundary functioning
- Hierarchy

Note that these categories are conceptually distinct but, in practice, they are correlated and may overlap significantly. Problems with boundaries are, for example, likely to be found in client histories in which there has been significant abuse. Similarly there is, by definition, a lack of caretaker availability in situations in which neglect has occurred.

How the team thinks about a family with these dimensions in mind will be partly a function of the type of data that emerges and a sense of its reliability and significance. Thus, for example, a single observation of a moment of parental unavailability will not be as compelling as multiple reports of a sustained pattern of parental unavailability resulting from chronic, severe substance abuse. At the same time, one of these dimensions of caretaking capacity may be much more salient in a family than others. In families who are referred for intensive services through the child protection system, it is often the case that traumatic factors will be strikingly evident and may be the critical data in understanding the child's working model of relationships. It is important to keep in mind, though, as noted elsewhere, that historical accounts found in the various documents that may arrive at the start of treatment are not necessarily factually correct or relevant. In adhering to a configural approach to assessment, hypotheses generated by different domains of data can be compared and their relative usefulness and predictive power can be assessed.

In those cases in which the child has not been in the care of the parents for some years and has had a series of caretakers before entering treatment, the clinician must make an effort to reconstruct the child's experience in any and all of these caretaking environments. The question becomes, "What has the child's experience of each of these dimensions been with caretakers *throughout her development?*" Obviously, data that are reconstructed are not as reliable as data derived from direct observation.

In the rest of this section, an effort is made to define these dimensions of caretaking more concretely. For each dimension some orienting questions, possible data points, or relevant risk factors related to the particular parental skill or capacity that is being discussed are listed. These lists are by no means exhaustive; instead, they are simply an effort to note some of the obstacles that are often encountered in practice that can disrupt the best efforts of parents to nurture and sustain their children. Note also that there are some issues that can always constitute barriers to or disruptions of "good enough" caretaking. These include extreme poverty and homelessness, physical and sexual abuse, and clinical depression in the caretaker. Ultimately, though, the quality of caretaking and the detail of the repeated exchanges between parent and child that constitute the content of their relationship will be strongly determined by the *internal working model of the caretaker.*

Availability

Here, attention is directed at the parent's physical and emotional availability to the child in response to his or her proximity seeking. To be *available*, the parent must be physically present enough of the time and with enough consistency that he or she can respond to the child's distress or needs (Bowlby, 1973). *Emotional presence* means that the parent is psychologically mature enough and relatively free of psychological distress so that he or she is able to suspend his or her own needs, apprehend the child's distress or needs, and respond in a more or less timely fashion. The clinician, then, might be looking at the data with these sorts of questions in mind:

- Are there any life circumstances that currently disrupt or that have historically caused significant disruption in the caretaker's availability to the child? These could include substance abuse, incarceration, health problems, abandonment, or military deployment.
- Does the caretaker notice and recognize proximity seeking by the child?
- Does the caretaker recognize the need driving the proximity seeking as valid?
- Does the caretaker make an effort to respond to the proximity seeking?

Some variants the clinician could see might include the following:

- Rejecting of proximity seeking
- Dismissive of proximity seeking
- Overavailability (trying to amplify the child's need), appears to need the child to be needy
- Intrusively available
- Available only in response to particular states or forms of proximity seeking
- Clearly dislikes "neediness" or views proximity seeking as a manipulation or a calculation of some kind
- Unpredictably available
- Caretaker reliably available given the family circumstances

Attunement or Contingent Responsiveness

Here, the clinician is focused on the parent's capacity to respond to proximity seeking and displays of emotion with a response that is actually correlated with the child's particular affective state. This requires an accurate reading of the child's state as well as a capacity to then generate a response that is emotionally connected with what the child is experiencing. (Stern [1985] has described the complex nature and effects of attunement during infancy.) A parent can be available (present and able to respond) but poorly attuned (misreading the child's state or showing a discontinuous emotional response). For example, a parent who responds to a child's anxious proximity seeking (perhaps the child is holding back and trying to cling to the mother's hand) on the first day of kindergarten with derisive teasing about being "such a baby" is showing poor attunement. Barriers to attunement often include personality traits in the parent that arise from rigid, skewed working models that create interpretive biases (viewing proximity seeking as a sign of excessive dependence) that disrupt open, accurate "reading" of the child's emotional state. Similarly, such rigid, skewed parental working models may also limit the parent's interpersonal behavior in such a way that the "good enough" response simply is not available to him or her. Possible presentations in this dimension include the following:

- The caretaker has difficulty accurately reading the emotion or need underlying some of the child's approaches.
- The caretaker has a limited range of emotional expression available for responding in a reflective, attuned fashion to the state presented by the child.
- The caretaker tends to read diverse approaches from the child in terms of a single emotional state; for example, the caretaker views most proximity seeking as related to fearfulness or anxiety, hunger, or fatigue.
- The caretaker's responses to the child suggest that she is correct often enough in reading the emotional state of the child and in responding accordingly. There is a quality of emotional resonance between caretaker and child.
- When inevitable misattunements occur, the parent displays a readiness and a capacity to reconnect with the child and engage in interactive repair.

Engagement

Here, the quality and emotional tone of the parent's interest and pleasure in and availability to the child at all times (not only in response to proximity seeking) is the team's focus. It is important to observe the parent's capacity to demonstrate rewarding pleasure and interest in the child's activities, accomplishments, and verbalizations. Engagement can be seen in delight, attentiveness, playfulness, and a readiness to participate in his or her activities, interests, concerns, and play. Barriers to engagement can include parental depression, substance abuse, and difficult work schedules. Some possible data points include the following:

- Engagement is strongly negative in some way; many interactions are conflictual or characterized by the presence of strong negative affect.
- Engagement is weak: There seems to be a diminished connection to the child; the caretaker is often unaware of the child's whereabouts or state.
- Engagement is excessive: The caretaker maintains an intrusive interest in the child's thoughts, emotional states, and activities.
- Engagement is largely positive: The caretaker shows a generally positive interest in the child's pursuits and can actively participate with the child about and in his activities and ideas. The general stance is pleasurable interest.

Regulatory Functions

Here, the focus is on the capacity of the caretaker to actively assist the child in returning to equilibrium from a state of distress or disorganization. Over the course of development this capacity in the caretaker will translate into a progressively increasing capacity for self-regulation in the child (Cassidy, 1994). These regulating interactions can include subtle affective exchanges with infants in which the caretaker reflects the child's emotional state back to the child and may be easily recognized as soothing. In older children this can include more complex interactions that begin to look like limit setting. A mother who becomes helpless and overwhelmed when a toddler becomes overstimulated, excited, and ultimately disorganized needs help understanding her importance as a regulating figure in the child's functioning and needs assistance in precisely what sort of stance will be most helpful to the child. A father who becomes furious and shut down when a school-age child is frantic over a lost toy also needs help thinking about what might work better and what he has done at other times that undoubtedly did work better. Barriers to successful emotional regulation can vary with the stage of development of the child but can include inexperience, parental personality traits, and trauma history. For example, very young, inexperienced parents of infants and toddlers who have little extended family support may need guidance with knowing when and how to respond to their children's states of distress, frustration, excitement, and so forth. Parents of older children may be inhibited in actively containing a tantrum because of their fears of their own anger. Some orienting questions include the following:

- Can the caretaker recognize those moments of emotional distress that call for an intervention to soothe, support, or contain the child?
- Does the caretaker demonstrate a reasonably wide range of emotional expressions? Are there any kinds of emotional expression with which the caretaker is very uncomfortable?
- When the caretaker does intervene, are his or her efforts clear and confident or tentative and cautious? Does the caretaker seem

intimidated or in any way uneasy with the task of handling the child in a state of distress? Does the parent persist in the face of resistance?

- Are the caretaker's efforts successful? Is the child's emotional state effectively downregulated, is there no change, or do the caretaker's efforts seem to escalate the child?
- Is the child somehow responsible for regulating the caretaker's states?

Hierarchy

Here, a set of caretaker capacities that are closely related to regulatory function are of interest. Instead of the regulation of emotional states, though, the concern is with the regulation of behavior. Such functions are sometimes referred to as "limit setting," "containment," or "behavior management." The term "hierarchy" is widely used in the family therapy literature to refer to the effectiveness of parents as authority figures (e.g., Walsh, 2002). In very general terms, the focus of this dimension is the parent's capacity to simply be in charge by setting expectations and rules, praising compliance, and disciplining noncompliance. Under this general heading are a great many exchanges between caretaker and child in which the caretaker tries to interrupt behavior seen as unsafe or negative and seeks to teach or amplify behaviors that are desired. Many factors will influence this part of the relationship between caretaker and child: the caretaker's own history with behavior regulation as a child, expectations and beliefs about the child's capacities at different stages of development, and the caretaker's own comfort with being an authority figure. Relevant orienting questions for this dimension include the following:

- Are there reasonably well-understood and reasonable standards of behavior that are communicated consistently?
- Is the caretaker sufficiently engaged with the child to be aware of the child's activities and compliance with the standards?
- Is there any significant antisocial activity occurring in the household that the child would reasonably be aware of? Or is there implicit or explicit permission conveyed to the child for antisocial activity?
- What is the balance between negative consequences and positive attention and rewards for compliance and generally good behavior?
- Is there a pattern of harsh, punitive, or abusive responding to negative behavior?
- Is there any significant inhibition on the part of the caretaker in setting limits on the child's behavior? These can include fears of one's own anger, worries about loss of relationship with the child, and fears of being depriving.

Tolerance of and Support for Autonomy

Here, the team looks for the flip side of the parent's response to proximity-seeking behavior. Recall that in attachment theory, in addition to the attachment behavioral system, there is a complementary behavioral system that supports or drives exploration of the environment. In the absence of threats to safety and when the child has a secure or confident sense of the availability of the caretaker, the exploratory behavioral system is activated and the child can move away from the caretaker and investigate and learn about the environment (Bowlby, 1969, 1988). Parents support exploration of the environment first by providing security in the form of reliable, attuned availability. By doing so, they make possible the development in the child of a "secure base" or an internalized feeling of confidence and safety. Additionally, though, they may support exploration through direct encouragement of actual exploration of the environment and through their interest and pleasure in the child's learning and developmental achievements, pursuits and projects, and proud displays of independence. Parents who rely on the child to meet their own emotional needs may have great difficulty supporting exploration and the independence it can bring. Data points of interest include the following:

- Does the caretaker notice the child's movement away and remain alert to situations that might be unsafe?
- Does the caretaker permit exploration?
- Does the caretaker maintain a flexible balance of intervening, teaching, and cautioning with encouragement, delight, and interest?
- Does the caretaker allow the child to "own" his or her discoveries or try to take over the discovery and make it at least partly his own?
- Does the caretaker, given the available resources, make an effort to provide a reasonably stimulating environment or exploration/learning opportunities for the child?
- Does the parent have any beliefs, fears, or other concerns that lead him or her to inhibit exploration and learning?
- Does the environment in which the family resides contain significant risks from which the child should be consistently shielded or protected?

Mentalization and Reflective Function

The capacities described by these terms have been the subject of considerable attention among attachment researchers in recent years. The concept of "mentalization" was first introduced by Fonagy and his colleagues (Fonagy and Target, 1997; Fonagy et al., 2002) and refers to the capacity to view others (and oneself) as intentional beings whose actions can be understood in terms of mental states such as wishes, motives, feelings, and goals. In the current context, it is the capacity of a parent to view a child (and her- or himself in relation to the child) in this way that is of interest. This ability allows a person to interpret and make predictions about the behavior of others by imagining or attributing the mental states that could be thought to cause such behavior (Gergely and Unoka, 2008). Thus, Allen, Fonagy, and Bateman (2008) define *mentalization* or *reflective function* as "attending to mental states in self and others and interpreting behavior accordingly" and distinguish it from the overlapping concept of "psychological mindedness," which is seen as a disposition to engage in mentalization (p. 41). When a child encounters this capacity in a caretaker, it enables him or her to then "see himself" in the mind of the parent as a complex being whose acts arise from wishes, beliefs, and feelings—mental states—and not only from immediate physical experience. Slade (2008), commenting on the developmental possibilities created by the mentalizing parent, writes as follows:

> *A mother's capacity to hold in her own mind a* representation *of her child as having feelings, desires, and intentions* allows the child to discover his own internal experience via his mother's re-presentation of it. *A mother's capacity to make meaning of the child's experience will make him meaningful to himself, and allow her to go beyond what is apparent, beyond the concrete, and to instead make sense of the child's behavior in light of mental states, of underlying, likely unobservable, changing, dynamic intentions, and emotion. This helps the child to begin to symbolize, contain, and regulate his internal experience, and to develop coherent and organized representations of self and other. This also helps the parent regulate her own internal experience* as well as her behavior. (p. 314)

In the absence of such a capacity, the parent may be unable to make *any* real attributions about the child's behavior and instead simply describe behavior in concrete terms: "He went off, completely off, and wrecked his room!" Alternatively, the parent may rely on fixed personality descriptions which stop short of an attribution based on thinking about possible internal states or emotions: "He's a lot like his father, stubborn, and he doesn't like it when he doesn't get his way." It is worth noting, in the quote immediately above from Slade (2008), her italics on the final phrase "*as well as her behavior.*" Thus, if restricted to "nonmentalizing" explanations that rely on such concrete, fixed theories about a child's behavior, the parent is much less likely to respond to this behavior and the states that underlie it in a flexible, attuned fashion.

In the course of completing a relational assessment, how is the clinician able to gauge the quality of parental reflective function? First, by attending to the parent's discourse about the child:

- In speaking of the child's behavior, does the parent or caretaker show a capacity for curiosity about the mental states that underlie the behavior?
- If an explanation for the child's behavior is offered that refers to possible underlying mental states, can the parent entertain or play with that theory?

- Are there regularly repeated, nonmentalizing attributions offered in response to the child's behavior? For example, "He's a bad boy." "He's just that way." "He's just like his father."
- In speaking of her own reactions to the child and her behavior, does the caretaker refer to her own beliefs, feelings, hopes, wishes, etc.?
- Does the caretaker use mental state vocabulary, referring to feelings, intentions, and beliefs?
- When she anticipates the child's behavior in response to a particular event or challenge, can the caretaker make reference to likely, hypothetical mental states that might drive that response?

Second, and somewhat more difficult, are the data that can be derived from either the caretaker's accounts of specific exchanges and interactions with the child or direct observation of these exchanges and interactions:

- In handling or responding to the child's behavior, does the parent's response refer to the mental states he might believe are driving the behavior?
- If there is no explicit reference to these states made in the response, can he, if asked immediately following the exchange to explain the response, refer to possible underlying mental states that he believes are associated with the behavior?

Traumatic Factors

Here, the team's attention is on hurtful events or patterns of relational trauma that result in significant disturbances in both functioning and the capacity for successful relatedness. These issues have already been addressed in the description of the population served in many intensive programs. The effects of childhood trauma on nearly all areas of development are well documented (van der Kolk, 2005; Nader, 2008) Similarly, the discussion of the disorganized attachment style and its relation to an experience of the caretaker as "frightened or frightening" (Main and Hesse, 1990) illustrates one specific mechanism by which traumatic experience in the caretaking relationship profoundly influences the child's working model of attachment. The range of hurtful experiences that may result in psychological injury or the derailing of development is very large. In the course of working with multiple clients with varied and complex histories of trauma, there is a tendency for workers to become numbed and to begin to generalize and equate these histories. This is an effect to be resisted; it is important to investigate the details of traumatic experience with care and precision. When (and sometimes this takes a very long time and is often never satisfactorily completed) a reasonably full picture of the child's (and, often, the parent's) traumatic experience is developed, one can more clearly understand some of the most troubling and difficult aspects of the behavior.

There are many things we want to know about when we are aware of a history (or continuing presence) of trauma in the family or the life of the child. Some key issues include the following:

- Trauma in the history of the caretaker:
  - What are the details of the traumatic events (or pattern of events)—age, nature of the trauma, length of exposure, etc.?
  - Did the trauma come from a caretaker or other attachment figure?
  - Was there support for disclosure or for the victim's version of events?
  - Did the victim receive any form of treatment or have other, less formal opportunities for integration of the traumatic events?

- Trauma in the child's life:
  - What are the details of the traumatic events (or pattern of events)—age, nature of the trauma, length of exposure, etc.?
  - Did the trauma come from the caretaker or other attachment figure?
  - Did the trauma involve threat or injury to an attachment figure?
  - What was the pretraumatic attachment environment like for the child?
  - Was there support for disclosure or for the victim's version of the events?
  - Have attachment figures acknowledged/recognized the occurrence and the meaning of the trauma for the child?

Was there a significant pattern in which an attachment figure failed to provide protection or safety? This domain of the child's experience is included in the category of traumatic factors for obvious reasons. Many traumatized children have experienced injury, neglect, or abuse as a result of what appears to be a failure on the part of one or more caretakers to provide reasonable care, safety, and protection. In this domain the focus is not on the caretaker as an active agent of hurtful experience but on the different situations in which the caretaker failed or was unable to provide protection or a reasonable sense of safety. The causes and contexts of these events are always complex. In some cases, the failure to protect seems to be part of a sustained pattern of neglect and disengagement; in other cases, the caretaker is herself a fellow victim with the child; and in still others, the failure appears to involve a reenactment of the parent's own early trauma. Each of these possible scenarios relates to questions worth pursuing in this domain:

- Was the failure to protect related in any way to trauma history in the parent?
- Was the parent also (concurrently with the child) a victim of abuse or violence?

- Was there a sustained pattern of failure to protect that reached across multiple domains of caretaking?
- Can the parent, in speaking of the hurtful events, acknowledge the failure to protect? Can the parent speak with the child in a way that is appropriate to the child's age and developmental level?

Projective Processes Directed at the Child

Here, interest lies in any ways in which the caretaker inaccurately attributes a variety of traits, wishes, or impulses to the child. The attributions that are of greatest clinical concern are those which are strongly negative and which have the potential to profoundly skew the developing child's sense of self. When the word "projection" is used, it usually implies that these attributed characteristics are warded off aspects of the parent's own personality. While it is important to reference this specifically psychodynamic meaning of the term, attention should be called to *any* ways in which the parent persistently misreads the states, intentions, wishes, or personality of the child. Lieberman (1997, 1999) and Silverman and Lieberman (1999) have described the workings and consequences of these attributional processes in detail. They point out, for example, the ways in which such attributions can influence caretaking behavior by directing attention to particular behaviors and affective states and by markedly skewing the caretaker's interpretations of the child's behavior. These projections can also intrude into the caretaker's exchanges with the child in ways that pressure him or her to then enact the projection. Leiberman (1999, pp. 744–745) describes the projections of aggression and violence toward male children observed in mothers with histories of relationships with battering partners. These mothers address their sons with aggressive epithets ("monster," "devil") and then subtly and unconsciously provoke them to actual aggression.

When these attributions are intensely felt, are rigidly held, and have striking or peculiar content, they may emerge in the very first contact with the caretaker. In some cases, though, it may be necessary to engage the caretaker in a collaborative treatment relationship in which she can more gradually share her image of her child. While the inaccurate or distorted elements of this image may be aspects of the parent's own personality that are unacknowledged, they can also reflect the effects of unintegrated traumatic experiences or unresolved relational difficulties from the caretaker's own childhood. The clinician alert to information relevant to this dimension can think in terms of the following questions and issues:

- Is the caretaker making any grossly exaggerated or inaccurate attributions about the child? In this domain there is some range of intensity. That is, there will be some caretaker attributions or beliefs about the child that are not so strongly held and may be understandable in terms of exaggerated perceptions of the child's real temperament. In other, more concerning cases, the attributions will be held with great intensity and will seem strikingly inaccurate or peculiar and of enormous personal importance to the caretaker.

- Does the caretaker make any attributions about the child that feel inaccurate, peculiar, or connected in some way to events or figures in the caretaker's own life?
- Can the caretaker reflect on these attributions and entertain the possibility of alternate views?

Generally, the content of these attributions may involve any of the basic human needs or urges. Thus, they may include beliefs about the child's capacity for aggression, sexuality, capacity for strategic manipulation of others, and need for emotional support.

Boundary Functioning

Here, the concern is with the parents' capacity to create and sustain flexible, appropriate boundaries within and around the family. As with hierarchy, boundaries have been a focus of interest of family therapists, particularly structural family therapists, since the work of Minuchin (1977; see also Walsh, 2002). This observational category very clearly overlaps with some that have already been considered. Maltreatment, particularly sexual abuse, represents a massive boundary violation. Similarly, families with very rigid, impermeable boundaries with the world outside the family have difficulty supporting exploration and autonomy. Some of the particular qualities of boundaries which need attention are as follows:

- Presence/absence
- Stability
- Permeability
- Rigidity/flexibility
- Consensus about the boundaries in the family.

The way in which parental capacities in each of these areas is evaluated will be greatly determined by the sort of program in which the family is encountered for the first time. Children placed residentially very often arrive with volumes of documentation that allow the construction of a chronological narrative of the family's journey through the system. This narrative may yield a variety of useful clues about the child's actual experience in early relationships with caretakers. A child seen on an outpatient basis in a public school is likely to have little documentation, and the parents may lack the resources of time and transportation and may have little interest in collaborating in the treatment. Therefore, data can come from various sources and, in some programs, there may be a great deal of evidence of one kind (say, documentary) and very little of another kind (say, direct observation of parent–child interactions). Utilizing the best data available and weighting it according to a sense of its accuracy will allow gradual construction of a picture of the child's experience in key relationships. This picture will, in some ways, always remain preliminary and be subject to revision as new observations are made and new data collected. The next task in arriving at a description of the child's internal working model of relationships involves directly observing the child's current interpersonal behavior or, as it has been referred to elsewhere, "response to the offer of relationship."

THE CHILD'S CURRENT INTERPERSONAL BEHAVIOR

In constructing a description of the child's internal working model of relationships, it is not necessary to be limited to narrowly defined observations of behavior that the child directs at others. Data may also be derived from the behavioral and psychological outcomes of the child's history of interactions with caregivers. The discussion of attachment theory has shown that effective, emotionally attuned caretaking results in more than simple reassurance or the provision of safety; it also drives development in areas such as emotional regulation and the sense of self.

Important dimensions of current functioning are as follows:

- Organization of behavior and self-regulation
- Proximity seeking and pursuit of relationship
- Exploratory capacity
- Sense of self
- Boundary functions
- Affective expression (range, intensity, and modulation)
- Emotions evoked in staff
- Themes of current relationships, including the presence of significant aggressive or sexual behavior

As with the observational categories that relate to the child's experience with caregivers, it can again be seen that these dimensions of functioning will yield overlapping and sometimes redundant information. Also, it is again important to be prepared to encounter variation and complexity and to realize that general characterizations of functioning may be impossible. It may be of critical importance to note exceptions and variations and then to pursue an understanding of the key settings, people, states, and environmental triggers which may be associated with this variation.

Organization of Behavior and Self-Regulation

Here, the team attends to a group of correlated functions, each of which relies to some degree on other, more fundamental capacities. The capacity for self-regulation is closely connected to that of emotional regulation. Self-regulation can be thought of as the broader construct, embracing the managing and controlling of (in addition to emotion) attention, thoughts, impulses, and behavior (Gross and Thompson, 2006). The growth of the capacity for self-regulation in infancy and childhood begins as a process that is fundamentally about interactions with caretakers (Siegel, 1999). As the young child becomes a toddler, this reliance on the immediate regulating presence of the caretaker gives way to what Sroufe (1995, p. 192) has called "caregiver-guided self-regulation." Now, the caregiver may leave the young child to manage emotional states of low or moderate arousal but will intervene in states of high arousal that the child is still unable to manage on her own and is likely to step in to interrupt aggression or help with impulse control (Sroufe, 1995, p. 193). Here, we are generally concerned with older children, but it is still useful to think about this capacity in terms of the relative balance of necessary dyadic regulation versus the possibility of true self-regulation. Thus, when one considers a child in almost any setting, be it a foster home, a classroom, a family, or a high-level residential facility, the following question might be asked: What level (amount and intensity) of supervision (dyadic regulation) is necessary for this child to participate more or less appropriately in this setting? The answer to this question will strongly reflect the child's level of internal organization. When children are spoken of as being "difficult" or "tough," it is often meant that they are disorganized and require high levels of supervision to move through their day. To answer this question, it is useful to look at the following kinds of data (note that any of these observations must be roughly weighted according to the child's age):

- The capacity to organize extended sequences of activity in play, academic work, or chores.
- The capacity to tolerate transitions from one activity to another, including from pleasurable activities such as play to less pleasurable activities such as academic work; from one setting to another; and from one state to another (for example, wakefulness to sleep).
- The capacity to delay gratification
- The capacity to tolerate frustration, envy, momentary disruptions of connection to a regulating figure, loss of a valued possession, etc.
- Impulsiveness: Can the child wait his turn, follow the rules of a game, stand still and listen to a direction and then follow it?
- Across all the settings in which the child must function, what is her capacity to inhibit motor activity and verbal output as required by the situation?

Proximity Seeking and the Pursuit of Relationship

In our discussion of attachment theory, proximity seeking was described as the fundamental expression of activation of the attachment behavioral system. Here, "proximity seeking" is utilized as a category for observation that can assist the clinician in describing the child's internal working model. Thus, the clinician and the treatment team can observe how the child goes about using adults for the various functions an adult can serve for a child. In the narrowest terms the focus is on the specific function of providing relief from feelings of distress. This distress may be related to fear or anxiety, injury or illness, or painful emotions such as intense frustration or sadness. To learn about proximity seeking, it is important to observe how the child uses adults to manage these states and the ways in which she pursues support or closeness with an adult. Finally, it is also important to observe the degree to which an adult's presence or efforts to provide comfort meet with success in relieving the child's distress. With younger children, such as those seen in therapeutic preschools or during home visits as part of an outpatient intervention, it is often possible to directly observe proximity seeking. With school-age children and adolescents the team may have to rely on briefer observations in family sessions or on descriptions provided by caretakers. In milieu treatment settings it is possible to directly observe the unfolding of relationships and proximity seeking with staff members who are functioning as surrogate caretakers. Some specific questions to have in mind include the following:

- Does proximity seeking occur in response to distress?
- Do other states (anxiety, ambivalence, anger, fear) appear to interfere with proximity seeking?
- Does proximity seeking seem to be intermixed with fear and retreat in any way?
- Does provision of proximity seem to provide relief?
- What forms of indirect, "inappropriate," or "nonadaptive" proximity seeking does the child show? These might take the form of provocative behavior, pestering, caretaking, oppositional, or controlling behavior.

One significant complexity about proximity seeking is that children in vulnerable populations have often been in settings in which direct approaches to caretakers fail to elicit the needed comforting, reassuring response. As a result, they may have learned that the only way they can secure any form of engagement with a caretaker is by less direct approaches that may not look like proximity seeking at all. Thus, for example, a child whose mother suffers from severe, chronic depression may seek proximity by being a caretaker or a child whose early experience with caretakers includes sexual abuse may seek proximity by being seductive. Thus, it is vital to attend to a variety of behaviors that strike us as problematic and to be open to the possibility that they are expressions of a need for proximity.

Exploratory Capacity

Here, the focus is on the presence and level of functioning of the exploratory behavioral system that exists in a complementary fashion to the attachment behavioral system. The general heading of "exploratory capacity" is an effort to summarize a great many activities that are all the things young mammals should be doing when their caretakers have provided them with a sense of safety. This external safety is then represented internally as a feeling of security that creates the necessary psychological conditions for moving away from the attachment figure and experiencing interest and curiosity in the environment (Bowlby, 1969, 1988). This, in turn, can lead to searching, playing, investigating, generating theories, and doing experiments—in a word, learning. As noted earlier, attachment theory argues that proximity seeking has become hardwired in the human species as a result of the adaptive advantage it conferred on evolving humans. Exploration is assumed to be similarly hardwired for exactly the same reasons. An organism that is able to actively explore the environment, examine its interesting and important features, and then represent this knowledge internally is better able to anticipate and deal with challenges to survival. What are the behaviors that allow us to assess the child's exploratory capacities?

Curiosity and interests

Does the child have any areas of special interest in which he has become an expert and that he identifies as part of who he is? These are usually subjects that have captured the child's interest and imagination. Some traumatized children may have traumatically driven preoccupations that may be efforts to, for example, compensate for feelings of weakness and vulnerability. These preoccupations may convey a presence of curiosity and exploration but may also reflect efforts to manage distressing, intrusive worries.

Academic functioning

While it is true that classroom performance is enormously overdetermined, it is one important indicator of the child's capacity to focus on the external world and take in new information. Is there pleasure in pursuing novelty, in mastering new skills or material, and in discovering how things in the world work?

Play

While play is not strictly a form of exploration, it is an expression of the child's efforts to master and represent experience and can be a measure of the resources she has available for activities not immediately required for survival. It can be useful, then, to look at the child's capacity for imaginative, pleasurable activities. These may be solitary activities or may involve collaboration (and competition) with peers. It is important to keep in mind that not all play is equal. Severely traumatized children are known to engage in grim, repetitive play in which they seem to endlessly revisit some aspect of their trauma. Such play may have an emotional tone that is driven and bleak and may yield little pleasure or sense of mastery for the child. Thus, it important to evaluate the richness and flexibility of the play, its emotional tone, and any themes that emerge.

Emotions or states that inhibit exploration

Is the child notably fearful in the face of new experience? Is fearfulness pervasive or situation-specific? Are there any other emotional states, preoccupations, or concerns that seem to have an inhibiting effect on exploration and curiosity.

Sense of Self

It has already been noted that the working model of attachment relationships includes a representation of the self. As Bowlby (1973) notes, "Thus, an unwanted child is likely not only to feel unwanted by his parents but to believe that he is essentially unwantable, namely unwanted by anyone. Conversely, a much-loved child may grow up to be not only confident of his parents' affection but confident that everyone else will find him lovable too" (p. 204). Thus, in working to arrive at a complete description of the client's working model, it is useful to include some account of the child's image of herself. This is not always a straightforward task. Consider, for example, the ways in which an adolescent may at times present a grandiose, inflated image of herself and her abilities and exploits. The exaggerated quality of such a presentation and its emergence in situations in which the child may be experiencing some narcissistic vulnerability are clues that this self-image represents, in part, a protective strategy aimed at avoiding painful feelings of inadequacy, weakness, or vulnerability. It is important for the clinician to make every effort to understand the workings of this self-image and to discover the meanings of those situations which activate it. In thinking about the self, it is of particular importance to remember that concern with and conscious representation of the self is something that changes in the course of development. Thus, younger children are not particularly interested in focusing on themselves and may not yet have the cognitive capacity to think about themselves and compare themselves to others (Harter, 1999). They may rarely make self-referential statements, while preadolescents and adolescents are likely to be much more concerned with evaluating their skills, competencies, and physical being and are in the process of using newly developed capacities for abstract thought to construct a more complex image of themselves that embraces their more complex roles, their relationships with peers, and their personal beliefs and values. In thinking about self-image or sense of self, several specific dimensions are of concern:

- *Valence*. Is the view of self generally observable in interaction with the child positive or negative?
- *Intensity*. How strongly expressed are emotions about the self?

- *Agency.* Is the self seen as capable, effective, an originator of action in the world, or more at the mercy of external events and circumstances?
- *Stability and coherence.* How reliable and unitary is the image of the self? Does it shift rapidly, and how vulnerable is it to change or disruption by external events or feedback?
- *Realism.* How accurate is the self-image? Is there notable self-inflation or deflation? (Again, in this regard, it is important to evaluate realism of ideas about the self with the age and developmental level of the child in mind.)

This process will rely on several data sources:

- *The child's observable readiness to engage with new challenges and unfamiliar environments or people.* Here, the team makes note of the child's energy and confidence in the face of experience that is outside his comfort zone. Among older school-age children and teens, a lack of confidence and energy may be observed in efforts to scornfully denigrate new activities and tasks as "stupid" or "weak."
- *The child's direct statements about himself in the course of daily life as he faces challenges and frustrations.* Some children will make strikingly clear statements about their own strengths and skills. These can be positive and very obviously exaggerated, or they may be notably negative and self-derogating.
- *The child's explicit story about himself.* In this category there are fewer incidental remarks elicited by events and exchanges in daily life, as just described, and more extended narratives the child may offer about him- or herself, family, and community. This may include identifications with important figures, cultural phenomena, or current events. Thus, the "story" can be delivered not only in words—"I'm a gangster!"—but also in behavior—acting like a gangster.

Boundary Functioning

The usefulness of considering the caretakers' boundary functioning has already been noted. Because of how the term "boundary" has been used in the family therapy literature (Minuchin, 1977; Walsh, 2002), it is typically thought of as a characteristic of relations among family subsystems or of the relation between the family and the outside world. In the current usage, *boundary* or *boundary functioning* is conceived of as a characteristic of the child that can be inferred from his or her behavior with others. The child's awareness of, understanding of, and capacity to respect and live within basic interpersonal boundaries can yield important data about what sorts of caretaking experiences she has had, about how she views the interpersonal world, and about her capacity to control impulses. The key data source in this domain is direct observation of the child's management of her own personal boundaries and her respect for the boundaries of others. Some examples of boundary data include the following:

- Persistent, personal questions directed at others that are not appropriate to their roles with the child
- Inappropriate self-disclosure
- An inability to maintain her own boundaries against, for example, intrusions by peers
- Inappropriate physical boundaries in the child's management of personal space, touching, and demands for hugs or other physical contact
- Overly rigid boundaries that inhibit the child's capacity for warm engagement with others, avoidance of physical contact

Affective Expression (Range, Intensity, and Modulation)

The expression of emotion is not, strictly speaking, an element in the working model of a child. It is, of course, possible to describe a child's image of the interpersonal world without much reference to his or her range of emotional expression or capacity to modulate emotional experience. Nevertheless, information from these domains can greatly enhance an understanding of the flavor or feeling tone of how the child lives in the interpersonal world. Three related areas of data are of interest: the range of emotions expressed, the intensity of expression, and the capacity to modulate strong feelings. In thinking about this domain, it can be useful to have Siegel's (1999) concept of the "window of tolerance" (p. 253) in mind. This concept refers to the ranges of intensity and types of emotion which different individuals are able to process without becoming dysregulated. Thus, some people must expend considerable energy avoiding particular affects (anger or shame, for example) or certain ranges of intensity to remain in a state of relative equilibrium. This may require efforts to avoid a range of triggering situations, people, or kinds of interactions. Even with such efforts, some individuals are still vulnerable to being regularly catapulted into states of intense disorganization. These states can then, in turn, create escalating distress. Siegel writes:

> Windows of tolerance may also be directly influenced by experiential history. If children have been frightened repeatedly in their early history, fear may become associated with a sense of dread or terror that is disorganizing to their systems. Repeated senses of being out of control—experiencing emotions without a sense of others helping to calm them down— can lead such persons to be unable to soothe themselves as they develop. This lack of self-soothing can lead directly to a narrow window of tolerance. When such a person breaks

through that window, the result is a very disorganizing, "out of control" sensation, which in itself creates a further state of distress. (1999, pp. 255–256)

The following more specific observational suggestions can assist in developing a picture of the child's affective functioning:

- Range of emotion: Observed in direct interaction with the child and from the reports of key informants, range. Range of emotion involves the degree to which the child expresses the various emotions that might be elicited in the interpersonal situations and contexts in which observers encounter her or him. Are there particular emotions that the child never or rarely shows?
- *Intensity of emotion*: Again, this is observed in direct interaction with the child and from the reports of key informants, particularly in expressions of emotions which are exaggerated in their intensity.
- *Modulation of emotion* This often overlaps significantly with the domain of self-regulation. In this category, the focus is on the child's capacity to tolerate strong emotion without it regularly or significantly intruding into and disrupting cognitive functioning, peer relations, and participation in the various settings (school, home, community) in which the child is observed. Examples of such disruptions might be regular dramatic temper tantrums, anxiety that makes participation in classroom activities impossible, or dramatic emotional displays in response to fairly typical frustrations, frequent bouts of extreme sadness, and disappointment. Modulation of emotion is also evaluated in terms of the antecedents and settings related to the incidents and the frequency and number of domains (pervasiveness) in which the incidents occur.

Emotions Evoked in Others

The key word in the title of this domain of data is "evoked." That is, the focus here is not those feelings that staff or other adults think they *should have* in relation to a child but the emotional responses they *find themselves having*. It is generally the case that program staff who interact with children and caretakers are individuals with good intentions who are generous, emotionally available, and easily engaged. In spite of this default posture, ongoing interactions with clients will inevitably evoke a variety of other emotions. Much of the time these emotions can be contained and do not intrude into a staff member's thinking about or reactions to the client or family. Nevertheless, they can be recognized, noted, and utilized as one element in the description of the child's internal working model. This way of exploiting emotional responses to clients arises from the proposition that the internal working model of the child involves an invitation to respond to him in particular ways that would confirm his implicit beliefs about both himself and the interpersonal world. These invitations are transmitted in real interpersonal exchanges that often have an intense emotional component. Some examples regularly seen in programs serving traumatized, very vulnerable children include the following:

- *Disconnection:* The child seems unable to engage in pleasurable contact with adults, "drifts off the screens" of staff members, and is allowed to not participate in what are usually required activities.
- *Fear:* The child's readiness to engage in aggression or the threat of aggression leads to uneasiness and fear of setting limits or maintaining basic expectations.
- *Annoyed retreat:* The child's persistent pursuit of annoying power struggles, "manipulative" negotiation, and off-putting, peculiar habits and behaviors causes adults to disengage and limit their contact with the child to very routinized, "correct" interactions.

Themes of Current Relationships

This category of data is placed last in the description of the child's current interpersonal behavior because it often serves as a summary or integration of all the other categories of data. Because these themes often incorporate observations from all the other categories, it also comes closest to being a functional description of the child's internal working model. It is not difficult to move from these observed themes to inferences about the child's implicit beliefs about how the interpersonal world works. Here, the concern is with persistent, recurring interpersonal scenarios that seem to characterize many of the child's relationships and come to be central to any description of him. In these recurring scenarios one can see that the child reliably approaches others in particular ways and that the interactions seem to always, or almost always, involve similar content. Description of these themes does not require sophisticated clinical vocabulary; their essential features are often captured in the everyday accounts provided by those who interact regularly with the child. Following are some examples:

- "She's very seductive."
- "He's a little thug ... always tries to be intimidating, always tries to get you to back down."
- "He's so needy. He just gloms on to the first person who comes through the door."
- "He's a con-man, always working the angles, trying to see what he can get."

- "He's a great kid, always trying to be helpful, see what he can do for you."
- "Yikes, he is so disgusting. It's as if he's trying to gross you out."
- "He's really eager to please, extremely compliant."

Each of these shorthand summaries of impressions describes important regularities experienced by people interacting with the child. Again, it may emerge in the course of further exploration that these themes are most pronounced under certain conditions, do not appear at all in certain settings or with particular caretakers, or gradually fade when the child is in a new setting. The themes encountered in the population of children and adolescents have generally been clustered along several dimensions of interpersonal behavior :

- *Lack of regulation:* This theme could be summarized as "desperate for help getting organized". Children showing this theme have often been diagnosed with attention-deficit/hyperactivity disorder and are pervasively disorganized.
- *Intense neediness:* This involves great interpersonal hunger and a lack of discrimination in seeking support, affection, and physical proximity from adults. The child often has very poor frustration tolerance and can easily be triggered into emotional crises by disappointments or frustrations.
- *Reliance on aggression and intimidation:* These children use aggression as the primary currency of their relationships. They are often preoccupied with size, strength, and who can physically dominate whom. Aggression may be used to connect with others, to inflate and thereby soothe the self, to relieve tension, and to avoid painful feelings.
- *Preoccupation with sexuality:* In this case, it appears that sexuality functions for the child in a way similar to how aggression functions for those children described previously ("Reliance on aggression and intimidation"). They are hypersensitive to and hyperaware of possible and imagined sexual meanings in interpersonal exchanges, visual images, and popular culture. They are at times explicitly seductive and may try to engage peers in sexual acting out.
- *Intensely negative self-image:* These children appear to have internalized strongly negative images of themselves, and they engage others with the assumption that they will come to the same view. They will often try to create or elicit this view in others with behavior that is annoying, disgusting, or somehow provocative.
- *Preoccupation with "manipulation" and other forms of coercive control:* These children's interactions often seem to involve elements of calculation and efforts to gain what they feel might be the "upper hand" in a relationship. Their connections with others can have a transparently instrumental quality, with an explicit focus on the

concrete gains they might realize, and as a result interactions often feel like tedious negotiations. They are often quick to learn the rules in any new setting and then set about trying to use those rules to annoy and to gain some imagined advantage.

- *Disconnection*: These children may have some elements of any or all the dimensions already described, but the fundamental feature of their interpersonal connections is that they are disconnected. There is an absence of pleasure in what might normally be joyful exchanges, and they do not seem to feel gratified by interpersonal engagement. In fact, adults will often note that they feel they don't know how to engage the child and that in the group he or she is peripheral, invisible, or in danger of floating away.

It is important to note that these examples of themes are not always present as pure types. That is, not all children perfectly and exclusively exemplify one of the relationship types. Instead, there are shadings, variations, and even combinations of types.

RELATIONAL INTERVENTION: USING THE DESCRIPTION OF THE CHILD'S INTERNAL WORKING MODEL TO DRIVE TREATMENT

Treatment utilizing the relational principles described here is based on providing the client with disconfirming experience that will lead to modification of the internal working model. This is not a new idea. A variety of writers have called attention to the importance of these issues in the psychotherapy treatment relationship. Alexander and French (1946), in their discussion of the "corrective emotional experience," argued that the therapeutic action of psychoanalytic therapy came from the analyst's ability to engage the patient in a way that is fundamentally different from earlier hurtful relationships. This possibility can then convert the usual transference manifestations into "one-sided shadow-boxing" (p. 67). In other words, the patient's efforts to engage the therapist in a repetition of an old relationship scenario do not evoke complementary or confirming responses. They elaborate this idea as follows:

> *Because the therapist's attitude is different from the authoritative person of the past, he gives the patient an opportunity to face again and again, under more favorable circumstances, those emotional situations which were formerly unbearable and to deal with them in a manner different from the old. This can be accomplished only through actual experience in the patient's relationship to the therapist; intellectual insight alone is not sufficient. (p. 67)*

To illustrate the workings of this process, they provide an example from literature, a pivotal scene from the life of Jean Valjean in Victor Hugo's *Les Mise?rables*. In this case, the corrective emotional experience is condensed into a single powerful moment when a kindly bishop saves Valjean from arrest and return to prison, even after Valjean has robbed him. This startling and unexpected act of compassion is a profound disconfirmation of both Valjean's life experience and his working model. He is suddenly thrown into turmoil and senses that he is at a tipping point in which he will either surrender to an existence filled with bitterness and hatred or undergo a transformation and begin a different life (p. 68).

More recent theorists within the psychoanalytic tradition have also emphasized the importance of "disconfirmation of pathogenic beliefs" (Weiss, 1993; Weiss and Sampson, 1986; Silberschatz, 2005). Weiss (1993) argued that much of psychopathology arises from pathogenic beliefs that are the result of traumatic experience in early relationships with caretakers. In the course of psychotherapy or psychoanalysis, the patient actively engages the therapist, seeking disconfirming experience in the therapeutic relationship. The therapy succeeds to the degree that the therapist understands the patient's efforts and responds with a stance and interpretations which disconfirm these beliefs. Bleiberg (2001), one of a few writers who has explored these ideas in work with children, makes use of the term "representational mismatch" to describe the disconfirming experience which he views as an essential ingredient in treating children and adolescents who present with personality disorders. The term "representational mismatch" was first introduced by Horowitz (1987) to describe discrepancies between experience in the external world and the contents of internal representational models. In explaining the role of such mismatches in treatment, Bleiberg (2003) observes,

> In the case of youngsters with dramatic personality disorders, a representational mismatch arises when parents and treaters demonstrate effectiveness and consistency in providing children with limit-setting, nurturance and support, generational boundaries and encouragement for mastery and autonomy... Thwarting children's self-defeating and self-destructive behavior challenges these children's view of their parents and other adults as unreliable, ineffectual, or indifferent— or as brutal and exploitative. (p. 469)

In its explicit attention to the importance of disconfirming experience in treatment relationships, the relational approach described here shares much with these ways of thinking. It should be noted, however, that the current approach, through its use of the working model assessment, provides a way for the treatment team to articulate a quite clear and specific relationship stance that is then available to and can become the basis for supervising or collaborating with caretakers, direct care staff, clinicians, teachers, classroom aides, and all the other adults who are participating in or supporting the treatment of the child. At the outset of this book it was noted that it is not often the case that the most challenging, high-risk children are served only in outpatient settings where they receive individual psychotherapy and perhaps some level of family treatment. Instead, they often make their way, via the path of multiple placement failures, to more intensive programs, in which they are served by interdisciplinary teams of collaborating helpers. It is in settings such as these—residential treatment facilities serving children in the child welfare and mental health systems, day treatment programs serving the more difficult children within a school district's special education population, treatment foster care programs and community-based wrap-around interventions—that the working models of high-risk children seem to be enacted most intensely. While psychotherapy is a key ingredient in the treatment mix in such settings, it is only one ingredient. Thus, these challenging young clients never fail a placement because they were unable to make use of a psychotherapy relationship. Instead, they overwhelm caretakers, teachers, and a variety of support staff with provocative, disruptive, and often disorganized behavior. A clinician seeing such clients in any kind of setting usually has some level of training, regular clinical supervision, and access to continuing education. Even with these supports, therapists can easily find themselves pushed over into frustration, anger, detachment, or complete withdrawal by the behavior of the child. It is, however, the large number of nontherapists who, for many more hours each day, are teaching, feeding, bathing, playing with, comforting, disciplining, and just hanging out with these very difficult children. It is these adults who are most likely to be persistently invited by the clients to reenact a variety of traumatic scenarios and who are most in need of a conceptual scheme that will allow them to understand and respond to the behavior that is being directed at them. A thoughtful description of each child's working model of relationships is the first step in providing such a conceptual scheme.

Once such a description is available, it is possible for the team to begin to think together about what responses the child's behavior seems to invite. In other words, they are beginning to think about the various ways in which they might be pulled to *confirm* the child's internal working model. Armed with even a preliminary review of the dimensions of "the child's experience with caretakers" and "the child's current interpersonal behavior" just described, it is not difficult for the team to generate a series of possible confirming responses to the child's behavior. When they reach the dimension of "emotions evoked in staff," they may well find themselves acknowledging some of the ways in which they may already be enacting confirming responses. Thus, in such a meeting team members may recognize responses like the following:

- "I'm afraid of him. I find myself avoiding setting limits."
- "I'm incredibly careful around her. The slightest question or demand can set her off."

- From a female staff member: "He makes me feel really uneasy. He stares at my body in a really intimidating way."
- "I don't take anything from him. I have to be really mechanical and just let him know exactly what I need him to do."
- "Sometimes I let her stay in her room after quiet time is over because I just don't want to deal with her. She can be so draining!"
- "He has to negotiate everything. I won't have it. I just cut him off and give him a time-out."

Some of these reactions to a client can be seen as confirming in that they are *the absence of a response.* That is, they confirm the child's internal working model by failing to resist the way in which the child's behavior structures a particular exchange or ongoing relationship. In these staff responses, uneasiness about or fear of engaging a client's use of intimidation exemplifies how this can work. The child's view of herself as dangerous, potentially violent, and invulnerable is affirmed by the failure of the adults in the environment to respond. This lack of a response is a de facto retreat.

Generally, the next step in the process of creating a relational intervention flows logically and directly from the last. Having deciphered the child's invitation, the team must now devise a way of responding that declines that invitation. This is often a reasonably straightforward task. Disconfirming stances can involve resisting intimidation and provocation and limiting seductiveness and expression of sexual preoccupations. It is also true that some disconfirming stances are generic while others are specific. Thus, all programs have or work to create structures which limit acting out, support engagement, and provide caring emotional support. These are all part of what could be called a "generic" disconfirming stance. It is these generic stances which can often collapse or gradually erode in the face of relentless intimidation, disturbing sexualized behavior, and constant provocation. Describing a specific way of responding to individual clients yields a specific disconfirming stance that can become the basis of collaboration and supervision and is then the core of a relational treatment plan. This approach is also strengthened when, as will be discussed in Chapter 6, relational intervention is combined with positive behavioral supports. Thus, modification of internal working models can also be advanced by teaching new behaviors that provide the client with new ways of relieving distress, new ways of gaining access to caretakers or other regulating figures, and new ways of regulating behavior.

The successful use of such an approach to treatment is dependent on having administrative, training, and supervision structures that support the regular discussion and revision of the client's internal working model. This necessarily includes collaborative team meetings in which time is given to review of the client's relational invitations and to reflection on successful and unsuccessful responses. The clinician must contribute to creating an atmosphere of curiosity and reflection in which there is room for staff to be aware of their emotional reactions to clients and to clients' families. Two key activities in this process are modeling reflective awareness of emotional reactions to clients and asking questions that encourage this awareness. At the same time, team members must see the clinician as a full collaborator in their process. This standing on the team is created when the clinician actively participates in the treatment milieu and is a regular presence at team meetings. (Thus, program designs in which clinicians function only as psychotherapists and do not actively participate in the treatment milieu can lead to splits between what comes to be seen as "therapeutic" people and activities and everyone else. In its most problematic version of this kind of split, clinicians can come to be seen as overly gratifying, even permissive figures, while direct care staff feel that they are "in the trenches" dealing with very difficult behavior with little understanding or support.) Additionally, the clinician will be most successful when he or she maintains a curious, collaborative, and respectful presence. While it is important in most team meetings to do the business of communicating and problem solving, the clinician can support an important alternative (but complementary) process by slowing things down and asking questions. Useful areas of inquiry can include what is working and what isn't and the details of very specific exchanges with clients and the feelings that they evoked.

Thus, the clinician must function as a "clinical informant" to the team. This may not involve explicitly prescriptive functions (hence, the term "clinical informant" rather than, for example, "clinical leader") but a combination of educative and interpretive functions in which the clinician gently and respectfully asserts the importance of the client's actual experience and family history in the development of the behavior and symptoms. Keeping these data present in team discussions is a powerful antidote to less reflective attributions that team members can adopt about "manipulation" or "needs for attention."

Often, clinicians must utilize similar clinical skills to those called on in work with clients to assist the staff to contain and make use of their emotional reactions to the clients. Thus, for example, the understandable anger, frustration, sadness, disgust, or helplessness that can be evoked by work in our programs must be recognized, processed, and understood as useful data about the experience and psychology of the client. This also requires that the clinicians know and see with some clarity the strengths and vulnerabilities of their team members. In other words, emotional reactions to the client's behavior are about not only the client but also the person who is having the reaction. Working effectively in this domain requires attention to issues of respect and safety— clinicians will implicitly invite their team members to be open to feelings and internal experiences that may be shameful, disturbing, or "unprofessional." Finally, it must also be acknowledged that while clinicians do have special training, they are as vulnerable to fear, confusion, and hopelessness as other members of the team. In this respect, clinical supervision is an essential arena for addressing these reactions.

The use of the internal working model assessment and the development of relational treatment plans will be discussed in more detail in Chapter 7 and then illustrated with two case studies in Chapter 8.

Chapter Six

Positive Behavioral Intervention

In order to be effective, programs serving vulnerable children and youth need to involve at least some elements in their approach to intervention that can be described as "behavioral." Using the word "behavioral" means nothing more than that the interventions come from the body of research and practice that is derived from basic principles of learning theory. In some programs, this emphasis is very explicit and visible. These programs have complex "behavioral systems" in which clients have behavioral goals and are regularly and systematically rewarded for progress toward them. In other programs, the focus on behavior is more implicit. In community-based or outpatient programs in which clinicians and support counselors work to support the efforts of parents or surrogate caretakers, the focus may be more on providing behavioral training and consultation to these caretakers so that they can be as effective as possible. Even in approaches such as these, in which the behavioral intervention is essentially indirect and carried out by others, it is enormously useful if workers are knowledgeable about implementing basic behavior-change strategies.

When these interventions are said to come from the body of research and practice derived from learning theory, several very simple things are meant:

- There is a focus on observable behavior.
- There is an assumption that all behavior is, at least in part, established and maintained by rewarding events or by escape from negative events that may follow it.
- There is curiosity about and systematic observation of the antecedents, settings, and consequences that are reliably associated with behaviors of interest.
- There is careful attention to the contingencies that may have established problem behaviors and may, in the current setting, be maintaining the behavior.
- There is a commitment to creating a treatment environment in which clients collaborate in developing behavioral goals for themselves and their

;roups. These goals represent new, more flexible, more adaptive behaviors cnat have been absent from their behavioral repertoires.

- All treatment settings should be as rewarding as possible and offer clients numerous, regular opportunities to feel gratified, cared for, and stimulated in exciting, interesting ways. Note that these are basic qualities of each setting and not reinforcements that are contingently available for the performance of positive behavior.
- In the context of work with families, there is a fundamental interest in enabling parents to become more effectively connected to the behavior of their children by helping them to understand the value and power of their interest, attention, and availability to their children.

BEHAVIORAL INTERVENTION AND RELATIONSHIP-BASED WORK

How does behavioral intervention connect to ideas about relationship-based treatment, and how does it also relate to an interest in the problems and processes of human attachment? Behavioral intervention must start with recognition of children's fundamental, biologically based needs for proximity and containment by emotionally attuned, unconditionally available caretakers. This means that the behavioral interventions (which are inevitably about the planned use of contingencies) must be carried out inside a bigger "container," or structure, that is fundamentally unconditional and noncontingent. In other words, a client may have a behavioral treatment plan in which he is *conditionally* rewarded for making use of new, more adaptive behaviors. But the client's continuing presence in the program and the readiness of staff to engage with and assist him are explicitly *unconditional.* Many traumatized children have learned in the course of their development that the only way they can secure this vital proximity from an adult is through a variety of interpersonally aversive behaviors (Lyons-Ruth, 1996; Lieberman and Pawl, 1990). These may include, for example, coercive or controlling behavior, defiance, recklessness, risk taking, certain kinds of sleep problems, and a variety of provocative and annoying ways of engaging with others. A commitment to working with these problems behaviorally cannot be based on any assumption that these behaviors will simply be "extinguished" by withdrawal of attention. Instead, the team must work from the assumption that children require proximity and attention and that one part of the job is to teach them successful ways of getting it. Of course, there are behaviors that can be ignored, but such an intervention should always be embedded in a treatment plan in which new, more effective behaviors are being taught and the reassuring proximity of an adult is available.

Another way in which an interest in the development of human relatedness informs and enriches this approach to behavioral intervention is attention to the child's working model of attachment relationships. As already discussed, this concept refers to the child's schemas or images of how the interpersonal world works and how she fits into it. The working model can be thought of as an "interpersonal operating system" that develops from the child's accumulated experience with caretakers. However, it is not only a representation of past relationships but also includes expectations of future relationships based on these earlier experiences. The working model is an implicit structure; its content can be inferred from the child's behavior with others, from her account of how she came to placement, and from how she makes use of the offer of relationship that is part of any intervention. Many clients have developed working models that result in very fixed, rigid patterns of relating which invite negative treatment from others. How does the concept of the internal working model connect to the use of behavioral intervention? First, it is important to be aware that part of the reason some of the problematic behaviors that a client presents are maintained is *because they are congruent with the internal working model.* Thus, the child's story of who she is, how she should be treated, and what she can expect from others comes to guide her behavior. In other words, these behaviors are being "reinforced" in the sense that they end up confirming the child's prior experience and expectations of the future. This is a form of reinforcement that is not typically described in behavioral literature but must be recognized by the treatment team. Second, a working model of relationships—and of the self—that is mainly negative may be strikingly impervious to language and to the effects of new experience. In other words, behavioral interventions that are aimed at positively reinforcing new, more adaptive behaviors often run counter to the child's powerful internal story about who she is and what kind of treatment she should expect. (For example, the child's implicit belief might be "I am not capable of learning new behaviors; I am not worthy of being cared for and rewarded in this way.") This should not derail an intervention team from teaching methods for regulating intense emotional states, more successful ways to get attention, and more effective behaviors for making friends. But it is important to know that this approach may feel piecemeal and may not proceed quickly.

In thinking about the connections between behavioral approaches and what has been described as a core commitment to relationship-based work, an acknowledgment must be made that the discourse in the field, in the culture more generally, and in programs often shows a duality between hard and soft, between relationship and structure, and between focusing on internal experience (thoughts and feelings) and external experience (behavior). This dichotomy, while familiar and understandable in some ways, is fundamentally misleading and unhelpful. Behavioral interventions in programs for very troubled children are an aspect of structure, but they also support relationship. They do this by providing a coherent set of methods that modify and constrain staff members' behavior and help to keep it within a particular emotional range. This contributes to consistency and clarity of expectations and provides a reassuring regularity to exchanges that might otherwise become highly charged confrontations between adults and children. All of these effects are critical to the maintenance of safety within a program, a group home, a classroom, or a family; and safety is, ultimately, the great creator of relationship. Thus, this "hard," empirically derived approach to intervention always ends up promoting relationship. Interestingly, the converse is also true: Relationship advances structure and amplifies the power of behavioral interventions. Proximity, praise, and attention from a valued adult who has repeatedly demonstrated availability to a child (even in the face of highly provocative, disturbing behavior) are undeniably more reinforcing than the same rewards from a caretaker with whom the child has little or no relationship. Structure and relationship (or behavioral and relationship-based interventions) operate in a synergistic fashion, each requiring the presence of the other.

There is also evidence that when caretakers become more effective modifiers and containers of behavior there is an upsurge of proximity seeking and expressions of affection from their children. Sutton (2001), working from a cognitive behavior perspective, undertook a relatively brief program of parent training that focused on providing parents of young children with basic behavior-management tools. She describes the parent–child connections in her sample at the outset of the study as strongly negative. Without seeking the information, Sutton found that many parents spontaneously reported notable increases in affectionate proximity seeking. Several parents even noted that other adults who knew the child commented on the shift in the emotional tone of their connection to their mothers. Such a result is entirely consistent with the perspective presented here. Effective, positive behavioral techniques inevitably displace negative, reactive, and coercive exchanges. This, in turn, leads to an enhanced sense of competence and control on the part of the caretaker and an amplified experience of regulation and safety on the part of the child. Both these shifts lead to enriched possibilities for connection and engagement between caretaker and child.

WHY DO BEHAVIORAL INTERVENTION?

It is certainly the case that some programs working with populations similar to that focused on here do not invest much time and energy in developing and implementing explicitly behavioral approaches to intervention. The fundamental rationale for including behavioral intervention in the treatment mix includes these very concrete processes that are, after all, at the heart of work with traumatized, high-risk children and youth:

- To teach new, more adaptive behaviors in a systematic way
- To understand, as much as the current data allow, the factors contributing to the maintenance of problem behaviors
- To interrupt and extinguish problem behaviors
- To avoid inadvertently reinforcing problem behaviors
- To support safety and structure

Whose Behavior Is Getting Modified, Anyhow?

In addition to these important goals, it is worth acknowledging that the effect of a behavioral system is almost always at least as profound on its practitioners as on its subjects. To put it another way, the team's behavior is also powerfully modified by any behavioral system they work from. This was noted earlier when it was said that behavioral interventions are "provide staff with a coherent set of methods that constrain their behavior and keep it in a particular range." This idea deserves elaboration. Earlier in this book it was observed that the behavior of many clients seems to be an invitation to others to repeat or reenact certain elements of hurtful experiences from their pasts. This is one effect of an internal working model in which a traumatized child, for example, is left with the expectation that he will inevitably reexperience mistreatment at the hands of caretakers. Treatment, then, consists in large part in defying this expectation and providing the client with relationships in which such invitations are declined and the expectations that drive them are disconfirmed. These invitations are sometimes easy to see coming and can be documented in a treatment plan so that everyone on the team responds in a consistent way. Sometimes, though, these invitations are enormously subtle, and a worker can suddenly find herself in a situation with a client that is full of surprising intensity. It is certainly also possible for strongly felt, unexamined emotional reactions to clients to overtake the thinking of an entire team in such a way that these responses skew treatment planning and infiltrate and distort daily interactions with the client. A behavioral system that provides staff members with a toolbox that prescribes a set of basic interventions and continually reiterates the relative importance of positive intervention is enormously helpful to this critical process of declining invitations and disconfirming expectations. This is why a behavioral approach can be thought of as constraining the behavior of staff and keeping it in a particular range. It is both a range of emotion (well-modulated) and a range of action (focused on maintaining safety, interrupting escalating chains of behavior, and relentlessly attending to the positive behaviors that are being taught). Simply knowing a child's antecedents and working with him in a collaborative way on developing alternative behaviors immediately positions clinicians, workers, and caretakers in such a way that they can more effectively resist the child's efforts to recreate familiar, negative patterns of engagement. Thus, positive behavioral intervention based on thoughtful assessment and attention to the (often proximity seeking) function of behavior can function as a barrier to repeated, unreflective reenactments of scenarios or relationship patterns from the child's traumatic past.

Positive Rewards for Adaptive Behavior vs. Negative Consequences for "Problem" Behavior

Another key insight from learning theory that is of general importance to programs that strive to serve severely behavior-disordered children has to do with the relative effectiveness of utilizing positive reinforcement to support the learning of new behaviors over employing negative consequences to suppress negative behaviors (Rushton and Teachman, 1978). Clients often present with behavior that is startling in its inappropriateness, intensity, and persistence. These are often the very behaviors that led to the repeated placement failures that brought them, ultimately, to the very highest levels of service. When programs begin to engage such clients, these behaviors have a way of "engulfing the field" (Heider, 1958). That is, they may be all that is noticed and quickly become the focus of all the attention of the interveners. In some ways this is right and appropriate. The children themselves sometimes seem to participate or conspire in this belief by the sheer volume of disruptive, provocative acts they direct at the adults in their environments. It would be incomprehensible to try to engage these children in a way that disregarded these behaviors. What can become problematic, though, is to then focus intervention only or primarily on reactive, consequence-based techniques aimed at suppressing these responses. Later in the chapter a more extensive rationale for this position will be offered; at this point, two explanations will be asserted. First, research in the applied field of behavior modification has shown that positive approaches that reward adaptive behavior are more effective than strategies which are primarily focused on suppressing negative behavior with negative consequences (Kazdin, 2001). Second, the use of reactive or negative strategies is often at risk of drifting into an increasingly punitive relationship dynamic in which the client's negative internal working model is repeatedly confirmed (Patterson, 1982). These dynamics can then be intensified by unacknowledged emotional responses on the part of workers who may be frightened, alarmed, or disgusted by the behavior of the client.

In fact, if caretakers, clinicians, and teams of support staff are clear that much of this provocative behavior developed in large part because it was an adaptive response to the relational environment in which the child found himself, then they must also be committed to establishing more successful, gratifying ways for the child to engage adults and to find reassurance, support, and emotional regulation. Thus, it is critical that teams develop behavioral treatment plans in which the new rewarded behaviors actually serve the same function as the "problem" behaviors.

One way of insuring that behavioral interventions continue to be *positive* is to regularly ask the following question with regard to every client and every treatment plan: What is being taught, and what is being learned? As has been noted repeatedly in the discussion of the attachment histories of many clients, they are experts at their own stories. That is, they have an uncanny, often relentless capacity to move an entire team (usually unconsciously but not infrequently explicitly) which is operating with the best of intentions in the direction of negative, punitive interventions. This drift toward unreflective, coercive interventions that are aimed at suppressing behavior is a familiar phenomenon to workers who seek to help traumatized

children and youth with difficult attachment histories. A commitme
positive behavioral intervention can be a key barrier to this drift.

METHODS OF BEHAVIORAL INTERVENTION

First, it is important to understand that the principles of learning theory are
operating at all times. They are not only in effect when doing an explicit,
intentional process called "behavioral intervention." In exchanges with the physical
environment, friends, coworkers, parents, and children, certain behaviors secure
outcomes that are desired, while others help evade outcomes that are not wanted.
Fundamental principles such as reinforcement, extinction, shaping, and generalization
are at work everywhere, all the time.

The unintentional and sometimes unfortunate efficacy of these principles can
be seen in the lives of clients and in many settings in which they have been placed.
The negative behaviors of clients have been established and maintained in precisely the same manner that workers are seeking to establish and maintain new,
alternative behaviors. In fact, understanding the extraordinary persistence of some
of these behaviors in the face of a variety of aversive consequences from the
environment is greatly supported by an understanding of some of the basic
principles of learning theory. For example, many children who display disruptive
or provocative behavior have been reinforced intermittently for this behavior,
meaning some proportion of the time the behavior succeeded in getting them
something they wanted. It is well established that this schedule of reinforcement
(which is also utilized in slot machines) produces very high rates of behavior that
persist even when no reinforcement is available. When the operation of these
principles is acknowledged in all human interactions, it must also be acknowledged that some clients are themselves extremely skilled modifiers of the behavior
of others. For example, a child may have learned that by having a tantrum and
stopping the tantrum when caretakers meet a demand or a need, she can gradually
assume control over some aspects of the behavior. Patterson (1982; see also
Patterson, DeBaryshe, and Ramsey, 1989) has described how this pattern is a
key element in the interactions of the families of predelinquent children. In the
somewhat confusing language of behavior modification, the child is using negative
reinforcement on the caretakers. That is, without any explicit knowledge of
behavioral principles, the child has rewarded the parents for submitting to her
demands or ceasing their demands of her by terminating the aversive tantrum. The
tantrum is a negative reinforcement in the sense that it increases the frequency of
the parents' submission behavior by its removal. In the development of children
living in benign situations with caretakers who have adequate resources for
effective parenting, the principles of learning theory are operating just as powerfully.
The results, however, are generally more favorable.

In contrast to these unfortunate demonstrations of the power of basic behavioral principles, it is the goal to make use of these same principles in a systematic program of intervention. Such a program will have the following elements:

- *To decide, for each client, on a limited domain of behaviors on which to focus efforts.* This domain will generally include negative behaviors that have caused problems for the child and for others in his environment, as well as positive behaviors that need to be taught and reinforced.
- *To understand as fully as possible both the historical and current forces in the child's environment that established and maintained negative behaviors or disrupted the learning and mastery of positive behaviors.* This is an assessment task that requires observation of the child in the environments in which he is currently operating, review of documents, and interviews with informants.
- *To define these behaviors very specifically and concretely so that they can be understood by the client and reliably observed by staff members*
- *To determine the degree to which the behaviors are currently present in the client's repertoire.* In many cases, this will be a simple measure of the frequency of the behavior in a specified period of time. For some behaviors, it will be important to assess other dimensions such as duration, latency, or intensity (Miltenberger, 2005).
- *To carry out a functional analysis of the behaviors of concern.* This part of the assessment task involves observation of the antecedents, settings, and consequences that currently play a role in maintaining the behavior (Watson and Steege, 2003; Bambara and Kern, 2005).
- *To plan an intervention which will include choosing the reinforcers, alternative behaviors, and schedules of reinforcement that will be utilized.* The plan could also involve changes to the child's environment (such as removing key triggers from the settings in which he operates or modifying an instructional approach) and explicit training in key behavioral skills such as distress tolerance or emotional regulation (Linehan, 1993; Miller, Rathus, Linehan, Wetzler, and Leigh, 1997).
- *To monitor the effectiveness of an intervention with follow-up observations that determine how much change has occurred.*

THE BEHAVIOR ITSELF

This process of positive behavioral intervention begins with an effort to describe or define the behavior of interest (Miltenberger, 2005). This requires that other ways of thinking about the client be suspended. These other modes of description may be equally useful and interesting but generally do not yield results that easily lead to behavioral intervention. Thus, while team members may have impressions of a client as "aggressive" or "immature" or "disorganized" or "sexualized," it is important that the first step in a behavioral assessment move beyond these diagnostic or trait descriptions. The team may, inevitably, start from these global characterizations of the client and his or her personality traits but then must ask a simple focusing question: What are the behaviors of the client that make this an accurate description? If this question is applied to our list of descriptors, the results might look something like this:

Aggressive: Strikes peers in conflict situations
Makes fists and angry facial expressions when frustrated
Uses threats of physical violence to get own way
Charges up to staff, shouting angrily when given a limit
Calls peers names, in a belittling, derisive tone

Immature: (Assuming an 11-year-old child)
Is unable to complete activities of daily living such as dressing and personal hygiene without adult supervision
Prefers activities of younger children
Chooses younger children as playmates
Has temper tantrums when frustrated—crying helplessly and rolling around on the floor when not immediately given what he or she demands

Disorganized: Unable to sustain sequences of organized activity such as play, chores, or academic work
Constantly distracted by events in the environment

Sexualized: (Assuming a 12-year-old girl)
Dresses in revealing, provocative ways—skirts too short, tops cut too low, and jeans too tight
Touches others in a manner inconsistent with roles or relationships, touch lingers too long, too much body contact when giving hugs to adult males
Stands too close to others, intrudes on personal space
Interprets neutral comments and exchanges with others as having sexual meaning and accuses others, in an excited and flirtatious tone, of being "inappropriate"

These examples are only initial efforts to specify the actual behaviors that might contribute to broad characterizations of functioning. The particular behaviors listed for each general descriptor could, for the purposes of observation or intervention, be specified even further. Take, for example, the behavior "touches inappropriately" listed as an example of sexualized behavior. If this behavior were defined as a target of intervention, it would be important to specify what that label includes and does not include so that the client, independent observers, and ultimately anyone carrying out an intervention would all be operating from the same definition.

The specific behaviors used in this illustration are all behaviors that would be targeted for suppression in an intervention plan. As noted earlier, though, it is vital that such a plan include equally concrete and specific descriptions of positive behaviors and skills that the team would want to see increase. So-called negative or negative target behaviors are those that are already occurring that have contributed to the client's difficulties. It is important to describe these behaviors so that their frequency can be assessed, those factors in the environment which are maintaining them can be discerned, and a plan to address them can be devised. Every plan of this kind should also include descriptions of behaviors that the client is not yet performing (or not performing enough) that will be taught or supported by the team. These are more functional replacement behaviors that will allow the client to meet some of the same needs that she has attempted to meet with negative behaviors.

USEFUL DIMENSIONS FOR DESCRIBING BEHAVIOR

This task of defining or describing behaviors of interest is important and too easy to gloss over with generalities or poorly specified descriptions. It is too easy to assume that those carrying out the intervention plan that is eventually developed—and they might include parents, support counselors, classroom staff, or a residential team—are in complete agreement. Effective interventions, though (especially those that are being carried out by multiple staff or caretakers), depend on clear agreement about what behavior is being reinforced or observed. What then are some useful dimensions for arriving at concrete, specific descriptions of behavior? Different descriptive approaches will turn out to be useful for different sorts of concerns on the part of observers. Capturing the most important aspects of the act of raising one's hand to ask a question in the classroom can be quite different from what an observer might focus on in describing a tantrum. In the first case, the concern might be with how "well" or how frequently the hand is raised: Does the child wave it about in a disruptive way, is it accompanied by verbal demands to be recognized, and what percentage of the time that the child makes a contribution does he raise a hand vs. simply shouting out? In the case of the tantrum, the team's concern might be with the intensity of the tantrum and the degree to which it involves verbal activity, particular kinds of emotion, and physical aggression. The following list of dimensions for observation of behavior comes from Martin and Pear (1999, pp. 242–251).

- *Amount of behavior.* This is among the most common concerns for observers or interveners: How much does the behavior happen? An accurate assessment in this domain allows the team to know if interventions are having an effect, that is, if positive behaviors have increased and if negative behaviors have decreased. Depending on the particular behavior, however, the "amount" of the behavior may be defined differently. Thus, if the behavior of interest is hand raising in the classroom, then frequency may be all that needs to be known. If the interest is in the child's interactions with peers on the playground, the team might be more focused on (among other things) the duration of the interactions.

- *Topography.* This refers to the actual physical execution of the behavior or its shape and expression as it's being carried out. For example, in working with a child who has very poor hygiene, workers may need to specify with some precision how he is to go about taking a shower, including a description of key body parts to receive attention, how to apply shampoo, and how long to massage it in. Sometimes this dimension overlaps conceptually with the idea of the quality of the response or the degree to which it meets some specified standard as it is carried out. The dimension of quality can also be quite simple, though, and can be applied to measuring behaviors such as academic progress through numbers of correct answers, percentage of homework turned in, and so forth.

- *Intensity.* This refers to the actual physical force, or "oomph," brought to the execution of the behavior. A good example is an effort to improve the functioning of a socially anxious, self-isolating child. In this case, the focus is on the volume of the child's speech in particular settings or interactions. The volume at which a child speaks is very much a matter of intensity. A different example might involve working with a child who uses menacing gestures or posture to intimidate others. In this case, the team's approach is in the opposite direction; that is, the intensity of his behavior needs to be lowered.

- *Latency.* For many behaviors of interest, the team is concerned with how long it takes for them to happen after a particular event has occurred. Again, though, depending on the behavior, the goal is to either increase or decrease response latency. For example, with resistant, passive–aggressive children the aim is to lower the latency of their responses to adult prompts or requests. Conversely, for a child who is impulsive and cannot inhibit a behavior in particular situations, the goal is to increase the latency of responses.

- *Stimulus control.* This term refers to those stimuli that may have some controlling influence over whether or not the behavior occurs. Assessing stimulus control is simply an effort to determine those conditions (or stimuli) that have been reliably associated with the behavior being reinforced or rewarded. The behavior is then more likely to occur in the presence of that stimulus. An event (situation, condition, etc.) is said to have stimulus control if the behavior occurs only in its presence. This issue can be of importance in both trying to reinforce desired behaviors (the behavior may need to occur in particular, appropriate settings) and trying to minimize negative behaviors (the behavior may not be pervasive but occur only in the presence of particular stimuli).

CRITERIA FOR EVALUATING DESCRIPTIONS

The sorts of behaviors that clients show or fail to show are truly manifold. Clients almost always present with some *behavioral excesses*, which are behaviors that should occur either not at all or with significantly lower frequency, duration, or intensity, and some *behavioral deficits*, which are behaviors that are developmentally appropriate but not present or not present in the right amount and at the right time (Martin and Pear, 1999). Once specific, concrete descriptions of the behavior have been determined, an evaluation of the definitions needs to be made to ensure that they will actually work.

In addition to these dimensions for describing behavior, it is possible to articulate criteria for behavioral definitions that will ensure, or at least improve the probability of, success in designing an effective intervention. Kazdin (2001; after Hawkins and Dobes, 1975) offers three useful criteria to apply to descriptions of behavior that may be the focus of intervention:

- *Objectivity.* Does the definition of the behavior refer to observable acts or observable events in the environment? For example, the definition of a child's aggressive behavior should refer to acts such as threatening gestures, assaults on others, or the use of intimidating postures that can be observed directly.
- *Clarity.* Is the definition of the behavior clear and simple enough so that a person new to the situation could understand it easily and restate it so that others could then understand it? Part of clarity, and ultimately of the utility of the description, is also economy. That is, minimal elaboration should be required to communicate the definition so that team members can readily use it. For example, in defining an assault, the team might specify that it includes striking, pushing, or spitting at another person. Or defining "initiation of a positive interaction with a peer" might include making a verbal statement that includes the peer's name and is a positive observation about an activity of the peer or a possession of the peer or is a direct request or invitation to participate in an activity. This criterion has also been referred to as "the stranger test" (Kaplan and Carter, 1995), that is, whether the definition of the behavior could be conveyed easily to a stranger.
- *Completeness.* Does the definition of the behavior specify those acts that are included in the behavior and those that are not? For example, with an aggressive child the definition of an assault might specify that verbal

aggression without a physical act is not considered an assault. Ultimately, of course, verbal aggression may also be engaged by an intervention. Initially, however, verbal aggression by itself might be considered progress and therefore not included under the behavioral definition of an assault. In defining "initiates positive interactions with peers," it might be specified that routine interactions, such as requests for food to be passed at the dinner table, are not included.

It is easy to see how this process of behavior definition might proceed with, for example, a client newly admitted to a program or at the earliest stages of outpatient treatment. Even before the child has been seen, intake documents and the reports of caretakers or other informants have often provided a sense of what the critical behaviors are that will need to be addressed in an intervention plan. Sometimes these behaviors are elaborated only in terms of the general trait or diagnostic descriptions like those used in the illustrations here. Sometimes the descriptions refer to particular behaviors with some specificity but do not convey a sense of their intensity or frequency. Fairly regularly, these descriptions fail to provide clues about those factors that may possess stimulus control over the behavior. Nevertheless, these sources provide general areas for initial, informal observation; and from these initial observations a definition is constructed of those critical behaviors which will be the focus of systematic observation and, ultimately, of intervention.

What then are some examples of definitions of critical behaviors that illustrate objectivity, clarity, and completeness? Here are two examples of such operational definitions of general categories of behavior. The first example defines a problem behavior that will be the focus of intervention, and the second example defines adaptive behaviors that might be part of a positive behavioral intervention.

- *Hyperactivity and disorganization:* This is defined as the number of times that the child leaves his or her seat in the classroom without permission (an objective behavior). Leaving his or her seat is defined as no longer being in physical contact with any part of the desk during any class period in which the clear expectation is completion of desk work (a clear description that can be easily communicated to team members and to the client). This behavior does not include leaving the desk when permission has been requested and given (the limits of the behavior are specified).
- *Supporting peers:* This is defined as the number of positive statements made to peers during the unstructured play activities including recess, classroom, and house play periods. Positive statements are further defined as compliments about a peer's performance ("Good shot!"), appearance ("You look nice."), or shared activities ("That was a fun

game."). Also included are explicit expressions of thanks for the positive acts of peers, defined as uttering the words "Thank you" or "Thanks for . . . ," and a brief description of the positive act ("Thanks for lending me your ball."). This behavior does not include verbalizations to peers that are neutral or are demands, requests, or questions.

A final note on behavioral description: Generally, it is a good idea to keep in mind the notion of describing observable acts either being committed or to be committed by the client. Using verbs (Kaplan and Carter, 1995) and avoiding judgments, diagnoses, and hypothetical underlying personality traits is a good rule of thumb in this process.

BEHAVIORAL ASSESSMENT I: HOW MUCH OF THE BEHAVIOR IS HAPPENING? DOES IT MEET A DEFINED STANDARD?

Once adequately objective, complete, and clear definitions of key behaviors have been produced, the clinician and the team come to the next part of the assessment process. This requires a more systematic approach than that seen in the less formal observations that are needed for defining behavior. Once again, it is important to keep in mind that behaviors of interest or target behaviors may be negative behaviors that the client can be helped to stop or reduce or positive behaviors that the client can be helped to learn or increase.

The first level of behavioral assessment very often involves determining how much the behavior is occurring (Miltenberger, 2005). This process provides baseline data that will ultimately allow the team to determine if any intervention has had the desired effect. The particular form that this assessment takes, though, will depend on the particular dimensions that have been used to define the behavior. This assessment may be as simple as counting the frequency with which the behavior occurs in a given time period. In many cases, though, it is important to focus the question "How much?" in more specific ways. Two examples can illustrate this point. In the first case, a withdrawn, isolated boy is helped to become more active with his peers. The behavior of interest that is decided on is "initiating interactions with peers." This target behavior is then defined more specifically to include the following behaviors, and the assessment procedure may involve marking a recording sheet each time that the behavior occurs: asking to join an ongoing game or activity, complimenting another child on his or her performance in a game or athletic event, or inviting another child to join him in a game or activity.

In the second case, a client who has poor personal hygiene is helped to bathe more effectively. In this case, the target behavior is defined more specifically to include the following component behaviors:

- Brushes teeth for 2 minutes before entering shower
- Places an appropriate amount of shampoo on hair, works up lather, and massages it in
- Uses bar soap to wash body in a head-to-toe progression, beginning with face and ending with feet

In this case, the team is not interested in making the behavior occur more than once per day, and therefore, a continuing frequency count would not be meaningful. Instead, the team is concerned with whether or not the component behaviors occur within a particular time frame in the client's day (evening hygiene time). Thus, the nature of the target behaviors will determine what workers focus on as the assessment is carried out. It is also true that behaviors vary in the ease with which they can be assessed, and this also determines how to go about answering the "how much" question. For example, low-frequency behaviors that are dramatic and therefore easily observed can be continuously recorded. An assault on a peer or a staff member does not usually happen more than a few times in a day, and each instance can be recorded. Other behaviors, though, may occur at very high rates and a continuous frequency count would require the full attention of an assessor at all times. Such an approach would place an unacceptable drain on resources and is usually not possible. Examples of these sorts of behaviors include off-task behavior, provoking peers, and self-isolating behaviors. In cases such as these, observers may need to specify particular intervals for observation that will provide meaningful, representative samples of the behavior. Thus, for example, a classroom teacher assessing on-task behavior might specify three 10-minute observation periods in the course of the school day for a staff member to focus exclusively on that behavior in a particular client. The actual timing of the intervals would be chosen according to the schedule of the school day, to increase the likelihood of capturing a meaningful sample.

As with the example of hygiene, the initial assessment of some behaviors of interest will not involve frequency but may require observation of duration or intensity (Kazdin, 2001; Miltenberger, 2005). A self-isolating child, for example, may successfully begin to initiate contact with peers but may limit those contacts to very brief exchanges. In this case, it will be necessary for the team to focus their assessment and intervention efforts on the *duration* of exchanges with peers. This may be a more labor-intensive process and would require some observation of the child in those settings in which social contact with peers occurs and actual timing of interactions. When the behavior of interest involves intensity, as with a child who is learning to modulate the volume of her voice, the team must create a simple but reliable rating scale of intensity. In this particular example, the team has no purely objective measure of intensity (volume) such as that provided by a decibel meter. Therefore, the rating scale must be simple enough that is likely to be interpreted similarly by the multiple observers who might use it. Thus, a three-point scale that goes from normal voice tone to raised voice to yelling might serve the team's purposes well.

BEHAVIORAL ASSESSMENT II: ATTEMPTING TO DISCERN THE FUNCTION OF BEHAVIOR

The approach to practice described here begins with an assumption that clients, and this includes children and their families, have been doing the best they can with the resources they have available. This idea can be restated in behavioral terms with a related meaning: All relationships with clients begin with the default assumption that their problematic behaviors worked for them in some way in other settings and relationships. "Worked for them" means that these behaviors may have been the only way in which they could successfully establish proximity with caretakers or create some sense of safety or control and predictability for themselves. In the earlier discussion of the importance of relationships with caretakers, it was argued that this drive to establish proximity is a biologically based, hardwired need existing in the child from birth. The difficulties in the lives of many clients, and this includes both parents and children, often involve some disruption or distortion in relationships with caretakers, which result in, among other things, the learning of problematic behaviors. These behaviors, while often puzzling and very vexing to others, can sometimes be understood as efforts to create proximity and safety or to lower anxiety about the whereabouts or well-being of a caretaker or as a response to trauma. Thus, a key ingredient in effective behavioral assessment involves a systematic effort to discern those forces and events in the life of the client that established the behavior and those forces and events in the current environment that may trigger, maintain, or have some control over the expression of the behavior. In the literature of behavior modification, this process is referred to as "functional analysis" (Watson and Steege, 2003; Bambara and Kern, 2005) and, at its best, it is a powerful, systematic expression of respect for the behavior and its meaning and curiosity about how it is triggered and maintained in the current environment.

It is not difficult to find treatment settings in which behavioral intervention is undertaken in the absence of a careful functional analysis. Various behaviors, both positive and negative, are targeted for positive or negative consequences; and not much thought is given to understanding the antecedents, settings, or other stimuli that may be associated with their occurrence. Unfortunately, failure to consider these issues in developing an intervention plan does not mean that one has no assumptions about the function and meaning of the behavior but only that one's assumptions are implicit and untested. This way of proceeding is, of course, possible; but because it usually relies on such untested assumptions about the client and the behavior, there is some likelihood that effort will be wasted and the client will be poorly served. This difficulty is often encountered with behavioral plans that rely primarily on extinction to reduce or eliminate negative target behaviors. (*Extinction* is the behavioral principle underlying strategies in which the reinforcement, or the assumed reinforcement, of a behavior is stopped so that the frequency of the behavior declines [Martin and Pear, 1999]. The use of extinction will be discussed in greater detail later.) In these situations, an assumption is sometimes made that the behavior is being reinforced by attention (even negative attention) that has been provided by adults. A plan is then devised to simply withdraw attention by having adults in the child's environment not respond to the behavior in question. Such a plan could be successful if the assumption is, in fact, correct and if some new behavior is taught to the child to secure the attention of adults through some more acceptable behavior. Kazdin (2001) describes similar difficulties with interventions that rely on "throwing consequences" at a problem without some hypothesis about the role of antecedents, settings, and consequences.

In order to illustrate the value of carefully investigating a behavior's function, two untested theories will be considered about a particular behavior. The behavior in question is seen in a 9-year-old girl who has recently been admitted to a group home. Once she has been put to bed for the night, the girl begins to call out to staff members, requesting drinks of water and permission to use the bathroom. Often, she engages any staff member who responds and will ask questions about the next day's activities and which staff members will be working. This behavior is then repeated multiple times and ends up being disruptive to her roommate and to staff routine. In one theory, the team hypothesizes that the girl is engaging in this behavior to "get attention from adults." They note that in the girl's last placement caretakers reacted to this behavior by allowing the girl to get out of bed, engaging her in conversation about whatever complaint or concern she had, and generally rewarding the behavior with attention. In another theory, the team notes that the girl has been a victim of sexual abuse in several settings and that in at least some cases this abuse occurred at bedtime. They hypothesize that the girl is experiencing significant anxiety at bedtime and that her calling out to staff is an effort to establish some feeling of control and safety. In this model the behavior represents an effort to escape from the aversive experience of anxious dread that she feels at bedtime.

It is easy to see that these two theories represent very different ways of thinking about the behavior in question and that they will likely lead to different approaches to intervention. The first group of staff feels pretty certain that they can reduce the frequency of the behavior by presenting the girl with a reinforcement environment in which her requests are met with minimal responses. If she escalates her efforts to engage staff (an "extinction burst" in this model), she will be moved from her bedroom to a time-out in the living room. The second group of staff feels that this behavior will diminish if the child's requests are met with reasonable reassurances and a comforting bedtime routine that reduces her anxiety. This might involve reading a story and then having a staff member sit in close proximity to her room until she falls asleep.

It should also be easy to see that these two approaches to intervention will yield quite different outcomes depending on which theory more fully captures the experience of the child. If the first theory is largely correct but the second intervention is utilized, then the staff will find themselves actually increasing the rate of nighttime requests and demands. Similarly, if the second theory is largely correct and the first approach is applied, then the child is likely to desperately escalate bedtime acting out in an effort to secure proximity from staff who are making every effort to disengage from her.

THE QUESTIONS THAT DRIVE A FUNCTIONAL ANALYSIS

The second example illustrates the importance of arriving at a theory of what function various problem behaviors may serve for a child. Watson and Steege (2003) note, "Only by identifying the relationships between the unique characteristics of the individual and the contextual variables that trigger and reinforce behavior can we begin to truly understand human behavior and work in concert with the person and those in his/her environment to develop interventions that lead to socially significant and meaningful behavior change (p. 5)." In attempting to generate useful hypotheses about the function of behavior, there are a number of questions that the team should pursue. These questions are in no way specific to a particular kind of setting; the child may be in a classroom, in a group home, or with his own family. These questions are concerned with eliciting information about events in the client's environment or within the client himself that are reliably associated with the behavior and can then be addressed in an intervention plan.

- What are the settings in which the behavior occurs? Are there some in which it always occurs? Are there any settings in which the behavior never occurs? For traumatized children being served in intensive treatment programs, it is useful to consider transitions, bedtimes, and other periods of reduced structure or proximity. Do events in the setting seem to elicit negative emotional states (anxiety, fear, frustration, humiliation) from which the client would be motivated to escape? Does the behavior reliably occur at particular times of the day but not at others? Can anything about other events which may be controlling or eliciting the behavior be learned from these temporal patterns?
- What are the antecedents of the behavior? These may include events in the environment and states in the client (such as fatigue, hunger, contact with particular individuals, and thoughts and feelings which the client reports). Antecedents may also involve behaviors of the client that are part of a chain of events that ultimately leads to the behavior of interest occurring. Thus, for example, verbal aggression by the client may be a reliable antecedent of physical aggression. It is also important to note that when trauma is an element in the child's history, certain figures in his life, certain kinds of physical settings, certain sensory experiences (smells, for

example), and certain affects are potential triggers of dysregulated emotional and behavioral states and dissociative episodes (Nader, 2008).

- What are the consequences of the behavior? Does the behavior reliably result in any particular outcome for the client? How do key people in the child's environment respond to the behavior? Is the behavior resulting in escape from or termination of any aversive states such as anxiety or humiliation?
- From the client's point of view, what function does the behavior serve?
- Does the team's knowledge of the client's history suggest any other factors that should be considered? Here, the investigation is being opened to more complex, not immediately observable factors that may have contributed to the establishment of problematic behaviors. In some populations of clients, these factors most often include the effects of trauma and neglect but may also include a variety of client variables such as health issues, learning disabilities, medication effects, or expressive or receptive language difficulties. (In this regard, see Appendix J, titled "Client Variables Form". This form may be used as a prompt for the team, ensuring that client factors will be assessed as possible contributors to the behaviors under review. It is adapted from a similar form offered by Watson and Steege [2003].)

If these are the questions that drive an investigation of the functions and meanings of a client's behavior, then what are the methods needed to go about answering them? In general, these methods proceed by systematic, direct observation of the client across those settings in which she lives and behaves. It is, of course, possible for a treatment team to assemble and share their less formal observations of a client. These sorts of discussions are, especially in a staff that has some behavioral training, enormously useful. Similarly, a clinician may meet with parents and pursue their theories and observations about the triggers and settings that they feel are related to the child's behavior. This sort of exploration almost always leads to important data and should be part of any initial work with parents. Such discussions, however, are best viewed as preliminary, as an initial effort to generate hypotheses about behavior that can then be evaluated through further observation. Thus, for example, members of the team might note that a behavior of concern seems to occur only at school or that it is more frequent at bedtime. Parents meeting with a clinician may contribute observations about the role of fatigue, the influence of particular peers, or the effects of a sibling's behavior. These hypotheses and observations can then be integrated into a more formal assessment plan in which the behavior is tracked, settings and antecedents are recorded, and the responses of the various adults in the child's life are noted. Once this sort of data is collected, the team is in a position to look for meaningful patterns which may shed light on the function of the behavior and then guide intervention. (In Appendix I, "Functional Analysis Worksheet," a series of prompts are provided to guide such collaborative discussions with parents, treatment partners such as teachers, and program staff members.)

In an earlier discussion of assessment processes, it was noted that it is not all that helpful to view assessment as entirely distinct from intervention. The current discussion of behavioral assessment methods illustrates this issue well. In working with parents or caretakers of children who present with various sorts of behavior problems, the approach discussed here can be enormously helpful in lowering emotional intensity, evoking curiosity, and creating a measure of optimism and hope. Not infrequently, caretakers, feeling overwhelmed by the difficulties of managing the child, may feel that certain behaviors are happening constantly and may end up with a variety of competing theories about the sources of these behaviors. They may be buffeted by the opinions of various professionals, of the child's teacher, and of their own parents. At times, they are mystified and at a loss; at other times, they may note the similarities of the child's behavior to a biologically based mental illness they saw described on the news; and at other times, they may feel that the child is simply bad, manipulative, or mean-spirited. Regardless of their theory, however, it is almost always the case that they possess a fair amount of data about actual events. Questions that bring these data forward and enlist the parents as coevaluators almost always help to create a treatment alliance and to convey to the parents a sense that things may actually make sense and that they can become more effectively connected to the behavior of their children. At this moment, assessment is indistinguishable from treatment. If the parents can be drawn into the more systematic collection of data by, for example, doing daily frequency counts or keeping a log of antecedents and settings, then they may discover that the behavior doesn't happen as much as they thought, that desirable replacement behaviors are already in the child's repertoire, and that there actually are some meaningful patterns to when problem behaviors occur.

In the earlier discussion of defining behaviors, the importance of arriving at descriptions of behaviors of concern that are specific and concrete and that possess the qualities of clarity, objectivity, and completeness was noted. A description that meets these standards will make reliable assessments of the behavior's function possible. There are a variety of approaches to tracking behavior once it is defined. Discussions of various methods may be found in Kazdin (2001), Martin and Pear (1999), and Bambara and Kern (2005). The most straightforward approach involves creating a simple chart, with the definition of the behavior noted at the top and a series of rows for recording each example of the behavior. The observer simply notes the time the behavior occurred, records the antecedents and settings related to the occurrence, and notes any consequence that followed the behavior. This approach works best for relatively low-frequency events that might happen several times in a school day or a residential shift. Here's a simple example:

Behavior: *Aggression toward peers, defined as making threatening verbal demands with an intimidating voice and posture, placing hands on a peer in a threatening way such as grabbing the front of a shirt, shoving or shouldering aside, and direct aggression in the form of a slap, punch, or kick.*

The data in Table 6.1 could then lead to the hypothesis that an important antecedent for Andrew's behavior is competitive situations in which there is less structure. It also seems that this boy's behavior is being reinforced by the submission of his peers. In any setting in which this sort of observational scheme is undertaken, it is possible to add further observational categories that will contribute other data. In a treatment milieu this might include the shift on which the incident occurred, the gender of the staff who are present, the actual identities of the staff who are present, the immediate "tone" of the milieu (as in calm, shaky with other kids in crisis, or in full crisis), and the child's current level on the level system. The categories that are included on the recording form will be depend on the very preliminary guesses that staff, caretakers, or other collaborators have offered about what might be related to the behavior. Sometimes the first few days of observation will very quickly point to fruitful areas for more detailed observation, and the tracking form can then be revised accordingly. The observations then have a way of systematically capturing the role of these other factors that emerged in the course of the earlier observations.

Table 6.1 An Illustration of a Simple Functional Assessment Scheme

Date and Time	Description of Incident	Antecedent/Settings	Consequences/Effects
2/6 1:45 p.m.	Andrew shoved Peter	Basketball game on playground	Peter retreats
2/7 10:00 a.m.	Andrew takes menacing posture toward Steve	Discussion of taking turns at Nintendo	Steve backs down
2/7 11:45 a.m.	Andrew pushes past several peers as they are getting into the van	Transition to van for an outing	Peers allow him to get ahead
2/8 8:45 a.m.	Andrew makes a fist and waves it in Sally's face while he is smiling	School day hasn't started yet, Andrew and Sally are arguing over who will get to pick up the lunches	Sally is silent

It is also important to note that sometimes, particularly in complex environments like milieu treatment programs, events may not have the meaning to the client that the team might assume. A very simple example of this involves the use of time-out strategies. Workers may assume that removal from a setting will function as a time-out from positive reinforcement when in fact, for the client, it is experienced as an escape from a situation which is in some way painful, humiliating, or simply unstimulating. This is why the data from any observational scheme must be evaluated with care. Recall the example of the little girl who acted out at bedtime. If she is removed from her bedroom for a time-out in the staff office where a staff member supervises her, that intervention may be a welcome relief from the anxiety she experienced lying in bed with no staff nearby. Another example familiar to school or day treatment staff involves the problem of relying on a special classroom for disruptive students. In some settings these classrooms are created to hold students who are being disruptive. The goal is to remove the child from a reinforcing situation in which she may be rewarded by the amusement of peers or the negative attention of teachers. At the same time, instruction in the regular classroom can continue without disruption. Typically, the student is permitted to rejoin the class as soon as she demonstrates a readiness to be compliant. These settings are generally designed to be nonreinforcing (no talking or social interaction is permitted). While they are often vital to maintaining a calm, productive educational milieu, they may inadvertently reinforce negative, disruptive client behavior by allowing escape from what the student may be experiencing as the humiliating failure of academic work or by providing an audience of like-minded peers who are also displaying disruptive or defiant behavior. In the worst-case scenario, such a setting becomes a much more gratifying one than the regular classroom and has the additional negative impact of confirming the student's implicit beliefs that she will inevitably be ejected from normal settings and that she is a bad, disruptive, and unwelcome presence wherever she goes. It will be important to revisit this issue when the use of time-out is discussed as a behavioral intervention; it is raised in this context because sometimes overly simple observational schemes may miss the most important data. In the example of Andrew, depicted in Table 6.1, the situation might unfold in the following way: A series of observations might show that he had been removed from the classroom after each incident of aggression. In spite of this use of extended time-out from the classroom, the behavior persists at very high rates. It becomes important then to be curious about why this intervention is not effective, and further inquiry might reveal that, rather than experiencing a negative consequence, Andrew is being intermittently reinforced for his aggression by getting to affiliate with other disruptive clients. An interesting variant on this problem involves the relationships that clients sometimes develop with the staff members who are in charge of settings to which disruptive students are separated. For some youngsters this may be the first real connection that they establish in a new school placement. After years of being disruptive and feeling out of control, unsafe, and too powerful in every setting in which they have been placed, these young people finally encounter a figure who is "up to the challenge" of providing them with consistent, neutral, nonretaliatory containment. After multiple settings in which the child has been successful in creating havoc and has intimidated and unnerved a series of adults, she now encounters an immovable force, an adult who is capable of setting limits in a resolute, calm way. This relationship often becomes very important to the child, and since these adults are staffing the setting where one is sent for being disruptive, it is necessary to guard against the possibility that the child will act out in order to have contact with them. The simple solution to this problem is to afford the child positive opportunities to spend time with these special staff members. Such a strategy can even be formally integrated into a child's behavioral treatment plan.

In carrying out any inquiry into the function of behavior, the search for reinforcing events should not be emphasized at the expense of the search for controlling or eliciting stimuli. Research on the behavior of aggressive children in their families shows quite clearly that the moment-to-moment occurrence of aggressive behavior in the home is determined by the presence or absence of key controlling or triggering stimuli and is only weakly related to changes in reinforcement (Patterson, 2002). When evaluating the function of behavior, it is also important to make every effort to look at all consequences of the behavior and not only those that are initiated by caretakers, staff members, or other adults in the child's life. Thus, for example, with older children and adolescents, the response of peers to their behavior may be far more reinforcing than any reaction from adults. The effects of peer reinforcement on antisocial behavior have been well documented (Snyder, 2002). This is a very important consideration in the design and planning of any treatment environment for these young people. It is of great importance that a reinforcement culture be created in which youth are challenged to be active participants in each others' treatment and to reward each other for progress toward personal and behavioral goals.

Finally, it is also important to acknowledge that there are some real limitations to functional analysis. Kazdin (1995, 2001) has noted these difficulties with regard to aggressive children, pointing out that such behavior has been related to a range of factors, such as the presence of aggressive behavior in the family, the child's emotional temperament at birth, and the parents' use of corporal punishment. Careful direct observation in a treatment setting may reveal only a subset of factors, such as the reinforcing reactions of peers, and yield no information about these important historical factors. Similarly, functional analysis does not provide access to internal factors that cannot be observed in behavior. These include the client's beliefs and assumptions about how the world works and are often knowable only from interaction with the client in the context of a relationship. Others (Carr and Leblanc, 2003) have pointed out that very low–frequency behaviors can be difficult to assess reliably since an adequate sample of observations may be difficult to obtain. In this case it may be possible to do a functional assessment of a higher-frequency precursor or antecedent that is regularly associated with the occurrence of the lower-frequency behavior (Kern, 2005).

KEY INGREDIENTS IN IMPLEMENTING POSITIVE BEHAVIORAL CHANGE

When these steps are followed, a number of behaviors of concern will have been identified and described and observations will have been made that yield hypotheses about the functions of this behavior. Thus, an initial behavioral assessment has been completed and a behavioral intervention can now be planned.

Any consideration of behavioral intervention begins with a discussion of the nature of reinforcement. This term appears to be simple, but its use in learning theory and behavior modification has some complexity. It is sometimes used interchangeably with the more common "reward," and this can lead to some confusion. In behavioral terms, *reinforcement* is something that either increases the frequency of a behavior by its presence (a *positive reinforcer* or a reward) or increases the frequency of a behavior by its removal (a *negative reinforcer*). Positive reinforcers are sometimes divided into primary and secondary categories, with *primary reinforcers* being those rewards that derive their power from biologically determined needs—typically food and sex but also, as we have seen, proximity to attachment figures—and *secondary* (or conditioned) *reinforcers* being those stimuli that derive their effectiveness in increasing behavior from their association with primary reinforcers—for example, money, tokens or points in a level system. A negative reinforcer is a stimulus that the organism is motivated to work to avoid or escape from. (It is important to keep in mind that a negative reinforcer is not the same as a punishment, which reduces the frequency of a behavior *by its presence*.) Examples of negative reinforcers would include a spouse's nagging or a child's tantrum. The parent might respond to the tantrum by, for example, giving the child a toy to distract her or him. The cessation of the tantrum at that point would reinforce the parent's use of distraction when the child is upset.

Lists of what constitutes useful positive reinforcers for the teaching of new behavior almost always include material reinforcement, social reinforcers such as praise and attention, and various token or "back-up" reinforcers such as points in a level system that can be used to gain access to privileges or to "purchase" material reinforcers. In addition to these familiar sorts of rewarding experiences, there are two categories of positive reinforcement worth mentioning. They include high-probability behaviors (Premack, 1959) and feedback (Kazdin, 2001; Van Houten, 1998).

High-Probability Behaviors as Reinforcers

The use of high-probability behaviors to reward low-probability behaviors may sound complicated and esoteric but is, in fact, the simple phenomenon behind a good parent's instruction to a child "No TV until your homework is done." In other words, watching TV, which for most children is a high-probability behavior, functions as a reward for a low-probability behavior—in this case, the completion of homework. Point and level systems, while they rely on the use of backup reinforcers as the immediate reward conveyed to the client at the time of performing a target behavior, often utilize high-probability behaviors as the real rewards. That is, points are, according to some more or less systematic method, converted into privileges such as a later bedtime and the opportunity to watch TV, to use the video game system, and to participate in outings. While these events are often powerfully reinforcing, they do have certain drawbacks that should be acknowledged (Kazdin, 2001). In most real-world settings (a classroom, for example), it is often not possible or desirable to immediately convey the reward of a high-probability behavior. Futhermore, such rewards are not easily divided into partial rewards and are typically things that can be either earned or not earned. Thus, the targeted behavior of initiating a positive interaction with a peer may happen a number of times over several days, but the reward of being able to participate in a weekly outing or special event may be days away. The issue of timing the reward is not a small one and will be discussed at greater length later. Points, which the client may understand will lead to the ultimate reward, may serve a useful intermediate function that helps to establish and maintain the behavior; but for clients who are younger, who have a shorter time perspective, or who are new to a point and level system, the issue of delay may be of real importance.

Feedback as a Reinforcer

Feedback about performance must also be counted as a useful addition to the list of reinforcing events. It is certainly the case that any reinforcing event contains information for the client about how he is performing, but it is also the case that such information, even in the absence of any other reinforcing event, can be an effective reward. This phenomenon is why biofeedback procedures have been effective in helping medical patients control a range of physiological functions, such as blood pressure, and explains the popularity of the complex feedback devices now attached to almost all new exercise equipment that busily provide the exerciser with information on heart rate, calories consumed, and miles cycled. These examples show clearly that feedback can also be harnessed as a useful part of a system of behavior change. The behavior modification literature outlines a number of very useful guidelines for effective use of feedback. Van Houten (1998) offers the following useful rules:

- Use a quantitative measure of performance such as rate of behavior or percentage of correct responses. Numerical feedback is most effective.
- Give feedback as immediately as possible. When delays in feedback are inevitable, it is sometimes possible to have clients score or evaluate their own performance and thereby provide the feedback themselves.
- Give feedback frequently. In general, the more feedback that is provided, the more rapidly new behavior is learned.

- Make the feedback positive; avoid giving feedback about failure or incorrect responses and praise correct performance.
- Provide group feedback. Set a goal for the group that will have the effect of improving individual performance. This approach will tend to create positive group and class effects that will amplify the reinforcing effect of the feedback.
- Post feedback results publicly. This guideline has the effect of prompting the behavior of both staff and peers to recognize and praise good performances.

Notes on the Use of Praise and Attention

Certainly, for a great many children, the most cost-effective positive reinforcer that can be used is praise and attention. It is readily available, requires no complicated arrangements to deliver, and has been shown by years of research to be very effective (Hall and Hall, 1998a). Praise and attention should be the most common positive behavioral intervention, and it overlaps significantly with what has been called "engagement." *Engagement* means that it is important to be curious about and attentive to the child's pursuits, projects, strengths, and successes as well as those moments in which he connects with adults in an authentic way. The word "praise" tends to suggest direct verbal compliments or encouragement, and certainly these can be useful reinforcers. It is also very valuable to ask questions, show interest and curiosity, and establish physical proximity. The systematic use of praise and attention that can be employed in behavior modification should include the following elements (many items follow the discussion of Hall and Hall, 1998a):

- It should be related to positive behavior.
- It should be varied and specific. Beware of stereotyped phrases that get used with every child or in every situation.
- Make eye contact and, when appropriate, physically touch to underscore the verbal praise.
- Enthusiasm should be varied according to the magnitude of the accomplishment. It is important to be authentic. Beware of "praise inflation."
- When possible and appropriate to the performance, show interest and curiosity about how it was accomplished.
- Praise the behavior and not the person.
- In general, praise is most effective when it is delivered immediately. Sometimes, though, attention to a good performance that is delayed can be very powerful. When a staff member tells a child "After I left work last night I was thinking about what a great job you did with . . ." that staff member is letting the child know that he continues to be an

important concern even when not immediately present. Many clients have not regularly and reliably had this experience of being held in the mind of another (see, for example, Pawl, 1995).

- Praise and attention can be public or private. Public recognition of a good performance can amplify rewarding effects by harnessing the attention of the whole group. Private or subtle acknowledgment of a child with a meaningful look, a smile, or some form of physical contact can be powerful because of the way in which it is unspoken and, hence, evokes some shared, private understanding of the relationship and of the child's effort or success.

In a treatment milieu such as a special education classroom or a day treatment program, in which staff are striving to be positive and to recognize and acknowledge good performances, there is sometimes a great deal of explicit, verbal praise being doled out. When this praise becomes too stereotyped or is elicited too easily, it can lose its value as a reinforcer—hence, the warning about "praise inflation." (Or, as a client once observed to a worker who had too readily offered some bit of praise, "You guys say 'good job' just for breathing!") In general, though, even a brief period of observation of a treatment milieu will reveal how difficult it is for staff to keep the economy of attention in the positive range. Often, there will be so much low-grade negative behavior eliciting staff attention that the tone will tilt decidedly in the direction of constant negative prompts, corrections, and time-outs. Many of these responses may be appropriate, but the result of failing to continue to recognize desired behaviors with praise and attention will be a gradual drift toward an increasingly negative atmosphere. This drift, once it begins, can be very hard to correct and may gradually result in increasingly negative (pessimistic, pathologizing) views of clients that are expressed both explicitly and implicitly by staff members. Another obstacle to maintenance of a rewarding environment in which positive behaviors are being recognized and praised is a feeling on the part of staff that they are rewarding behavior that the client should already be able to perform. This concern may be expressed as worries about infantilizing clients or failing to prepare them for the real world. This worry is understandable as it is certainly the case that a worker can easily find her- or himself in the position of praising behavior that is typically well established in many children of the same age as a client. Nevertheless, if careful assessment has shown that a key behavior is not established, then that is where the team must begin its intervention.

The Basic Elements of Behavioral Intervention

In moving from the assessment stage to the intervention stage, a number of ingredients that are part of any behavior-change strategy need to be attended to. These elements are all related to reinforcement and include contingency, timing, magnitude (or satiation), selection, and schedule. This discussion of factors that must be considered in planning a program of positive behavioral intervention follows that of Kazdin (2001). Depending on the setting in which the clinician or the treatment team is operating and the resources that are available to them, it may be more or less difficult to control all these variables in exactly the way that would render intervention optimally effective. Nevertheless, decisions that the treatment team makes about each of these variables will determine the specifics of a plan and how the client will learn new behavior.

Contingency of reinforcement

In considering the impact of reinforcement on behavior, the concept of "contingency: is critical. In this context, *contingency* simply expresses the idea that in order for the reinforcement to occur, the behavior must occur first. A perfect one-to-one relationship between the occurrence of the behavior and the delivery of the reinforcement would be complete contingency. A completely noncontingent relationship would require that the reinforcement never occur after the behavior. Many efforts to develop and implement behavioral plans in which specific behaviors are to be reinforced fail because the delivery of the reinforcement is not reliably connected to the goal behavior. This reliable connection ("If I do the behavior, I will earn a reward") is especially important early in the process of learning a new behavior. It is also important to keep in mind that many clients have developed or received treatment in settings in which reinforcement was unpredictable or almost completely noncontingent. For some of these children, their persistent provocative, negative behavior has been an attempt to wrest some sort of predictability and coherence from the environment. It may have been the only thing they did which secured a reliable response from caretakers. The bottom line, then, is very simple: Contingent reinforcement establishes behavior, and noncontingent reinforcement results in little or no change.

Timing

The next property of a reinforcement that determines its effectiveness is its timing in relation to the target behavior. Is the reinforcement delayed or immediate? It is a well-established principle of learning theory that immediate reinforcement produces more powerful results than does delayed reinforcement (Kazdin, 2001; Martin and Pear, 1999). A great many unfortunate behaviors of children and adults owe their existence to the fact that they result in an immediate, short-term positive reinforcement, while any negative consequence may not occur for months or even years. The immediate rewards establish and support behaviors more effectively than the delayed negative consequences can reduce the behaviors. In families or treatment settings more immediate reinforcers will establish behavior more quickly and closer to standard than if the reward is delayed (Kazdin, 2001). Immediate reinforcement is especially critical when a new behavior is being learned for the first time. After a behavior has been established and occurs in the desired settings on a reliable basis, it is possible and even desirable to introduce an element of gradual delay of reinforcement. Timing of reinforcement is also an important variable to keep in mind when working with clients of varied age or developmental level. Obviously, more mature clients may be able to wait for a reward until the end of an academic period or the end of the day. Younger or very disorganized clients may, especially in the early stages of treatment, need regular, more or less immediate positive reinforcement to remain engaged and to master new behaviors.

Magnitude or amount

The role of the magnitude of the reinforcer in determining its effectiveness is related to the concept of "satiation." Thus, while rewards of greater magnitude generally result in more frequent behavior, this effect declines when satiation has been reached. In practical terms, this means that any program of behavior change must arrange for reinforcement of the right magnitude so that it can continue to be rewarding. Excessive rewards will result in satiation and a drop in motivation to earn the rewards. The young client who noted that staff members give praise for breathing was observing, in part, that the rewards were too big for the behaviors that were being displayed. As a result, these efforts by staff to reward behavior had begun to lose their reinforcing power.

In general, professionals and paraprofessionals who work with highly vulnerable children are well aware that many of their clients have experienced both physical and emotional deprivation. Not infrequently they have fairly strong personal needs to gratify their clients, and they may be uneasy thinking in terms of deprivation as a driver of treatment effectiveness. Nevertheless, it is certainly the case that children who participate in treatment programs in which they may earn privileges or opportunities to use highly desirable resources (video games, for example) can satiate on these reinforcers if they have free access to them in other settings. Thus, children in school programs may be unmoved by reinforcers they can easily obtain at home each afternoon, and many residential workers have observed that their clients are not highly motivated after a weekend pass spent at the movies and playing video games or watching television. This problem is a very strong argument for close collaboration on behavioral intervention between treatment programs and the families of their clients.

Selection or choice of the reinforcer

Treatment teams implementing behavior-change plans with clients must also attend to the selection of the reinforcers being utilized. This variable is concerned with determining what things or events or kinds of interpersonal exchanges are likely to be rewarding to a particular client. It could be said that reinforcement is in the eye of the beholder. Or, to put it more accurately, reinforcement is in the eye of the recipient (see, for example, the discussion of selecting reinforcers in Axelrod and Hall, 1999, and Hall and Hall, 1998b). Some clients respond almost immediately to praise and attention, and others are intensely interested in amassing points and moving through a level system. Some clients are highly motivated to earn less structured time with peers; for others this might actually be aversive. At any given time program staff who are implementing a behavioral intervention may note that some percentage of the clients are not responding or have not yet "caught on" or been captured by the system. The reasons for these treatment impasses are usually complex, but in some cases they are due, at least in part, to a failure to discern what sorts of reinforcers might be most powerful with particular clients. This problem can also occur in a family setting in which caretakers undertake similar efforts to systematically reward particular behaviors. In the case of milieu programs, there is often a practice of utilizing generic reinforcers that have worked with most clients. Such an approach is fine—for most clients. Success with the "stuck" minority may require greater curiosity and investigation about what is reinforcing to the "non-responders." Sometimes this inquiry can be as simple as a brief conversation with the client about what sort of rewards she would like to be earning, while in other cases it may require some observation to discern what it is that seems to interest and motivate the client and what his preferred activities are. This issue reveals one difficulty with point and level systems: Such approaches to behavioral intervention are typically somewhat generic and assume that certain privileges, such as later bedtimes and freedom to go on outings or to use the video game system, will actually be reinforcing for all clients. When it is discovered that this is not the case for a particular individual, it is important to adjust the system to include special rewards or to make these rewards available to the client through specific behavioral contracts.

Schedules of reinforcement

A *schedule of reinforcement* is the scheme that determines the occurrence or timing of the delivery of the reinforcement (Masters, Burish, Hollon, and Rimm, 1987). Different schedules of reinforcement produce different and distinctive patterns of responding, and behavioral scientists have studied these effects in great detail. The simplest schedule of reinforcement is referred to as "continuous reinforcement" (Kazdin, 1995). In *continuous reinforcement*, the reward is delivered every time that the behavior occurs. Because this schedule produces very high rates of responding when behaviors are first being learned, it is most useful when new behaviors are being established. The problem with such a schedule of reinforcement is that once continuous reinforcement ends, the behavior also drops off quickly. (In other words, the individual has learned that every time a particular response is produced he will receive a reward. When the reward is not forthcoming, the behavior, unless it is rewarded by some other source of reinforcement, will decline rapidly.)

The other general category of reinforcement schedules is *intermittent schedules*, in which, according to some rule or scheme, only some instances of a particular behavior are rewarded. In this case, new behaviors that are rewarded intermittently will be mastered more slowly, but they will be sustained longer in the absence of reinforcement. (In behavioral terms, it would be said that behaviors learned under

intermittent schedules of reinforcement are more resistant to extinction.)
Intermittent schedules of reinforcement come in four basic types (Axelrod and
Hall, 1999):

- *Fixed ratio*: In this case, reinforcement is delivered after a specific exact
  number of responses have occurred. Thus, for example, every fifth
  instance of a behavior might be rewarded.
- *Fixed interval*: In this case, a specific, fixed time interval must pass before
  the next instance of a behavior can be rewarded. Thus, for example, at
  least 5 minutes would need to elapse after a reward has been delivered
  before the next reward could be delivered.
- *Variable ratio*: In this case, the reward is delivered after an average
  number of responses have occurred. Thus, for example, such a schedule
  might specify that a particular behavior will be rewarded on the average
  of every fifth occurrence. One effect of this is diminished predictability.
  After one instance of a behavior has been rewarded, the very next instance
  might be rewarded; but then the next reward might not come until 10
  behaviors have been observed. Slot machines run on variable ratio
  schedules of reinforcement, and they have the effect, to the advantage
  of casino owners, of producing extremely high rates of responding.
- *Variable interval*: In this case, an average time interval must elapse before
  the next instance of a behavior is reinforced. Thus, for example, the target
  behavior is rewarded only when intervals averaging 5 minutes have
  elapsed. As with variable ratio schedules, this means that some rewards
  will be delivered very soon after the last reward but that some might not
  be delivered for very long intervals.

While there are circumstances in which each of these schedules of reinforcement can be useful, some require greater attention to detail and, hence, significantly more resources. For example, using a fixed ratio schedule of reinforcement
requires a continuous exact count of every instance of the target behavior so that
the reward can be delivered after the correct number of behaviors. In most real-
world treatment settings such an investment of resources would be impossible. In
planning a behavioral intervention, it is probably most important to keep the
following ideas in mind:

- When working with a client to establish a new behavior, always begin
  with a generous ratio schedule of reinforcement, preferably continuous.
- As the client begins to master the behavior and it is showing some stability,
  shift to an intermittent schedule of reinforcement, such as variable ratio.

These two guidelines capture what occurs in naturalistic settings all the time.
Successful parents, teachers, coaches, and supervisors will closely monitor and

continuously reward performance when their children (or students, etc.) are first learning a new skill. As the skill is mastered, they will gradually fade this high level of engagement with that particular behavior (Esveldt-Dawson and Kazdin, 1998). With a great many prosocial positive behaviors, the environment then takes over the reward of the behavior. That is, the individual begins to reap naturally occurring rewards in the form of greater autonomy, more gratifying relationships with peers, or other forms of enhanced performance. Baer (1999) speaks of planning intervention with an eye to the "natural community of reinforcement" that will "maintain, extend and refine" (p. 16) behavior change that is initiated by intervention.

Additional Elements of Behavioral Intervention

Shaping and chaining

Often, a treatment team is in the position of selecting a target behavior for reinforcement that is not yet present at all in the client's behavioral repertoire. The process of developing these completely new behaviors is called *shaping*, and it begins with a search for some behaviors that the client already shows that in some way resemble or contain some element of the desired target behavior. These partial performances can then be reinforced through a process of rewarding successively closer approximations of the desired behavior until the client gradually masters the complete performance (Martin and Pear, 1999).

An illustration of this process would be a client with very poor social skills. The treatment team agrees that a key goal for the client involves cooperative play with peers. They define the behavior as having several possible components:

- Making a positive comment to a peer about any performance or behavior
- Asking to join a game or to take a turn in an activity
- Inviting another child to join in a game or to use one of his possessions

The client, though, has never been seen to do any of these particular behaviors, actually tending to isolate himself from peers and typically engaging only adults. There is agreement on the team that there would be no real opportunities to praise or otherwise reward the desired performance. In using shaping to address this problem, the team might focus first on the behavior of physically approaching peers and reward the client for increasing physical proximity to the group during activities. The successive approximations that would follow might start with the client simply remaining in the same setting when peers are present, then moving to the periphery of group activities such as games and group play, and then moving to some form of actual involvement in the activity.

In other situations the team may find that there is a particular behavioral goal that actually consists of a series of component behaviors that must be organized in a sequence. Room cleaning is a familiar example of this *chaining* process. It might typically proceed from picking up laundry to putting away personal items to making the bed to vacuuming. With some populations this strategy for teaching more complex series of component behaviors is undertaken in a very structured, systematic way. Children who may have spent their early years of development in very chaotic environments with little supervision often have little sense of how to break down a task and carry it out in a logical sequence. When given a direction to clean their room, they will react with a predictably disorganized approach. While caretakers may not need to use highly sophisticated chaining strategies, it is important that they understand the concept and be prepared to support the child in developing a more organized approach to what for her may be complex tasks.

Using positive reinforcement to reduce negative behavior: Differential reinforcement

At the outset of this discussion of behavioral intervention, emphasis was placed on the use of *positive behavioral practice* and the teaching of new behavior. It is also the case, though, that in work with children with histories of disrupted attachments and severe trauma many are referred to treatment not for trauma but for behavioral difficulties. Observing some of these children in any treatment milieu will quickly show that there is far more provocative, disruptive behavior to manage than there is positive behavior to reward. It is very easy in the face of this sort of very well-established, unrelenting negative behavior to move in the direction of negative intervention strategies that rely on equally stubborn efforts to extinguish the behavior or to suppress it with aversive consequences. There are, however, behavioral approaches to the reduction of negative behavior that are based on the utilization of positive consequences. The key element in this approach is a reliance on the simple fact that performance of other, alternative behaviors will leave less room for the performance of the established, often highly practiced behaviors that the client first presents. Furthermore, when intervention proceeds from an understanding of the function of a child's behavior, it is almost always possible to conceive of a more adaptive, more successful, and more acceptable way for the child to accomplish that function.

The general term for this sort of approach is "differential reinforcement," and it relies on systematically applying very different levels of positive reinforcement for two different behaviors (Masters et al., 1987). One behavior, which the team aims to eliminate, receives no positive reinforcement and a second behavior, which the team aims to increase, receives reinforcement on a continuous schedule. The simplest approach of this sort is referred to as "differential reinforcement of other behavior" (Kazdin, 2001) and involves the reinforcement of almost any alternative behavior that the client presents. Such an approach is sometimes necessary when young clients have been in settings in which negative behavior was the only way in which they could secure any sort of attention or engagement from adults. Having learned the lesson well, these children may present us with a blizzard of negative behaviors—striking out at any child who comes within arm's length, grabbing at objects, and ignoring or defying directions. Other children who are enormously disorganized and present with highly impulsive, distracted behavior can also benefit from this approach. For these children, very high levels of one-to-one engagement in which virtually any positive, compliant behavior is praised and attended to with interest can be a useful opening phase of treatment. A more focused version of this strategy can be seen in interventions referred to as "differential reinforcement of alternative responding" (Martin and Pear, 1999), which is also sometimes called "reinforcement of incompatible alternatives." This procedure is more focused in that a target behavior is chosen for positive reinforcement that is an incompatible or competing alternative for a particular negative behavior of concern. The new, rewarded behavior is incompatible with the old, problem behavior in the sense that if it occurs it is much less likely or even impossible for the negative behavior to occur. Thus, the behavior being strengthened directly interferes with or replaces the behavior targeted for reduction. It is not difficult to think of a variety of negative behaviors that can be targeted in this way. Consider the following examples:

Targeted behavior	Rewarded Alternative Behavior
Off-task behavior	On-task behavior
Shouting out in the classroom	Raising hand to be called on
Physical retaliation in response to teasing	Ignoring teasing
Teasing peers	Making positive comments to peers
Encopresis	Using toilet for bowel movements
Persistent questioning and interrupting	Attentive listening

It is, of course, not always possible that the team can define an alternative behavior that will directly interfere with the performance of the negative behavior that has been targeted for elimination. It is, however, often possible in these cases to define alternative behaviors that accomplish the same function as the target behavior, or "functionally equivalent behaviors" (Watson and Steege, 2003). Thus, for example, a treatment team wishes to reduce a little girl's persistent physical aggression toward the adults working with her. A review of her history and observation of antecedents, settings, and consequences of this behavior suggests that she is among those children who have been in an institutional setting in which the only way to secure attention and engagement from adults was to engage in some form of negative behavior. Thus, it could be said that the function of her behavior was to seek proximity with and attention from her caretakers. At this point, the goal is to simply devise a behavioral intervention that assists the client in accomplishing the same function. Sometimes this can be as simple as teaching the client that he can ask for a reinforcer rather than having to engage in some negative way in order to provoke it from the environment. A very striking example of this process can be seen with neglected, emotionally deprived children who engage in highly disruptive behavior to provoke physical restraint when they enter foster or residential placement. When these children are taught that it is possible to simply *ask* for a hug and a moment of physical contact, their disruptive behavior often declines significantly.

Extinction

Extinction refers to the decline in frequency of a behavior that occurs when the reinforcement that has maintained it is no longer available (Hall and Hall, 1998c). Extinction is another method available for the reduction of negative behavior without resorting to negative consequences or punishment. It is a process that is important to understand very well and should not be used in isolation. Sometimes a behavioral intervention is based on an assessment that a particular reinforcing event has been maintaining the behavior. The obvious strategy might then consist of simply interrupting this process or in some way preventing the reinforcement from being delivered. This can be a risky or unproductive way in which to proceed since so many complex behaviors exhibited by children and teens are often maintained by a variety of reinforcers all operating in the client's environment more or less simultaneously. Consider, for example, all the reinforcers that may contribute to a pattern of aggressive behavior on the part of an adolescent. The behavior may have originally been modeled by powerful figures in the life of the child, then may have been directly reinforced by the responses of peers, and now may be supported by the relief from anxiety which such behavior affords the youth. It is virtually impossible for a program of behavioral intervention to insure that all these sources of reinforcement will be removed. At the same time, any effort to do so is likely to meet with poor results if it does not also include an effort to teach new behaviors that can serve some of the same functions that aggression served for the client.

In addition to striving to understand all possible sources of reinforcement when considering the use of extinction, it is critical that an effort be made to understand the schedule of reinforcement and the magnitude of the reinforcers that have been maintaining the behavior. These factors determine how long it will take for the now unreinforced behavior to be extinguished. Recall that intermittent schedules of reinforcement can produce very high rates of behavior and patterns of responding that are quite resistant to extinction. A great many of the behaviors seen in clients referred for intensive services have been maintained for very long periods of time on intermittent schedules of reinforcement and are likely to be maintained by multiple reinforcers in the child's environment that caretakers or treatment teams may not be able to control. Similarly, if the particular behavior has been successful in achieving high-magnitude rewards, then the behavior will be more persistent when the reward is no longer forthcoming. These issues are particularly important to keep in mind when a treatment team is providing behavioral consultation to a family that is working to reduce a child's negative behaviors. Often, parents know that they should not give in to stubborn demands, whining, and other forms of aversive control. Nevertheless, they may find it very difficult to resist these pressures and end up giving in some of the time. This means that they are intermittently rewarding such behavior and that reducing the behavior through extinction will be more difficult than if the behavior had been continuously reinforced.

(These problems sometimes play out in treatment programs when a team arrives at the, usually unsupported, determination that a child is engaging in a particular behavior "just to get attention." This formulation often leads to an ill-fated effort to mount a program of extinction in which staff working with the child simply ignore the behavior. When such an intervention is undertaken in the absence of a careful functional assessment and without making some educated guesses about the nature of the schedules of reinforcement that may have maintained the behavior, it almost invariably fails. The child may escalate the behavior significantly, and the team may then be caught in the undertow of coercion and countercoercion and soon find themselves arriving at increasingly negative attributions about the child.)

Other properties of the extinction process are also important to take into account, especially when the team is engaged in collaborative behavioral consultation with parents or other caregivers. Generally, when the reinforcing events in the environment are curtailed, the behavior being targeted for extinction demonstrates what is called an *extinction burst* (Axelrod and Hall, 1999). This phenomenon is an initial increase in the frequency (and, often, intensity) of the behavior that occurs when the behavior is no longer reinforced. It is not difficult to identify a great many naturally occurring examples of the extinction burst. Consider the frustrated flicking of light switches when a bulb has burned out or efforts to start a car when a battery has died. (Note that in both of these examples the behaviors of switch flicking and key turning are normally on continuous schedules of reinforcement. This tends to result in relatively rapid extinction processes, in contrast to the intermittently reinforced behaviors of many children.) Another element in the extinction process is called *spontaneous recovery*. This refers to the sudden reappearance of a behavior that is no longer being rewarded and had seemed to be on the way to extinction. Finally, extinction can produce a variety of reactions that go under the heading of "emotional responses." Personal computers which suddenly refuse to comply with their owners' demands (i.e., cease to reward typing behavior) often elicit these emotional responses. These reactions are also illustrated by the frustration at encountering the burned-out lightbulb. In that case, one knows how to fix the problem and usually has the necessary resources (a lightbulb) at hand. Clearly, the agitation, anger, and frustration will be proportionally more intense when the unreinforced response is a complex, long-standing behavior that has been intermittently reinforced with relatively high-magnitude rewards.

In collaborative work with families and other caregivers, it is essential that all these issues be explored before a plan utilizing extinction is implemented. In the absence of this sort of preliminary educative work, there is a real risk that as they encounter the child's emotional reaction to the withdrawal of reinforcement and a discouraging intensification of the behavior at the outset of the intervention, the parents will resume reinforcing the behavior in some fashion. This result would likely further extend a pattern of intermittent reinforcement and further strengthen the target behavior. Three other general guidelines regarding the use of extinction should always be kept in mind:

- Every effort should be made to carry out a thoughtful, curious functional analysis of the target behavior. This will help to clarify both the sources of reinforcement currently maintaining the behavior and the antecedents and settings controlling its expression.
- Successful use of extinction may depend on the degree to which the treatment team can remove the child from the current setting or control that setting in such a way that all reinforcing events are curtailed.
- Extinction should always be carried out with a parallel plan for the teaching of new, alternative behaviors that afford the client an adaptive alternative way of meeting the same need.

Negative consequences
Up to this point in the discussion of behavioral intervention the focus has been on positive methods of changing behavior that involve effective approaches to teaching new behavior. These techniques can be especially effective when they are specifically aimed at supporting the development of behaviors that are alternatives to problem behaviors or "compete" with them directly. The reduction of negative behavior can also be facilitated by the careful use of some negative consequences.

As noted earlier, the terminology used within learning theory regarding negative reinforcement and punishment is somewhat confusing. To repeat, *positive reinforcement* is an event that follows a behavior and causes the frequency of that behavior to increase. A *negative reinforcement* is an event that increases the frequency of a behavior by its removal. Thus, the term "negative reinforcement" describes the phenomenon that occurs when a behavior is strengthened when it results in avoidance or escape from an aversive event. This concept is best understood with examples:

- A parent surrenders to the whining demands of a toddler and buys him candy at the supermarket checkout. The parent's giving in is reinforced by the removal of the aversive event of the child's annoying, embarrassing behavior.
- A teenager cleans her room after stubborn nagging from her parents. The behavior of cleaning up is reinforced by the termination of the nagging.

Many of the young clients served in intensive treatment programs are quite skilled in the use of negative reinforcement and regularly deploy a variety of aversive behaviors such as whining, temper tantrums, and persistent demands and questions in their exchanges with caretakers and other adults. It is also worth noting that in many families parents unknowingly intermittently reinforce a variety of negatively reinforcing behaviors used by their children. This schedule of reinforcement leads to very high rates of behavior that are quite resistant to extinction. Thus, in the first example, if the parents give in and buy candy on the average of every five trips to the supermarket, then they should expect to be dealing with whining every time they do their grocery shopping. It is interesting to note here the reciprocal nature of these patterns of reinforcement. Each actor in the exchange is modifying the behavior of the other. The child is rewarding the parent for giving in (by terminating their persistent demands) and the parent is rewarding the child for being demanding (by giving in to the demands).

In order for negative reinforcement to effectively strengthen a behavior, there must be a continuing aversive stimulus, the removal of which can be used to reinforce the target behavior. There are many reasons, not the least of which is ethical, that make negative reinforcement a poor choice for an intervention strategy. Negative reinforcement often produces negative side effects, such as anger and avoidance of the person associated with the negative reinforcement. At the same time, it is very difficult to effectively control aversive events so that they are removed or terminated at the precise moment that the target behavior occurs.

In the terminology of learning theory, the direct presentation of an aversive event to reduce a targeted negative behavior is called *punishment*. Kazdin (2001) notes that while the experience of aversive events that reduce behavior is a fundamental part of social life, its practice in everyday life is often associated with a variety of problems. These include emotional reactions such as anger, wishes, and efforts to escape from the punisher and the situation in which the punishment occurred, as well as negative attitudes toward the punisher. Fortunately, there are approaches to the use of punishment that are based not on the presentation of aversive stimuli but on the removal of positive reinforcement, and these can be effective additions to a behavioral intervention plan. The two techniques of this kind used regularly in the real world and in many treatment programs are time-out and response cost.

Time-out

Perhaps the most commonly used form of punishment is referred to as "time-out." In more technical behavioral vocabulary it is called "time-out from positive reinforcement," and this longer name is an important reminder of how it works and what conditions are necessary for it to be an effective intervention tool. *Time-out* is a method of behavior modification that involves the withdrawal of positive reinforcement for a brief period of time. Its defining characteristic is a brief interval in which positive reinforcement is not available to the individual. This suspension of reinforcement can be accomplished in a number of ways, including removing the client from the situation or activity, simply having the client sit away from the group, or even directing the client to put his head down on a desk for a brief period. Time-out is, of course, a procedure that is used contingently; that is, it is a response to a particular behavior that is targeted for reduction. The delivery of the time-out should occur immediately after the occurrence of the targeted behavior.

The discussion of time-out began by calling attention to the full name of this simple procedure, "time-out from positive reinforcement," to emphasize the importance of the general economy of reinforcement in the setting in which it is used. Thus, if the treatment setting is not relatively rich in opportunities to earn positive reinforcement, then the client will not experience the time-out as a particularly notable experience and behavior change is unlikely to occur. In the worst-case scenario, the client given the time-out is in a setting in which she is experiencing few reinforcing events and may even find some characteristics of the setting distinctly aversive. In this case, the time-out backfires completely and reinforces the targeted negative behavior by enabling it to function as an escape from the aversive situation. Observation of learning-disabled youngsters in classroom settings sometimes reveals just such a pattern. The child is having little or no academic success, is suffering considerable humiliation and discouragement, and begins to show disruptive behavior. Removal of the child to a time-out room, rather than punishing the negative behavior, rewards her with an opportunity to escape.

Response cost
Another approach to punishment based on removal of positive reinforcers rather than presentation of aversive events is response cost. This procedure involves the loss of some, usually specified, amount of positive reinforcement; and this removal of reinforcers is contingent on the occurrence of some targeted negative behavior. Like all methods of behavior modification, response cost is a method that is widely utilized outside treatment settings to control behavior. Fines, grounding, loss of recess, and penalties in sports are all examples of the use of response cost to reduce or eliminate particular negative behaviors. In treatment settings, response cost is often embedded in larger schemes of behavior modification such as point and level systems. When these methods are being used, response cost may consist of loss of points or levels contingent on the client displaying a targeted negative behavior. This sort of intervention, which is often explicitly built into a system of rewards and consequences, is no different from the loss of privileges that might be utilized by the parent of a teenager who violates curfew and loses the use of the family car.

GENERAL CONSIDERATIONS ON THE USE OF NEGATIVE CONSEQUENCES

Just as there are a variety of factors which determine the effectiveness of any plan to use positive reinforcement, so too are there a very similar set of factors which influence the effectiveness of negative consequences:

- *Delay.* Just as with positive reinforcers, negative consequences delivered immediately following the targeted behavior will be more effective than negative consequences that are delayed. This effect is a good argument for treatment settings to have quite specific and explicit guidelines for behavior that detail the response cost for a variety of frequently encountered negative behaviors. This sort of system empowers every staff member to make treatment decisions and avoid the delays that come with needing to find supervisors or convene a meeting of the team.
- *Schedule of punishment.* Negative consequences that reliably follow every instance of a targeted behavior are more effective than punishments that follow only some instances of a negative behavior. Thus, behaviors that elicit a time-out only 50% of the time that they occur will decline more slowly than those that elicit a time-out every time that they occur.
- *Conflicting positive reinforcement.* Behaviors that are the focus of negative consequences but are also being positively reinforced from some other source will decline more slowly than those receiving only negative consequences. The most familiar example of this is seen in group treatment settings in which the staff are busily utilizing negative consequences such as time-out and response cost while the peer group is equally busily rewarding the same behaviors with attention, laughter, and even direct encouragement. These sources of unwanted positive reinforcement should not be underestimated, and every effort should be made to limit them. For this reason, many settings will systematically reward clients who ignore the negative behavior of their peers.
- *Using time-out early in response chains.* Negative behavior is almost always one unit of behavior in a chain of behaviors that only become critical when they are completed. Thus, for example, a temper tantrum may begin with a demand for a desired object or activity, move toward increasingly intense expressions of emotion, and finally end up in a screaming, flailing display. Time-out can be especially effective as a preventive intervention that disrupts the chain before it escalates to the fullest, most problematic form of the behavior.
- *Parallel use of positive strategies.* The reduction of behavior will always be most effective when it is part of a unified intervention plan that includes the positive reinforcement of desired behaviors.

Chapter Seven

Phases of Treatment and Key Activities

Having reviewed some fundamental concepts and methods from both attachment and learning theory, it is now necessary to describe how the clinical processes that flow from these ideas might be woven into a coherent sequence of activities that can organize the efforts of clinicians, caretakers, teams, and programs. This description is necessarily somewhat general in that implementation will look quite different in varied settings and service-delivery models. Thus, for example, a clinician providing outpatient services to children in a public school setting will utilize these concepts in a different way from a clinician who is directing a team of support counselors delivering wrap-around services in a community-based mental health/child welfare collaboration. In this regard, it is useful to think of a continuum of implementation "looks" that roughly parallel the continuum from pure outpatient interventions to intensive, 24-hour, milieu treatment settings such as high-level residential treatment programs. At the least intensive, outpatient end of the continuum, implementation will involve a mix of possible direct services such as individual, family, and group therapy and a significant consulting function in which the clinician utilizes elements of the model to provide developmental guidance and behavioral consultation to caretakers, teachers, and other key figures in the life of the child. At the most intensive, milieu-based end of the continuum, the clinician will be one part of a team made up of other professionals and direct care staff. In these settings, the team of residential and/or day treatment staff will typically implement the behavioral and relational treatment plans. As children and teens prepare to transition out of these settings and move to lower levels of service such as family placements or treatment foster care, the team must shift from a direct treatment role toward a support and consulting role.

In the appendices, worksheets and forms are provided which can guide and support the various assessment and intervention activities that are described here. Some of these documents are essentially data-collection forms that can be modified to meet the requirements of the particular child, family, or program, while others are intended to lead the clinician through a particular process such as developing hypotheses for a functional assessment.

A note on sequential and parallel or interdependent tasks and processes. What follows is a description of key tasks and processes that represent the implementation of an approach to working with children, youth, and families that is both behavioral and relational. Some of the tasks are sequential; later ones cannot be carried out without the completion of earlier ones. For example, one can't complete a valid functional assessment without specific, operational definitions of target behaviors.

> Assessment starts when we say "hello" to the child. It continues until we say "goodbye."

Some of the tasks, though, are parallel or even interdependent; they are going on at the same time and support each other. For example, the data gathered in the course of interviewing parents to develop a history of a particular problem of the client do not have to be used only for that purpose. It should also find its way into the child's table of life events. Unfortunately, it is impossible to point out all these convergences and overlaps among the tasks described here. Nevertheless, it is critical that the reader think of these processes, even though described separately, as integrated. As indicated earlier, it is important to know that the length and overlap of these processes will vary by program or service-delivery model.

PREINTAKE AND INITIAL SCREENING

I. *Overview*: In this phase of treatment, contact is typically with the referral source and the child's caretakers. The amount of time required and the depth and complexity of this initial screening will vary by program. The data gathered in this initial meeting or conversation may well contribute to both the behavioral and relational assessments that will begin once the child is formally admitted. The ways in which a parent approaches these initial contacts, the questions they ask or don't ask, and the concerns they raise all yield information for both assessment streams.

II. *Task*: Receive and evaluate initial inquiry, screen for appropriateness of placement for the child.

A. *Behavioral*: Begin to *compile list of behaviors of concern* that are driving the referral. The concerns of the parents or caretakers may not be identical, and these differences should be noted. Should the client be admitted, these are likely to be among the behaviors targeted by the behavioral treatment plan.

B. *Relational*: This task is much more implicit than the behavioral task. Workers are asked to *respond with interest, respect, and curiosity* and should view this inquiry as the first opportunity to provide the client with a different experience of a treatment program. It may be necessary to spend a significant amount of time with

When planning to observe a child's behavior, ask:

When?
Who?
For how long?
What method?

implementation of the assessment strategy. Such a collaboration must always be based on a respectful appreciation of all the challenges and demands parents may be facing in their daily lives. Procedures, recording forms, and reporting methods should all be designed to ensure ease and convenience of use. Some treatment approaches utilize daily telephone calls to caretakers, built around a structured reporting form, for the regular collection of behavioral data (Chamberlain, 2003).

c. *How long* will the data collection go on? This will be determined, in part, by a team's informal assessment about how frequently the behavior occurs so that a meaningful baseline is obtained. If the behavior occurs many times every day, then an observation period of a single day may provide an adequate assessment of base rate. (It will still be advisable to collect data across several days to insure that a meaningful sample has been obtained.) On the other hand, if the behavior occurs only once or twice a day, it may be necessary to carry on the observation for as long as a week to obtain a meaningful evaluation of its base rate.

d. *What method* will be utilized in recording the data? The choice of a method for recording data will be determined in large part by the nature of the target behavior. In brief, for some behaviors—say, hitting peers—the team will be interested in frequency. With other behaviors—cooperative play with peers, for example—the team will be interested in duration. In general, based on the nature of the target behavior, the team will be choosing from this list of variables:

Frequency. Best for behaviors that are discrete acts with clear boundaries

- hitting
- initiating play with a peer
- running away
- leaving the classroom without permission

Duration: Here, the length of time the behavior is performed is key

- cooperative play with peers
- time spent in class

Intensity: For when the strength or force of the behavior is of interest

- voice tone/volume
- angry outbursts
- depressive emotion

the family to adequately understand their concerns, respond to their questions, and, if necessary, assist them in finding a more appropriate setting for their child. Contacts with referring professionals can also be an opportunity to become educated about their services and programs and to educate them more fully about the services available to the child and the family.

III. *Outcome*: Arrive at a decision on whether or not to admit the child.

ASSESSMENT

I. *Overview*: Assessment includes behavioral and relational components, both of which comprise several phases. The very first assessment data are simply those preliminary, tentative observations gathered during the initial screening and intake. As the clinician and the team move into the assessment proper, in addition to behavioral and relational domains, they must attend to issues of context, those issues outlined earlier (see Chapter 2, "Problems with Concrete Resources and Other Risk Factors Present in the External World Surrounding the Family").

II. *Task*: Conduct both a behavioral and a relational assessment and integrate into one clear assessment for treatment planning. Include a review of external risk factors that are present and need to be addressed.

A. *Behavioral:*

1. *Identify and prioritize problem behaviors.* This initial phase of assessment should be carried out in a collaborative fashion among the clinician, the client, caretakers, and referral sources. It is not necessary that all these parties meet at once, but implicitly or explicitly, they should all have input into the process. Additionally, the clinician may utilize documents such as discharge notes, court reports, and descriptions of behavior in other settings that are available upon the child's admission to the program. Finally, and of great importance, are the data derived from the child's behavior during the first days and weeks in treatment. These data are collected from direct care staff or caretakers who are engaged with the child in day-to-day life. This process should yield a list that can then be prioritized according to the dangerousness of the behavior to self and others, its disruptiveness to settings in which the child operates, and the degree to which it prevents the child from taking advantage of opportunities for learning, play, and positive social engagement in the milieu. Workers should choose an appropriate number of behaviors from the final prioritized list to be ultimately

> Assessment is based on behavioral and relational observations, but also involves attention to the context in which the family is living.

addressed in the treatment plan before moving on to the next step in the assessment process.

The forms and worksheets in the appendices are offered as organizing guides for both the assessment and treatment planning processes. Some may be used as templates for creating forms that can be employed for data-collection activities, while others are intended to be guides for the processes themselves, walking the clinician through a logical sequence of activities leading to a particular outcome. For example, Appendix C, Target Behavior Definition Form, proceeds from collection of general concerns of the various participants in the process (client, family, referral source, treatment team) to the development of objective, clear, and complete definitions of target behaviors. The use of that particular form is described in the next point.

2. *Define behaviors in terms that lead to clear assessment and planning* (see Appendix C, Target Behavior Definition Form): Arriving at a clear and objective

Criteria for good behavioral definitions:

o Objective

o Clear

o Complete

definition of the behavior is essential to reliable communication about the behavior among team members and reliable measurement of the behavior by team members. There are a number of descriptions of criteria for good behavioral definitions, such as those offered by Kazdin (2001, p. 75) and Bambara and Kern (2005, p. 109). In these accounts effective definitions of target behaviors meet these criteria:

a. *Objectivity*. The definition of the behavior should include observable, measurable characteristics. A useful rule of thumb is to rely on action verbs and to avoid any use of general labels, traits, or diagnostic categories.

b. *Clarity*. The definition is unambiguous and can pass the "stranger test"; that is, it is easily accessible to and can be immediately used in a reliable fashion by someone new to the client and to the behavior. No extra or unusual explanation beyond the definition itself is required for the "stranger" to begin to know the behavior when he sees it.

c. *Completeness*. This criterion is concerned with insuring that the definition includes information on all specific expressions of the behavior that are to be included and details what is *not* included in the definition that might, if not mentioned, drift into a series of observations.

3. *Initial direct observation/baseline determination* (see Appendix D, Behavioral Assessment Planning Worksheet): Once the three target behaviors are chosen and defined according to the above criteria, the team should initiate a process of systematic observation and assessment. The particular form that this assessment

takes will depend in part on the nature of the target behavior. decisions must be made:

a. *When* to carry out the observations. It is important to make at times when meaningful data can be collected. Some of a (behaviors may occur at almost any time of day. Otl particular settings or at particular times of day. In collection should follow the team's initial sense of whe occurs: If it is typically seen at home in the evenings, the the behavior should be collected. If it is typically seen acre settings, then it is ideal if observations are made in all of

b. *Who* will carry out the observations? It is important t member who will be in a position to observe the behav the terms of the assessment plan. The key issues here client at the appropriate times and understanding procedures so that reliable data are gathered. If multi be contributing to the observations or one observer is baseline and another obtains data later in treatment, tl rater reliability are of even greater importance. Obvi greatly enhanced by adhering to the criteria for defini outlined earlier and by training observers to the clien at the same time and having them collaborate in the definitions. It is still necessary to conduct some eval when multiple observers are involved in the data observers rate the same samples of behavior and agreement of ratings can yield useful data on this (for inter-rater agreement (see Kazdin, 2001, for exa Results below 80% indicate a need for greater spe definitions of target behavior or a need for retra reliability is acceptably high, it is useful for the te the definitions of a client's key target behaviors a criteria.

In some treatment settings, certain kinds o regularly collected to meet various regulator depending on regulation in the particular state being accessed, day treatment programs, treatment foster homes, and residential settin progress notes and incident reports. It is integrate formal behavioral assessments wi collection and -recording processes in such a: are rendered more efficient.

When the behaviors are occurring in the useful to include the parents or careta

Quality: The degree to which the behavior is performed in relation to some standard

- hygiene behaviors
- academic performance, as in correct answers on an assignment

Latency: The amount of time it takes for the client to begin to perform the behavior

- beginning work when asked

The methods used for the first stage of behavioral assessment are determined by the nature of the behavior – the frequency of the behavior is not always the key variable.

Depending on the variable identified in the behavioral definition, workers will choose from among the following observation approaches:

Frequency counts (see Appendix E, Observation Form—Frequency): counting how much the behavior occurs in a given time period

- when time units of observation are not the same, calculate rate of response per unit time

Intensity measures (see Attachment F, Observation Form—Intensity): requires construction of a measurement scale in which each point is anchored with a clear behavioral description.

Duration measures (see Attachment H, Observation Form—Duration):[1] directly measuring the length of time that the behavior is performed with a watch or stopwatch.

Latency measures: Here, workers focus on how long it takes the client to initiate a particular act, such as compliance with an instruction. This can be implemented in a meaningful way only if the particular event (such as the giving of an instruction or some other signal) is defined and included in the measurement strategy.

Outcome measures: Measuring performance of a behavior by measuring the frequency of a result or event that signals that the behavior has occurred. Examples would be percentage of completed assignments as a measure of academic engagement or an aggregate of outcomes such as bed made, no clothes on floor, and laundry in hamper as a measure of the behavior "keeps a clean room."

In addition to these essentially straightforward approaches to assessing variables determined by behavioral definitions in which each instance of the behavior is assessed on some dimension, the following methods of data collection may be used in the initial baseline assessment. These methods are sometimes referred to as "sampling" approaches and offer some convenience

Recording behavioral data does not have to be hugely time consuming. Every behavior does not require constant monitoring. Many behaviors can be captured in efficient sampling methods.

when the observer is "multitasking" by recording data while also, for example, supervising the group in which the client is currently functioning. This approach involves recording only if the behavior did or did not occur in a given sample of behavior. The samples may be defined by simply dividing the day into a series of continuous intervals or by observing the client at separate but regular predetermined intervals.

Interval recording: The day, or a class period or any other defined period of time, is divided into a series of continuous intervals of meaningful length. In a day at school, for example, this might be the six class periods that normally occur. In the course of an evening at home it might be 30-minute intervals. If the target behavior occurs during that period, the observer simply enters a check in a box corresponding to that interval. The final "score" is simply the percentage of intervals in which the behavior occurred.

Time sampling: Workers define when a series of observations will be made. This schedule of observations is not continuous; so, for example, the team might decide that they will make observations of whether or not the target behavior is happening for 1 minute every 30 minutes. A simple timer or wristwatch alarm is then set accordingly. When reminded of the start of the observation period in this way, the observer enters a check on the recording form only if the behavior is occurring.

Outcome: The team will now have made a systematic assessment of the key target behaviors on which intervention will be focused. Most frequently, the key piece of data provided by this initial assessment is a measurement of the base rate of the behavior—or how much it is happening in the child's total behavioral repertoire. In the next phase of behavioral assessment, the team will further sharpen its focus and begin to explore why the behavior is happening and what forces in the environment are related to the behavior.

4. *Functional assessment* (see Attachment I, Functional Assessment Worksheet): This phase of behavioral assessment is concerned with the ways in which three domains of the client's experience are related to the development, occurrence, and maintenance of his or her key problem behaviors. Since understanding these three elements is key to carrying out successful functional assessment, they will be briefly defined and elaborated:

- *Settings* or "setting events" can be understood in the general sense of the word, as in the "setting in which the behavior occurs." A little more specifically, though, settings are events or environments that are associated with the target behavior through their influence over antecedents and consequences. They can include actual settings, vulnerability states in the client such as fatigue or anxiety, and events that produce particular internal states in the client such as missing a visit with family, getting a bad grade on a test, or the loss of an important staff member with whom the child is connected.

- *Antecedent events* or those events that seem to be reliably associated with the target behavior as more or less immediate triggers. While settings could be thought of as the background or context in which the behavior is likely to occur, antecedents are usually immediately present right before or when the behavior is occurring. Antecedents can be acts of others such as requests or directions, a condition of the environment such as someone else getting to be first in line, or the loss of proximity from an important adult.
- *Consequences* are events in the environment in which the behavior is occurring that follow the target behavior and seem to be associated with maintaining it. In other words, these consequences are reinforcing the behavior *in some way*. The reward may be in the form of access to something desired by the client, such as proximity to a valued adult, the chance to be at the head of the line, or the approval of a high-status peer. The reward may, alternatively, be in the form of avoidance of or relief from an undesired state or event, such as the anxiety of being in a bedroom alone or having to do a problem set that is beyond one's ability.

a. *Stage 1*: Gathering information. The team will begin the functional assessment once the target behaviors are adequately defined according to the standards described. The first step in the functional assessment is an interview or a collaborative meeting of client, parents or caregivers, treatment partners such as other professionals, and program team members. Very often it is difficult to have all informants meet together, and the clinician or team supervisor may need to conduct a series of meetings to obtain everyone's thoughts and ideas. These conversations are a first round of data sharing that will allow the team to develop hypotheses about settings, antecedents, and consequences that have been observed to be related to the occurrence of the client's target behaviors. These initial hypotheses can then guide the next round of inquiry, which is focused on more systematic observation and data collection. The informal observations and theories gathered from the participants in this process will allow

Three Stages of Functional analysis (FA):

1. Gather information
2. Observe behavior in natural setting
3. Review and analyze data and develop hypothesis

the team to develop more educated guesses about the functions of the target behaviors that can then drive more direct, systematic observation. These observations are the core of the functional assessment and should yield reliable data regarding settings, antecedents, and consequences that will, in turn, permit the development of functional hypotheses.

While this meeting, or series of meetings, is part of an assessment process, it is also very much the beginning of intervention. It should be viewed as an opportunity to begin to connect more effectively and thoughtfully to the behavior of the client and to support the development of curiosity in all team members. In general, discussions that focus on the context and function of behavior move participants away from stances that are concrete, unreflective, and reactive. This discussion also provides additional sources of data other than the observations directly offered by the participants. Thus, for example, the meeting may also reveal important observational or interpretive biases on the part of any of the participants. Note that very often parents, teachers, and program staff members are excellent observers of behavior and that not uncommonly such an initial sharing of information may provide excellent information about the function of target behaviors that could actually allow the team to immediately develop a reasonable treatment plan. Nevertheless, it is still necessary to confirm these hypotheses with direct, systematic observation. Appendix I, the Functional Assessment Worksheet, provides a series of prompts and spaces for recording participants' input.

Another kind of data will also emerge in this early stage of treatment. These are the sorts of factors that are listed in Appendix J, the Client Variables Form. This form directs the attention of the team to those variables or issues that can be thought of as internal to the client but may be associated in some way with the occurrence of the target behavior. These can include factors such as specific learning disabilities, medication effects, cognitive ability, and particular beliefs or preoccupations.

b. *Stage 2*: Direct, systematic observation of target behaviors. The initial discussion among the participants should yield data that suggest patterns in the occurrence of the behavior that, in turn, will provide the basis for developing a plan for systematic observation of the behavior. The team will choose from the following observational schemes or develop, as necessary, their own data-collection form:

- Behavior Log (see Appendix M)
- ABC Observation Form (see Appendix L)
- Functional Behavior Assessment Form (see Appendix K)

A specific plan will be developed for the collection of these data, with timelines and clear roles assigned to each participant based on the behaviors in question and the setting in which he or she engages the client.

c. *Stage 3*: Data analysis and hypothesis formation. The final outcome of the functional assessment process is a summary of the data collected in the form of a clear, concise statement of the relationship between the behavior in question and the settings, antecedents, and consequences that have been observed. Such a hypothesis is a simple, economical conclusion about the function of the behavior, which can then guide the development of an appropriate, effective behavioral intervention. The hypothesis can be of the following form:

The fundamental purpose of the hypothesis is to provide a rationale that will connect the information generated by the assessment process with the specific methods utilized in the intervention process.

"When participating in PE, David becomes disruptive and provocative so that he will be excluded from the activity as a way to avoid feelings of humiliation when he is teased about his poor gross motor skills by his peers."

Or

"When preparing for bedtime, Sally becomes silly and disruptive so that she can receive a higher level of caretaker proximity because she is anxious about being alone in her room."

In the first case, the function of the behavior is escape from negative feelings associated with being teased. In the second case, the function of the behavior is to draw staff into closer proximity to relieve feelings of anxiety. Undoubtedly, the history and learning of these behaviors are complex and worth understanding. From the point of view of behavioral intervention, however, this simple statement of function can allow the team to move forward and begin planning.

Some general guidelines (Bambara and Kern, 2005) for evaluating hypotheses are as follows:

1) The hypothesis should refer to context, to environmental events that can be addressed in an intervention.
2) The hypothesis should include a description of the function that the client could achieve with an alternative behavior.
3) The hypothesis should grow logically from the data that were collected and avoid returning to theories or hunches that were generated in the initial information-gathering phase of the functional assessment.
4) All participants in the assessment process should feel that the hypothesis is reasonable.

BEHAVIORAL INTERVENTION

Positive behavioral intervention is positive because it focuses the efforts of the team away from negative or punitive responses to problem behaviors and toward

Interventions are much more likely to be successful if they are linked to the variables that are reliably associated with the target behavior.

the development of new, more adaptive behaviors. Note the use of the word "responses" in the previous sentence. In positive behavior plans the team should be spending less time and effort *responding* to problem behaviors and more time altering antecedents and settings, teaching new behaviors, and sustaining them with systematic reinforcement strategies (see Attachment O, Behavioral Treatment Plan Worksheet).

In constraining the efforts of the team in this direction, a positive behavioral treatment plan can specify activity in five primary areas:

- Modifying settings or antecedents
- Identifying appropriate replacement behaviors
- Reinforcement strategies
- Reactive procedures
- Provision for some ongoing collection of data

Positive behavioral intervention focuses the efforts of the team toward the development of new, more adaptive behaviors in the child.

I. *Modifying settings or antecedents*: Functional assessment should yield (and confirm by observation, to the extent possible) a set of initial hypotheses about variables in the child and in the environment that are related to the occurrence and maintenance of target behaviors. The factors ultimately identified may fall into a variety of categories:

- Physiological states in the child (fatigue, hunger)
- Emotional states in the child (anger, anxiety, fear)
- Interpersonal events or behavior by family members, peers, teachers, and other staff, such as

    o Parents: unavailability, excessive availability, poor limits
    o Peers: teasing, "set-ups," intimidation, threats of aggression, sexual overtures
    o Teachers/staff: inappropriate time-outs, failure to respond to behavior, responding to behavior

- Environmental events and activities, such as

    o Overly difficult academic work
    o Overly easy academic work
    o Transitions between activities

    o Loud noises, other children being in crisis

    o Stimuli that function as posttraumatic reminders, such as being in certain neighborhoods, people yelling at each other, certain kinds of physical contact

These factors are obviously varied and where one event (overly difficult academic work) may function as a trigger for one child, the opposite (overly easy academic work) may have similar results for another child.

The goal of this process is to provide the team with clear directions for intervention that arise in a straightforward way from the outcome of the assessment process.

Interventions in this domain are as varied as the settings and antecedents that might be associated with the occurrence of any target behavior. In general, these interventions are efforts to address underlying states or needs that are inferred from the data yielded by the functional assessment. Some general categories with specific examples to address are as follows:

- Physiological states that contribute to the occurrence of the target behavior: insure adequate sleep, provide snacks
- Need for proximity contributing to the occurrence of the target behavior: increase proximity to client, provide hand-to-hand supervision, schedule one-on-one supervision
- Need to escape from tasks experienced by client as aversive: alter difficulty of task, use "behavioral momentum" (providing easier tasks first and gradually building to more difficult tasks), alter task length, break task into smaller tasks
- Efforts to exert control in task completion: allow for maximal acceptable level of choice on the part of the client
- Negative reactions to transitioning from or stopping a preferred activity: provide a series of warnings or begin the next activity with a preferred task
- Settings that contribute to the occurrence of the target behavior: provide greater supervision on a school bus ride, shorten a bus ride, alter parental visitation schedules or supervision of visits
- Antecedents related to settings when the settings can't be altered: when the problematic bus ride cannot be altered, increasing structure around integrating the child into program after arrival

II. *Learning alternative behaviors and skills.* While striving to alter antecedents and settings may be a key ingredient in mounting a behavioral intervention for a client, these efforts will only have the effect of reducing the target behaviors seen as most problematic. Real change and success for clients will, inevitably, be strongly associated with the development of new skills and capacities that enable them to meet important needs without resorting to the problem behaviors that led to their placement in the first place.

As it did with modifying antecedents and settings, the material generated by the functional assessment should again inform intervention as the team selects and describes alternative behaviors for the client to learn and use in his or her daily life. The hypotheses yielded by the functional assessment should contain clear statements about the meaning or purpose of the behavior; and in selecting alternative behaviors for the team to work on with the client, these statements should guide the process. The team should consider the following questions in this planning process (see especially Appendix N, Replacement Behavior Worksheet):

- What is the function of the target behavior? What need or purpose does it express?
- What replacement behavior will enable the client to meet the same need and still preserve his or her safety and continued development?
- Does the client already show the proposed replacement in another setting or show behaviors that include components of the replacement behavior?
- What method will the team utilize in teaching the behavior? Will it need to be broken down into teachable components or taught in successive approximations (shaped/chained)?
- Is there anyone in the client's environment who is a skilled practitioner of the replacement behavior and could function as a model or "consultant" to the client?
- What training or support will any members of the team need to implement the teaching of this replacement behavior?
- How will the team monitor the client's mastery of the replacement behavior?

It is also critical that the team understand the importance of clear operational definitions of the replacement behavior. This is necessary for all the same reasons that it was critical that the original target behavior be defined objectively, clearly, and completely. In the absence of such definitions, team members will easily end up rewarding and observing the progress of somewhat different behaviors.

Teaching alternative behaviors that directly support the client's efforts to more adaptively meet the needs and functions of the target behavior will always be the centerpiece of the behavioral intervention for many clients. Nevertheless, it is also clear that there are a variety of skills and capacities that many clients will benefit from developing that are, strictly speaking, not replacement behaviors. Instead, they can be described as more general coping and tolerance skills (Halle, Bambara, and Reichle, 2005), emotion regulation skills (Linehan, 1993), or even general life skills such as hygiene and good manners. These skills, while not immediately related to the target behavior in the same way that a replacement or incompatible alternative behavior should be, will increase the client's ability to manage difficult, potentially disruptive emotional states that arise in the face of situations that are inevitably encountered in many environments in which they will need to function successfully. Some of these behaviors have been taught successfully in curriculum-based approaches in which structured, sequential materials are utilized, often in a group setting. These skills may also be noted in the behavior treatment plan.

III. *Reinforcement strategies*. In this section of the behavioral treatment plan the team will identify the reinforcers to be used, the schedule of reinforcement that determines the timing of rewards, and how the behaviors will be rewarded in the specific context(s) or setting(s) in which the child is placed. Thus, for example, the plan for a day treatment child might specify how the behavior will be rewarded in the context of the classroom utilizing praise and attention, support from peers, behavioral contracts, and/or the point and level system. Additionally, though, the plan might specify how the child's caretakers could reward the behavior with praise and contracts. The material in this section of the intervention plan could include, but would not be limited to, the following:

- Components of the replacement behavior and plan for chaining, if necessary
- Need and, if necessary, plan for rewarding successive approximations
- Schedules of reinforcement to be utilized
- Specific reinforcers found to be effective with this client
- Role of point/level system in rewarding the replacement behavior
- Use of behavioral contracts in reinforcing the behavior
- Timing of the delivery of reinforcement
- Any specific roles for particular members of the team, such as caregivers, teachers, community members, peers, milieu staff.

IV. *Reactive procedures*. It would be very nice indeed if positive behavioral intervention successfully interfered with all of a client's target behaviors and he or she never engaged in those problematic activities as soon as new behaviors began to take hold. Unfortunately, this does not occur. Inevitably, target behaviors do persist; often, they have been acquired under extremely powerful learning paradigms such as unpredictable, intermittent reinforcement and will take a long time to be effectively extinguished and/or replaced with more successful alternatives.

Because of this, it is necessary to specify what reactive measures will be utilized when the behavior occurs. In most intensive treatment programs for vulnerable children, the most common reactive procedures utilized and taught in the behavioral training involve the use of time-out strategies and various forms of response cost (see Chapter 6 for definitions).

A. *Milieu programs*. In milieu programs there has generally been a great deal of thought devoted to these issues and explicit, complex procedures have been created that detail precisely how instances of target behaviors will be responded to. In these programs there is an effort to create a consistent approach that avoids the pitfalls of moralistic, punitive strategies but still adds a needed layer to the overall program of behavioral intervention. In these programs there will be very little need for describing any additional or different responses beyond identifying those reactive procedures that have been particularly successful in managing the target behaviors.

The overall standard that should be applied to these procedure is as follows: The procedure should assist in reducing the frequency of the target behavior while not minimizing "down time" in which the child is out of program and losing out on opportunities for new learning. This is precisely the risk of extended periods of time-out in which a child or youth is separated from the treatment milieu as a negative consequence for highly aggressive or disruptive behavior. On some occasions, the use of these strategies may be an expression of quite strong unacknowledged, negative emotional reactions such as fear, anger, or helplessness on the part of the treatment team. At these moments, there is real risk of the "treatment" becoming an unconscious confirmation of the child's internal working model.

B. *Community- and school-based programs.* In community- or school-based programs, in which program staff may be collaborating with caretakers and other providers, the development of specific guidelines for reactive procedures may be of great importance. To some degree, this may be a training issue; and in this context, clinicians and direct care workers can function as behavioral consultants who work to understand the strategies that have been used and then, when necessary, assist in developing alternative or additional strategies. Because the team will often not be the direct implementers of the behavioral treatment plan, it is of great importance that any reactive procedures be described in considerable detail on the Behavioral Treatment Plan Worksheet and that the program staff work closely with program partners, caregivers, teachers, etc., to provide support in the use of these strategies.

V. *Provisions for ongoing collection of data.* Finally, it is necessary that the team include a component of the plan that outlines a timeline and a process for collection of further data. The purpose of revisiting the assessment process is simple: to measure the impact of interventions and determine if they require any adjustment. For the most part, these will be frequency data of the sort that were collected once the target behaviors were defined operationally. In many cases it will be necessary for comparison purposes to use the same method or approach to assessment that was used at the outset of the intervention-planning process. The timeline for this continuing assessment can be based on the team's estimate of what a meaningful period in which to see effects might be. In some programs, where treatment plans include measurable goals for performing replacement behaviors, a particular level of progress toward the goal can trigger the reassessment process.

Sample timeline for further data collection on target behaviors:

TIME FRAME	STAFF RESPONSIBLE	OUTCOME
Monthly	Milieu staff	**Reassess frequency of target behaviors using methods from original baseline determination**

RELATIONAL ASSESSMENT AND TREATMENT

As with behavioral intervention, treatment via relationship occurs only after there has been a thorough assessment of the client and the family and some initial hypotheses have been generated about the causes and meanings of their difficulties.

It is important to reiterate that the behavioral and relational are two important domains of treatment that overlap and should support each other throughout the child's and the family's engagement with the treatment team. The reader is referred back to the Introduction for a discussion of a way to conceptualize how these two modes of treatment can work in concert.

I. *Relational assessment.* It should be noted at the outset that assessment of the child's attachments to caretakers and his or her capacity for and use of relationships *proceeds in a somewhat different fashion from behavioral assessment.* It is necessarily less systematic and less rigorously empirical and not only relies on direct observation but also utilizes some less reliable, more complex data sources. These will usually include the client's own stories; the experiences of those who interact with the child, in the sense of both their "factual" narratives ("This happened and then this happened . . . .") as well as their reflective accounts of the thoughts and feelings that the client evokes in them ("During this interaction I felt this and thought . . . ."); a historical reconstruction of the child's key relationships with important adults in his or her life and observations of what can be called his or her response to "the default offer of relationship" (see Appendix A, Relational Assessment Worksheet).

A. Procedure FAQs

1. Who is responsible for carrying out this assessment?

While the clinician leads the process of relational assessment, all members of the team who are working with the child and the family contribute data. The child and the family (or caretakers) are also participants in this process and are invited to tell the story of their histories of relationships and to assist in constructing a chronology of those relationships.

2. What are the data sources for relational assessment?

a. Historical material from, for example, review of records, narratives provided by the client and family members, reports of key informants who have been involved with the child and the family

   b. Direct observation of interactions between the child and key caretakers

   c. Direct observation of the child in program

   d. The worker's own experience of interacting with the client and the family

3. In general terms, how is it carried out?

Rather than using a fixed or predetermined diagnostic algorithm, relational assessment relies on a *heuristic approach*, in which questions are raised or asked and the next question is suggested by the answer to the last one. A heuristic approach to gathering information resonates with the value of curiosity; it is based on the asking of questions and allows the data to lead the way, avoiding a checklist approach to understanding. (This distinction between algorithmic and heuristic assessment was suggested by John Franz, 2006, personal communication.)

Unfortunately, this means there is no cookbook that can walk the team through a sequential process to a conclusion. This is due, in part, to the fact that the relational data rarely arrive in a sequential fashion; they arise from interactions with the client, from her own story, from the way in which she tells that story, and from what is learned from sifting through records and reports.

4. In specific terms, how is it carried out?

Effective completion of relational assessment requires some baseline knowledge on the part of the clinician in areas such as child development, trauma studies, and family dynamics.

> A description of the "Internal Working Model" is a statement that shows the child's beliefs about the interpersonal world, his recurrent interpersonal invitations, and the flexibility of such a model.

The Relational Assessment Worksheet is provided as a guide for collection of data and presents the clinician with 18 categories of data. Ten of these relate to the child's experience with caretakers, and eight are concerned with the child's current interpersonal behavior.

In the first weeks of the child's placement the clinician inevitably has interactions with the child, interviewing care-takers, reviewing records, and hearing accounts of other staff members' experiences with the child and the family. *As data from these sources emerge, they can be entered on the worksheet in the form of brief notes or narratives.*

The data that end up filling the 18 domains are not ends in themselves but provide the basis for completing the final section of the worksheet: Description of the Internal Working Model.

5. What is the outcome of the process?

The result of relational assessment is a description of the child's internal working model of relationships. This description should be a brief, one- to two-paragraph account of:

- the child's implicit beliefs about the interpersonal world
- the recurrent interpersonal invitations he or she directs at others
- any other important details concerning, for example, the flexibility and pervasiveness of the working model

The Relational Assessment Worksheet provides several questions or prompts for the clinician to use in completing this section.

6. What is the timeline for completion of the relational assessment?

It should always be kept in mind that the relational assessment is a part of clinical work that is ongoing; it is, in a certain sense, always provisional and always subject to revision as new data are developed. Nevertheless, the first relational assessment can usually be completed within 30 days of the child's placement.

7. How does the relational assessment connect to and support other assessment or documentation requirements?

The content of the relational assessment should be useful in completing the various intake documents that may be required in different treatment settings. The description of the working model should greatly facilitate the writing of a case formulation for the typical initial assessment. At the same time it will extend the value of such documents by moving discussion beyond simple determination of a diagnosis.

II. *Relational treatment planning.* The process for developing a plan for relationship-based treatment grows directly from the contents of the Relational Assessment Worksheet. This material now becomes the basis for a new discussion that is focused on the sorts of relationships that the child is working to establish with others (see Appendix B, Relational Treatment Plan).

As discussed at length in earlier chapters, clients regularly engage in behavior that evokes or seems to invite particular responses from others. These responses, if they were to occur, are very often likely to confirm the child's beliefs about him- or herself and the interpersonal world. A useful relational treatment plan then begins by simply listing the responses that the child's behavior seems to evoke or invite.

The Relational Treatment Plan begins with a concise restatement of the description of the child's internal working model. For treatment-planning purposes, it is very helpful to elaborate this description in the form of a series of statements of the child's implicit beliefs about the interpersonal world.

A. *Example of internal working model:* For a 9-year-old girl who has been sexually abused, these statements might look something like this:

"*Being close to others always has to involve sexuality. To feel good about myself, I need to see that others find me sexually attractive. Even if they don't look like it, other people are always thinking about sex and are trying to find ways to have sex with each other.*"

Once this series of statements has been constructed, the team moves on to develop a list of the ways in which they might be at risk for responding that would tend to confirm the child's internal working model or implicit beliefs. It should be noted that these "confirmatory stances" can be just as complex and subtle as the invitations or enactments that the child directs at the adult. Thus, for example, the content of what an adult says to the child may seem to be disconfirming, but the emotional tone in which it is said may in fact be highly confirming of the child's internal model. Similarly, the child may also experience confirmation of the internal working model when, in a particular interaction, the adult does not respond at all and, for example, fails to set a limit.

B. *Countertherapeutic confirming stances:* Using the implicit beliefs just given, it is possible to illustrate what these confirmatory responses might be:

- Failing to adequately support generational boundaries with the child
- Responding to the child as older than she is, as more of an adolescent
- Permitting dress, makeup, or music that is adolescent
- Permitting subtle boundary violations such as "deniable" violations of personal space
- Sharing adult information or allowing the child to hear adult interactions.

In this example, the general principle is stated first and involves the risk of failing to adequately attend to and support the issue of generational boundaries with the child. Some more specific examples then follow that detail some of the domains in which generational boundaries might be blurred or crossed.

Having identified these "interactional risk factors" in which adults could find themselves responding in countertherapeutic ways to the child's behavior, the team must now try to define a series of disconfirming stances in which responses that would be likely to promote what is referred to as a "representational mismatch" are described. Developing such disconfirming stances can often proceed in a very straightforward way from what the team has determined would be the problematic confirming stances.

It is often good to start by stating the obvious: that adults interacting with the child must work to avoid the confirming stances that have already been described. Having done so, it then becomes necessary to state ways in which adults may interact with the child that actively disconfirm the internal working model and support the development of new, happier, and preferred narratives.

C. *Therapeutic disconfirming stances:* For the little girl whose implicit beliefs were described this list of disconfirming stances might include ideas such as the following:

- Support all generational boundaries; always remember that she is 9, not 19.
- Buy age-appropriate clothing and watch for subtle adjustments to or improvisations with clothing that make it more revealing or sophisticated,
- Support play with age peers.
- Teach age-appropriate games and activities.

It is worth noting that in this example many of the behaviors that would be supported in the relational treatment plan, such as age-appropriate play and interaction with age peers, could very likely be among replacement behaviors that would be listed for reinforcement in the behavioral treatment plan. Again, the behavioral and relational strategies support each other.

III. *Relational treatment:* In order for the relational treatment plan to effectively inform the child and the family's experience, it is important that every member of the team be familiar with it and that it be available and regularly reviewed in any discussion of the child's treatment or in formal treatment reviews. Those who work directly with the child and the family will always have new and useful information about the child's interpersonal functioning that can enrich the plan as treatment progresses. It is the responsibility of the clinician to formally integrate this new information into the plan as it becomes available. Thus, over time the team will encounter new challenges and invitations from the child and discover new ways to respond.

It is also true that despite an understanding of the child's interpersonal invitations and of the risky responses that workers might make, it is easy to regularly fall into patterns that, even if they aren't confirming, fail to effectively and clearly disconfirm the child's working model. This is a basic fact of life in work with children whose important attachment relationships have been disrupted or who have been otherwise traumatized. For this reason, it is very important that teams meet regularly in a setting in which staff can reflect openly and safely about their responses to the child.

THE TREATMENT PROCESS FLOWCHART

The flowchart shown in Table 7.1 is intended to provide a general overview of how the various processes in work with a client unfold. The reader should consider the following ideas:

1. The left-hand column is included to simply orient the reader to how the processes detailed in the practice guide fit with familiar phases of treatment generally encountered in the field.
2. There are two "streams" or components to treatment: behavioral and relational. They are described by the two main columns in the flowchart.
3. The behavioral stream is, in general, more sequential and more structured. The relational stream is more "clinical" and more inferential. It requires that the clinician make multiple connections among diverse domains of data and then generate a satisfactory unifying formulation. Behavioral assessment relies on structured observations of well-defined target behaviors; relational assessment is going on in any interaction with the child and the family.

Table 7.1 The Treatment Process Flowchart

Preintake Screening	Receive and Evaluate Initial Screening, Screen for Appropriateness	
	Behavioral Stream	*Relational Stream*
Preassessment	Identify and prioritize behaviors of concern (Appendix C)	Conduct relational assessment activities: Review documents Interview caregivers Interview other informants Interview client Review experience with client "The client's response to the default offer of Relationship."
Assessment planning	Plan behavioral assessment strategy (Appendix D)	Collect relational data, enter in Relational Assessment Worksheet (Appendix A)
Assessment	Carry out initial assessment/ baseline determination Utilize observation forms for: Frequency (Appendix E) Intensity (Appendix F) Duration (Appendix H) Frequency/duration (Appendix G) Carry out second stage of behavioral assessment: Functional analysis: Collaborative meeting, informal data collection (Appendix I) Complete Client Variables Form (Appendix J) Utilize direct observation of target behaviors (Appendices K, H, M) Formulate final hypothesis for guiding intervention	The child's experience with caretakers: 1. Availability 2. Attunement or contingent responsiveness 3. Engagement 4. Reflective function— mentalization 5. Regulatory function 6. Tolerance of and support for exploration and autonomy 7. Traumatic factors 8. Projective processes directed at the child by the caretaker 9. Boundary function 10. Hierarchy The child's current interpersonal behavior: 1. Organization and self-regulation 2. Proximity seeking and the pursuit of relationship 3. Exploratory capacity 4. Sense of self 5. Boundary functions 6. Affective expression 7. Emotions evoked in staff 8. Themes of current relationships

(Continued)

Table 7.1 (Continued)

Intervention planning	Plan behavioral intervention Develop replacement behaviors for each target (Appendix N) Complete Behavioral Treatment Plan Worksheet (Appendix O)	Plan relational intervention Describe client's internal working model (Appendix B) Complete Relational Treatment Plan (Appendix B)
Intervention	Implement behavioral treatment plan	Implement Relational Treatment Plan
Maintenance	Reassess behavioral treatment plan	Reassess Relational Treatment Plan

A key feature of the flowchart is the dotted line down the middle. It is meant to convey that the boundary between the behavioral and relational streams is not fixed or rigid. Teams should not proceed as if they are two separate, entirely distinguishable domains of data or methods. Thus, the team should not proceed in a cookbook fashion and work their way through the behavioral stream and then think, "Now we're done with that and we can start on the relational stream." Instead, data and insights from each side of the line should be flowing back and forth between the streams and enriching the thinking and activity of the team in both areas. For example, in the course of initial meetings with the family in which key behaviors of concern are identified, the team members may learn a great deal about regulatory functions and hierarchy in the family. Similarly, a good description of a child's internal working model (the outcome of the relational assessment) is likely to confirm or enlarge the team's ideas about what key replacement behaviors could be.

Chapter 8

Case Illustrations of the Model

In this chapter two case illustrations are presented. They are intended to illustrate the use of some of the forms and worksheets that have been referred to in the discussion of relational and behavioral intervention and are included in the appendices. In order to protect confidentiality, the cases presented here are composites of many cases which are typical of the lives and experience of clients seen in intensive treatment programs. The first case, David S., is an 11-year-old boy who has recently been placed in high-level residential treatment; and the second, Sarah P., is a 14-year-old girl who has recently been placed with her maternal aunt after several foster placements and psychiatric hospitalizations. In the case of David, a table of life events has been constructed to provide a sense of the histories and the journeys through various systems of care that these children often experience. For the sake of brevity, in the forms and worksheets related to behavioral work, only one target behavior is addressed. For complete versions of the forms and worksheets (which are formatted for three target behaviors), the reader is directed to the appendices.

THE CASE OF DAVID S.

David S. is an 11-year-old boy who has recently moved to a level 14 residential facility. (In California, residential programs are ranked according to the level of service they provide. Level 14 is the highest level of service and typically involves a staff-to-client ratio of 1:2 and a full range of treatment services. Often, these programs include an on-grounds day treatment program that serves as the school placement for clients.) David is tall, wiry, and strong. His position in the house quickly becomes very much that of alpha male. He announces both verbally and by physical presence and gestures that no one can tell him what to do, force him to do anything he doesn't want to do, or stop him from doing the things that he does want to do. During the earliest months in residential treatment David would convey the idea that his submission to rules and requests was by his own choice or the result of some specific and generous reward that he had extracted from the other. With some regularity, David's need to resist authority leads to physical confrontations and restraints. These containments are sometimes messy and difficult, and afterward he has been known to brag about how many staff were required to finally get him into the quiet room. He tends to see others primarily in terms of the dimension of strength and weakness. New staff are quickly sized up according to this yardstick, and David almost always enters these new relationships with a frank attempt at intimidation. During this period his vocabulary for describing others is very much a reflection of this preoccupation with power and intimidation. Thus, terms such as "weak," "gay," or "feeble" are commonly heard. In moments of confrontation, he has been known to tell staff, "You're nothing, I don't have to do what you say!" The only adults to whom he shows even grudging respect are extremely experienced, large, calm men who are not pushed off their mark by his challenges. He has not yet shown an interest in associating with these staff and instead seems mainly interested in keeping an eye on them and avoiding confrontation. As one staff notes, "David picks his battles."

In his interactions with peers (and with some adults) he is very alert to exchanges which result in the other being one-down, humiliated, or exposed as wrong or diminished. When another child fails at something or is placed in an embarrassing spot, David will laugh and make sure that everyone else is aware of the other's defeat. He is excited by public figures who are notable for exaggerated displays of invulnerability and strength or outrageous disregard for basic rules of conduct. When David is sick, he seems unable to enjoy or allow the one-to-one ministrations of a caretaker. In the classroom his very good cognitive ability is limited by his inability to ask for or receive help from his female teachers and aides. In therapy David is generally disparaging of the idea of "talking about his problems" and will deny any suggestion of dependency or attachment to his therapist. He spends many of his sessions sprawled on the couch, watching the clock, playing with a small stuffed monkey in a way that mimics physical abuse or cruelty, and asserting contemptuously that his therapist knows nothing about him or his experience.

David shows some noteworthy strengths and exceptions to the patterns just described. With children who are very obviously younger, smaller, or of lower status and who pose no threat to David as rivals, he is often kind and even, on occasion, protective of them. He is also known among staff for having a very reliable streak of honesty and integrity. He can be counted on to give truthful accounts of conflicts and confrontations and to report on events in the house with a fair degree of accuracy.

Table 8.1 is a table of life events that provides the details of David's history prior to his recent admission to residential treatment.

Table 8.1 Table of Life Events: David S.

Age	Date		Events
Pre	5/6/72	B	Birth of father, Bud S., in Tulsa, OK—called by family members "Little Bud".
			His parents separated when he was 2 years old, and he was raised by mother, who had a serious drinking problem. She was often with abusive boyfriends but did not marry again.
			During Bud's teenage years he was often in and out of juvenile hall. He struggled with school.
			He was arrested for petty theft at age 16 and then rearrested several times for violating parole. He defied authority, he did poorly in school, had a bad temper, and was seen as "highly explosive".
			Eventually, he was imprisoned after he tried to kill another man
	10/22/78	B	Birth of mother, Elizabeth B., Tacoma, WA, third of seven children. Her mother was from Texas, and father was employed as a construction worker.
			Her parents separated when she was a few months old, after father physically attacked her mother with a knife. Her mother became increasingly delusional and violent and was addicted to alcohol and drugs. She was institutionalized for 2 years in the state of Oregon after attempting suicide. She describes her mother as unpredictable and often absent for days at a time.
			At age 8 a boyfriend of mothers beat her severely, causing her to need a visit to the ER.
			At age 12 Elizabeth ran away from home and came under the supervision of the courts. She ended up in a series of foster placements. She never felt well cared for in any of them.
			Elizabeth returned to her natural mother for 3 months at age 15. She then got involved in a shoplifting ring and spent 4 months in juvenile hall, going on to other foster homes. Now has ongoing, intermittent relationship with her own mother. Her mother has been sober for some years and has sometimes provided care for David when his mother's partners wanted him out of the house. Length of these "visits" with grandmother unclear.

(Continued)

Table 8.1 (Continued)

			She graduated from high school and spent 1 year in junior college.
	1996	R	Mother met father in a bar, and they quickly began living with each other.
			Mother became pregnant with David; but their relationship quickly became abusive, and mother ended up living back with her own mother.
0	1/19/97	B	Date of birth—7 lb, 10 oz
			Mother reportedly drank heavily in the last month of her pregnancy.
		A	At time of birth, mother had completed twelfth grade. She ended relationship with father when she found out he was selling drugs. She then became involved with a succession of boyfriends, who were abusive to her and not connected to David.
		P	Mother reported that initially he was a relatively easy baby and she was able to manage his distress without too much difficulty. Later, he seemed to cry inconsolably; and she would turn up the TV or lock him in his room, and he would cry himself to sleep.
2–1	2/99		Initial behavior problems.
		P	Mother reports that as soon as he started running he had increased behavior problems. At home he would often run out of the house and not stop when an adult chased him.
2–2	3/99		Three reports to Child Protective Services.
		A	Neighbors reported screams and were sure that David was being beaten by mother's boyfriends.
			Reports were investigated but are labeled "unsubstantiated."
3–0	1/16/00		Began preschool.
		P	Bit other children, and teachers were unable to contain his aggression. Reportedly tried to intimidate older children.
		P	David tried to hit animals with his hand or a plastic bat or run over them with his toy car.
			Mother felt helpless to stop David's behavior.

(Continued)

Table 8.1 (Continued)

Age	Date		Events
3–9	10/00	P	David began to exhibit increases in destructive and depressed behavior.
			He destroyed his artwork and anything that held value to him. He would do such things as getting on a tricycle and riding it with his eyes closed down steep hills. At one point he ran into a mailbox, splitting his nose open and requiring stitches.
4–7	8/01		Seen by Dr. Serra, child psychiatrist.
		m	Started on dextroamphetamine (Dexedrine), which he took for 2 months—resulted in severe anorexia.
		m	Soon after began thioridazine (Mellaril) up to 25 mg daily, which was ineffective at helping his aggression and overly sedating. Subsequently was given divalproex (Depakote), but behavior deteriorated.
4–9	10/10/01		Hospitalized at James Hospital.
		P	History of "out-of-control behavior" including severe aggression and threatening to kill peers. He was also kicking and hitting himself. He had thrown things at his mother. Grandmother reported better success in controlling him.
		m	On admission on Dexedrine 5 mg twice a day, Depakote 125 mg twice a day was added but discontinued when it seemed to have no effect. Pemoline (Cylert) was then started 37.5 mg Q AM, resulting in a generalized red body rash; he also became very anorexic on it. Imipramine was then added 10 mg HS, increased to 20 mg. Appetite and insomnia seemed to improve on this, but electrocardiographic changes prevented further dose increases. Bupropion (Wellbutrin) 75 mg was then added (mother was informed of seizure risks) and increased to twice a day.
	10/25/01		Returned to mother.
			Continued on above medications, but behavior did not improve.
		R	Mother felt that grandmother was interfering in her mothering, while grandmother felt mother was ineffective.

(*Continued*)

Table 8.1 (Continued)

	11/01		Mother met new boyfriend.
		S	This boyfriend was more engaged with David and provided some measure of stability in the house for almost a year.
			Because of increasing domestic violence between mother and her current boyfriend, the relationship finally came to an end.
5–9	10/02		David began kindergarten in special education and for some time managed better at school than at home.
		P	Began to run away, leaving the house unsupervised, going to different places in town. Mother reported he would take the metro to nearby communities. She reported he always returned home unharmed after several hours. If David acted out when he and mother were about to get on a bus, she would not let him get on and he would run along the side of the bus crying. He would always find his way home.
			Special education assessments were initiated, and home tutoring was considered. He continued to decompensate.
4–0	2/03		Psychological assessment—Gerard Hemmings, PhD
		e	"Medication interventions appear to have been only marginally helpful. However, his maladaptive behaviors appear to be learned and he needs a highly structured environment over a period of time so that he can incorporate the notion that he cannot be a six-year-old 'omnipotent king' within the family."
6–8	9/03		Began first grade.
		P	Had increasing incidents of being out of control, hitting other kids, and challenging teachers.
	12/19/03		Hospitalized at the local county mental health unit.
		•	He had gotten in a fight with a peer at school and then proceeded to punch and kick his mother and hit the walls, required restraints to get back into the car. He was evaluated at the outpatient clinic and required restraint.
		e	Discharge diagnosis: Intermittent explosive disorder, attention-deficit/hyperactivity disorder combined type, R/O psychotic disorder NOS.
7			Decision was made to remove him from mother's care and make him a ward of the court as mother acknowledged that he was totally beyond her control.

(Continued)

Table 8.1 (Continued)

Age	Date		Events
7–4	3/15/04		Placed in foster care with Stella J.
		m	When discharged from hospital was on Mellaril 135 mg four times a day in divided doses, clonidine 0.1 mg twice a day, risperidone (Risperdal) 0.5 mg twice a day, and carbamazepine (Tegretol) twice a day.
			Initially, placement seemed to go well, but he then became defiant and was cruel to her pets.
		P	At this point he was referred to a day treatment program, where he had ongoing difficulties and threatened other children.
			Foster mother gave a 7-day notice, saying David was unmanageable and she was being called to the school too much to deal with his behaviors.
7–8	7/10/04		Placed in new foster home, Mr. & Mrs. R.
		P	The Joneses had their own boy, age 10, and one other foster child, a girl 7. David gradually became highly resentful of the other children and physically attacked them. This led to his being placed in yet another home.
8–1	2/05		Placed in foster home of Elaine H.
		m	Currently on amantadine 100 mg, Depakote 250 mg, Mellaril 25 mg, and nefazodone (Serzone) 300 mg.
			Within a month foster mother found David's behavior beyond her capacity to manage.
8–2	3/13/05		Placed in foster home of Maddy M.
		P	This was a single-parent home with no other foster children. Maddy felt that she was beginning to make a relationship with David and that he tried to make many demands on her and claimed that he was "the man of the house."
8–8	9/4/05		Placed in foster home of Viola C.
			Initially, this placement seemed more successful and David seemed to have an emotional connection to his foster mother.
		P	This placement had to end when the foster mother's own mother developed terminal cancer and she had to devote herself to her mother's care. Foster mother has written to David and called several times since he left her care, and she has indicated that

(Continued)

Table 8.1 (Continued)

			she would consider having him return to her home. She is somewhat alarmed by his behavior since leaving her care.
8–11	12/22/05		Admitted to Sterling Hospital for acting out, assaultive and aggressive behaviors.
		P	Aggressive outbursts occurred daily. He was prone to throwing furniture, assaulting staff, and hitting his fists against the walls. He became calmer during the later part of his hospitalization.
			He denied that he was angry that his last placement had to be terminated and said that he was "no sissy."
9–0	1/10/06		Placed in level 12 residential care.
		m	By this time was on 300 mg lithium three times a day, Depakote 250 mg twice a day, guanfacine (Tenex) 2 mg a.m. and 1 noon and 2 mg late afternoon, thorazine 50 mg three times a day, and Wellbutrin 75 mg twice a day.
		e	He now was given a diagnosis of bipolar disorder.
			Aggressive outbursts occurred daily. He was prone to throwing furniture, assaulting staff, and hitting his fists against the walls. He became calmer during the later part of his hospitalization
9–11	12/14/06		Admitted to Sterling County Children's Psychiatric Unit.
			He repeatedly ran away from his residence and attacked counselors and peers.
			At this time he was taking thorazine and imipramine.
			Aggressive outbursts did not subside, and his medications were changed to Tegretol and Mellaril, with little decrease in outbursts.
			Neurological and electrocardiographic exams were within normal limits.
			On the same day he was to return to residential care he said he didn't want to return, argued, began hitting the wall with a broken table leg, and failed to calm down. The police were called, and he was kept at the Sterling Unit until arrangements could be made for a higher level of care.
10–0	1/25/09		Transferred to a level 14 residential care facility.

(*Continued*)

Table 8.1 (Continued)

Age	Date	Events
		Over a several-month period he was gradually titrated off all psychotropic medications for thorough assessment.

Note on the findings in this table of life events: This information was gathered solely for the purposes of describing important events in this child's life as well as highlighting actual and potential strengths within the child and his family. It was drawn in large part from documents that were supplied by other agencies or through unrecorded interviews. The fact that something is reported here does not necessarily mean that it is true but simply that it was reported in these documents and interviews. A great deal of information may also be missing because we do not have access to it. This information is sensitive and should be treated as confidential. Recipients of this information should not release it to any third parties without obtaining appropriate consent.

Relational Assessment Worksheet

Client name:	David S.
Date of admission:	1/25/09
Clinician name:	Anna F.

Domains of data

Use the spaces provided to enter notes on each of the categories listed. An entry can be thought of as a key piece of data, an observation, or a discrepancy in the material as it emerges. Some categories are highly overlapping and correlated. Some are not as salient as others and some may not seem relevant at all.

For children with complex caretaker histories, provide a brief summary of their experiences. For example, "with biological parents from birth to age 3," "emergency foster care for 3 months," "long-term foster care for 3 years," "residential treatment."

I. The child's experience with caretakers.

Summary of caretaking stability: Provide a brief summary of the child's caretaking history. Include, for example, estimated numbers of placements, average length of placements, and the placements that seem to have been the longest or most important.

David lived with his mother, Sally, from birth to age 7. Throughout these years, however, there were periods in which David resided with his maternal grandmother for up to 1 month. At age 7 he was removed from the care of his mother, following evidence of physical abuse by his mother's boyfriend and a sustained pattern of failure to protect on the part of the mother. David was then placed in foster care, going through a succession of five foster placements until it was decided that he could not be served in foster care, and he was then placed in a level 12 residential facility at age 9. This placement was stormy, and it seems to have been a chaotic place. He was moved before his eleventh birthday to a level 14 placement. A former foster mother is interested in maintaining contact with David and might be a placement option for him in the future. She had some success managing his behavior, but the placement ended after 5 months when the foster mother's own mother became terminally ill. Until that time the placement had seemed that it might succeed.

1. Availability:

David's mother's own history of caretaking was quite compromised, with two placements in foster care and disruptions of attachment due to maternal illness and addiction. By her own account, her availability to David was problematic as she was a regular victim of domestic violence and very much at the mercy of violent partners, who had no attachment to David. These men sometimes demanded that David be left with his grandmother. Mom's challenges also included clinical depression and physical illnesses (somatization disorder?). Recent visits with mom are notable for mom's preoccupation with her own and David's health and a passive, fearful relation to David. His former foster mother was quite available; she had taken David on as a project and "worked with him."

2. Attunement or contingent responsiveness:

Observed interactions with mom show problems of attunement, with mother interpreting David's states in terms of physical symptoms or other concrete theories that restate his complaints ("He feels bad"). Early attunement is hard to assess with no specific data. Former foster mom's attunement may have been pretty good but sometimes seems to have gone sideways with her worries that David is "getting over on her" (i.e., manipulating her), which tends to skew her view of his needs, approaches, etc.

3. Engagement:

Mother's engagement with David has been intermittent, disrupted by her own life struggles and concerns and her repeated subordination of her relationship with David to her relationships with her often violent partners. His former foster mother seems to have been highly engaged with David and seemed to know where he was and what he was up to at all times. David seemed to have liked this about her.

4. Reflective function—mentalization:

Mother's capacity to see David as an intentional being acting from feelings, wishes, or mental states is highly variable and subject to disruption by her own needs and immediate states. Thus, she will regularly utilize unreflective attributions, such as "He's just like Scott" or "He just liked to hit sometimes." Much of the time it seems very difficult for his mother to think in terms of feeling states and she will stay with concrete behavioral accounts instead of efforts to understand based on feelings or intentions: "He wrecked the place" instead of "He got really frustrated and was out of control."

5. Regulatory function:

Mother reports relative comfort and ease in her early relationship with David. She states that he was an easy baby and that she was able to manage his distress without great difficulty: "He was always hungry and I fed him. It worked pretty good." Later, things got more difficult, and mom has described David as having periods of frustration and inconsolable crying that she did not know how to handle: "I tried everything. Sometimes I just had to turn up the TV and lock him in his room till he cried himself out and fell asleep. Afterwards, it was like it never happened." Or, at another point, "A few times I lost it at him and just screamed louder and louder. It would shut him up . . . he would just go sort of blank and freeze. I didn't like doing it, but what a relief."

6. Tolerance of and support for exploration and autonomy:

Mom's helplessness resulted in a certain de facto "tolerance" for David's autonomy, though she was generally fearful about the environment and often worried about a variety of dangers (many real, some imagined) in the succession of apartment buildings they lived in. David seems to have been almost counterphobic in his ventures out into the world. His maternal grandmother kept him on a short leash most of the time, but there seem to have also been notable, alarming lapses in her monitoring; and on several occasions, at a very young age, David was sent on errands and got lost. He still tells the story of one of these incidents with a certain amount of pride.

7. Traumatic factors:

Multiple, pervasive (see Table 8.1). David was exposed from an early age to repeated bursts of unpredictable violence in which his mother was battered by her partners. This occurred throughout the time that he resided with her. Additionally, he was a victim of physical abuse by some of mother's partners. Mother continues to deny that significant physical abuse of David occurred, and as a victim herself, she lacked the capacity to protect him from her partners. In one of his first foster placements he was removed following unsubstantiated disclosures of harsh physical discipline. Another foster child in the same home later made a strikingly similar allegation.

8. Projective processes directed at the child by the caretaker:

Not striking but mother does tend to see her own issues (physical fragility, illness and general health concerns) in David. Also, there is a drift toward hanging a persona on him that is derived from her view of men and their propensity for violence. She will observe, for example, that he reminds her of Scott, her longest off again–on again partner.

9. Boundary function:

Not clear, mother inclined to view David through the lens of her own issues and needs and to utilize him as a support for herself. Life circumstances also contributed to difficulties in this area: Family mostly lived in very close quarters, where David regularly witnessed adult activity (fighting, sexual activity, and some drug use).

10. Hierarchy:

In early relationship with mom, problematic: "He just wouldn't listen and it made me feel so helpless. Some of my boyfriends would try to act like a dad and were pretty rough with him. They never hurt him but the school found bruises on him and called the social workers. It was from a fight with another kid. He got into lots of those." By report maternal grandmother was a more effective authority: "You just have to be clear that you're the boss. Sally could never do that. She was a rug and he walked on her." Hierarchy with former foster mom seems very good indeed and seems to be a key ingredient in their relationship. David will say, "Viola gets me to do stuff. She stays on me. She's tough but she's nice too. She's a good cook."

II. The child's current interpersonal behavior

1. Organization and self-regulation:

History provided by mother and maternal grandmother suggests that there were periods of good functioning punctuated by dramatic collapses of self-regulation, with rages and periods of inconsolable crying. Mother reports a long history of sleep difficulties, with David often becoming agitated and restless at bedtime. This was a significant problem in all placements. Emotional self-regulation is now difficult to gauge: David is very invested in maintaining a posture of invulnerability that may mask self-regulatory difficulties. That is, there are places "he won't go." His access to intellectual abilities is gradually improving, with academic functioning now near grade level. In residential placement he has been seen as among the higher-functioning kids and, unless in a power struggle or confrontation, he did not need a high level of supervision to be maintained. He is able to follow through on complex tasks. His residential counselors comment that he is "independent" and that some of his capacities seem like the competence of a child who has had to fend for himself.

2. Proximity seeking and the pursuit of relationship:

Functioning in this area is very much compromised by David's need to maintain an invulnerable self. He is dismissive of any notion of connection or dependency and generally "cool" to involvement. Many staff note that David would not ask for help after falling on the playground, when he clearly needed assistance. He tried to wave off staff who approached him. He is very gradually developing connections to the residential staff who stayed engaged with him and who were the most consistent presence in his house. David is also showing signs of connecting to a very large, extremely calm male staff who walked him through the intake process, got him settled in the house, and has worked consistently with him since the beginning of his placement. David also shows signs of becoming connected to his interpersonally cool but demanding teacher. (She is very professional and demands little but work; there is no expectation of a relationship or a need on her part for any particular response from David.)

3. Exploratory capacity:

Apparently good but hard to assess. Has a counterphobic orientation to the environment, as though announcing all the time, "Nothing scares me!" So there is a readiness to be in the world and gestures of exploration, but he is too busy being invulnerable to be curious and admit that he doesn't know things. His teacher has had some success in getting him past this, and he has gradually become more open to learning and has progressed academically. His avoidant, counterdependent stance gives him a veneer of independence, but the real depth of this unclear. David has interests in predictable areas: rappers, wrestlers, and muscle cars. David prefers sports and competitive games. His imaginative play, which does not happen all that much, is driven by themes of power and aggression toward the weak.

4. Sense of self:

David is very careful to avoid any situation or experience in which he might feel "one-down" or at the mercy of others and will often make grandiose claims about his athletic prowess, his appeal to "the ladies," and his "skills" in almost any area. If challenged, he will respond with a laughing "Just playing!" and admit that he has to keep his reputation up. In other words, there is not a profound lack of realism about the self. There has been some growing pride in his academic gains or at least a reduction in what seemed to be an intense shame-related avoidance of academic challenges. David's need to maintain his sense of invulnerability can also be seen in his response to a handful of situations in which he encountered his own limitations in a very stark way. One involved the brief, temporary placement of an older, stronger version of himself in the group home; and the other involved a rejection by a girl in his class in the day treatment program. In the first case, he seemed to feel threatened and that he was losing his position in the peer group, and he withdrew and became sullen and depressed and derogated all the peers who he saw as gravitating to a new alpha male. In the case of his rejected interest in the girl, he also shut down and dismissed her as "stupid."

5. Boundary functions:

Superficially good, in that David presents himself as expecting little of others and tends to keep his distance. He never asks personal questions, intrudes on staff physically with requests for hugs, or sits too close to staff. He may intrude on another's space to assert power and control and will stand too close to staff who he is defying, conveying a looming, vaguely threatening presence. When confronted about this, he will respond with injured innocence and may try to blame the victim: "What are you so uptight about?"

6. Affective expression:

David's range of emotional expression is limited; he seems to favor contempt, arrogance, and disinterest. He cannot tolerate sadness or anxiety but does anger with some fluency. He has been known to enjoy and call attention to others' discomfort or embarrassment: "You got punked!" Intensity of expression is generally muted with a held-back quality that seems consciously cultivated. Modulation seems adequate but, again, emotional control seems to come from a defensive exclusion of strong emotion rather than real flexibility, distress tolerance, or self-regulation.

7. Emotions evoked in staff:

Staff seem to feel a mixture of distanced indifference from David ("Most of the time he doesn't demand much.") or a kind of mild intimidation ("I just feel off-balance, like I'm just not sure how he'll react to stuff and I won't know what to do next. It's not comfortable."). Some staff members describe this state as gradually becoming a feeling of "walking on eggs" and avoiding engagement with him. The more honest staff note that this sometimes leads them to "not notice" low-grade acting out such as intimidation of peers or unsafe physical posturing. They can then avoid setting a limit and the risk of an escalating confrontation. A related issue noted by staff does not involve an emotion but an idea. Several milieu workers and his therapist all noted that they are consistently surprised to remember that David is only 11 years old. He seems able to create in them the idea that he is really an adolescent. This is consistent with some descriptions of him as "pretty independent."

8. Themes of current relationships:

Power, intimidation, strength/weakness, avoidance of connection, dependency, vulnerability.

Description of the Internal Working Model In providing a useful description of the child's internal working model of relationships you may organize your thinking with questions such as:

How have important experiences with caretakers influenced the child's capacity for connections with others? How have they influenced his or her own interpersonal stance as well as his or her general functioning in the world?

What are the child's implicit beliefs about how the interpersonal world works?

How does he or she seem to expect to be treated or responded to in that world? In behavioral terms, what sort of treatment does he or she seem to invite from others?

To what degree and in what way is he or she able to make use of caretakers and other important adults in his or her life? To increase feelings of safety and security?

To learn about his or her environment? To comfort him or her when he or she is sick, hurt, or upset?

What are the key themes in his or her relationships with caretakers and other important adults?

David's implicit beliefs about relationships could be summarized in the following statements:

- I can't rely on others to meet my needs; therefore, I don't have (or can't let myself know about) any needs of my own.
- I'm on my own.
- I don't need other people (and if I ever feel like I do, I better not show it).
- Others are either weak and, therefore, legitimate targets for intimidation and exploitation or strong and, therefore, must be approached with care and calculation.
- I will never allow anyone to control me; I will always try to control the other.
- If I show any sort of weakness or vulnerability or if I show that I don't know something, then others may take advantage and humiliate me or try to control me.
- I am not afraid; I will make others afraid.
- I will not be humiliated; I will humiliate others.
- The world is a dangerous place and I need to be vigilant and even dangerous myself to survive in it.

Relational Treatment Plan

Client name:	David S.
Date:	2/10/09

Description of the child's internal working model of relationships (from the Relational Assessment Worksheet). Give particular attention to the "interpersonal invitations" that the child seems to direct at others; what sorts of relationships does he or she seem to try to establish with others?

- I can't rely on others to meet my needs; therefore, I don't have (or can't let myself know about) any needs of my own.
- I'm on my own.
- I don't need other people (and if I ever feel like I do, I better not show it).
- Others are either weak and, therefore, legitimate targets for intimidation and exploitation or strong and, therefore, must be approached with care and calculation.
- I will never allow anyone to control me; I will always try to control the other.

- If I show any sort of weakness or vulnerability or if I show that I don't know something, then others may take advantage and humiliate me or try to control me.
- I am not afraid; I will make others afraid.
- I will not be humiliated; I will humiliate others.
- The world is a dangerous place, and I need to be vigilant and even dangerous myself to survive in it.

Describe the responses that seem to be invited from or evoked in adults who are working with this child. In other words, how might staff members or other adults find themselves inadvertently confirming the child's implicit beliefs about the world? Try to be detailed and include descriptions of unsuccessful interactions in which the child's functioning declined. Information about the failure of prior placements is often useful in this regard; that is, what sorts of responses to the child seemed to lead to declines in functioning and, in turn, to placement failure?

David is working to have others experience the fear, helplessness, and confusion he regularly suffered in the course of his own development. This helplessness and confusion might be experienced as

- Not knowing how to respond.
- Finding yourself looking away from his negative behavior
- Being literally afraid of injury.
- Finding yourself avoiding setting limits.
- Trying to avoid being in David's presence, especially without backup.

David is working to avoid connection with others and the risks that that engagement can carry with it. People in relationship with him may feel or do the following:

- Overestimate his independence and capacity for self-management
- Assume that he needs nothing in the way of support or nurturing
- Forget that he is around
- Rely on him as a "junior staff" when other kids are getting unregulated
- Feel "nothing": indifference or neutrality

David is working to avoid any feelings of shame or humiliation and is making exaggerated efforts to cause or call attention to those feeling in others. The resulting states/actions in others might include

- Shame and humiliation
- A "closed-down feeling" in which one defensively avoids any statement or action that might elicit ridicule or shaming
- Feelings of intense anger in response to actually being made to feel shame

David is intensely preoccupied with the theme of power and strength vs. weakness and vulnerability. He will work to work to create relationships driven by this theme. The resulting states/actions might include

- Feelings of incompetence, inexperience, and being "off-balance"
- Wishes/urges to retaliate with intrusive overcontrol or excessively harsh regimes of behavioral control or consequences: a "break the mustang" mentality

Describe a disconfirming stance for staff to use in working with this child. This should include a general posture staff should take in response to the "interpersonal invitations" detailed above, as well as specific statements and behaviors that can be directed at the child in specific situations that are repeatedly encountered in the work. Try to include scenarios from all the settings in which staff engage the child.

Generally, resist the pull to avoid or not engage with David.

Specifically, work to create engagement by always remembering that he is a boy who needs nurturing and support in spite of his efforts to project a very different image. Thus, for example, create a bedtime plan so that he is read to or is provided with proximity as he is falling asleep. Avoid the appearance that this is "for David" as he will almost certainly reject it, seeing it as nurturing and infantilizing. Instead, make it about his roommate or just a matter of standard procedure. In the classroom, do not wait for him to ask for help but offer help in neutral ways that he may be more able to accept. Try asking him to show his own problem-solving process. Unlike many residents, David avoids asking for one-to-one engagement with staff members. The team should resist this avoidance of connection by creating opportunities for one-to-one activities with key staff members. Sharing in staff chores such as yard work and light maintenance work seems to have greater success than something that he may see as a special time or a special privilege.

In working to connect to David, keep in mind the value of fun and playfulness. He is more resistant to being cared for than he is to being delighted by play. More athletic and competitive games quickly turn into alpha male opportunities, so try to avoid them. He has had a lot of fun when the younger kids are involved in group games. Their presence seems to make the activity more fun for him, and it's not so grim.

Construct a list of critical behaviors that staff must intervene on. This list would describe all the "ignorable" behaviors that have been sometimes passed over in the interest of avoiding escalating confrontations. Some of the most important of these will be fairly subtle and may involve his use of physical posture and voice tone for intimidation.

Contain with neutrality. When David is contained, either in the general sense of limit setting or in the specific sense of seclusion or restraint, it is his expectation that the interaction will be an attempt to render him powerless, weak, and generally at the mercy of stronger adults. Even as he strives to give the interaction this quality, it is critical that every effort be made to offer him choices, to emphasize the choices that he is making, and to generally avoid a coercive response to his coercive behavior. Generally, prompts are more successful than moving rapidly to time-outs for noncompliance. Following any seclusion and restraint, it is most important to state in very simple terms why it was necessary to do the containment and to avoid any debate about these matters. Do not ask David to explain why he was restrained; he experiences this approach as an effort to essentially make him "say uncle." Our experience is that he knows very well the reasons for any given containment. We want to underscore that we are not out to just push him around. When you make a mistake about a rule or a consequence, always admit that you blew it and apologize—he has had very little of that sort of experience with adults.

Manage embarrassment. David often teases or points out failures, oversights, and anything else that might reflect inexperience or inadequacy on the part of staff members in an effort to cause embarrassment. Staff should respond to these provocations with comfortable self-deprecating humor and frank acknowledgment of the situation, thereby demonstrating that it is possible to tolerate and manage these emotional states.

Emphasize our resources and capacity to contain him. David will sometimes confront staff, especially those he sees as less experienced or less "strong," with direct verbal challenges, such as "What are you going to do? You can't restrain me!" While it is important to have adequate resources to actually contain David, it is also true that we need to be able to quietly, calmly, and neutrally communicate our confidence about that capacity.

(*Note.* These examples of possible disconfirming stances are fairly general. Inevitably, actual engagement with a real child allows a more fine-grained description of multiple settings and exchanges in which the child regularly attempts to elicit confirming responses. Once the team begins to understand the essential elements of the child's implicit beliefs and the "interpersonal undertow" that follows from those beliefs, they begin to generate increasingly specific examples of the child's regular efforts to create confirmatory interpersonal scenarios and events. This, in turn, permits the description of more specific disconfirming actions and postures that can be implemented in multiple treatment settings.)

Target behavior definition form

Date:	2/18/09
Client name:	David S.

Note: Input to this form may occur across several different meetings of the various participants in the treatment team. Please date each entry as it is added for each participant in the planning process. If necessary, use more than one form.

Part I. Areas of concern

List all behaviors/issues/concerns that each participant feels is important for the team, the client, and the family to address together. These initial entries may be of any form—this is a no-fault brainstorming process. (Please enter names of all participants in this planning process.)

(Example: "Defiance.")

Family:

"Violence, pushing people around, not listening to what adults tell him to do, having an attitude all the time."

Current caregivers (if other than the family):

Former foster mother: "Trying to get over on people all the time with his big personality, not minding, having to be told 10 times to do everything."

Client:

"Nothing really . . . anger management I guess. Anything to get out of this place."

Referral source (if relevant):

Child welfare worker: "Aggression, defiance, oppositional behavior."

Treatment team partners:

N/A

Residential team members:

"Use of intimidation, acting like the rules don't apply to him, refusing directions, noncompliance, stuck in being a certain personality who's all about pushing other people around or away. He has no idea how to be a little kid."

Behaviors known to have contributed to difficulties in prior placements:

Aggression (frequently needed physical management after escalating confrontations that usually began with David resisting directions or adult authority.

Other notes, thoughts, reflections, objections, or concerns:

Client is very concerned that compliance is a submission.

Part II. Prioritize behaviors

Among the various concerns raised by participants, what are the most important areas for the team to begin to address in its initial efforts? The following considerations might be important: risk of injury to self or other, disruptiveness in important settings in which the child must function. Try to focus on three areas of concern and give a brief "headline" summary of each one, such as "running away" or "losing temper" or "has a bad attitude."

1. Aggression in escalated confrontations with adults. Use of physical intimidation, verbal aggression in the form of sarcasm, derision.

2. Physical intimidation, "pushiness," defiance.
3. Difficulties asking or help. Avoidance of support from adults.

Part III. Moving from concerns to target behaviors

Here, we are going to bring a sharper focus on actual behavior—we want to move from what may be fairly general areas of concern to specific behaviors that are observable and measurable. For each area of concern listed above, ask the question "What does the child actually do that makes this a good description of him or her? Try to think in terms of verbs, not adjectives (e.g., out of seat and talking out rather than "hyper"). For each area of concern, there may be several (or even more) specific behaviors that the child has that make the items above good descriptions of things to work on. Some of the areas of concern may already be expressed in terms of pretty specific, concrete behaviors. If so, that's fine, just write them below. Examples of the level of focus that we're looking for here might be "doesn't complete homework," "steals food from the kitchen," "calls out for staff at bedtime," or "shouts angrily when given an instruction."

(Example: "Defiance." Shouts curses when given an instruction, puffs up chest and moves into the personal space of the adult, balls up hands into fists, tries to negotiate the instruction by pointing out that peers are not being given the same instruction.)

1. Physical and verbal aggression: moves forward into the space of the adult, uses his open hands to push the adult away as though he is going to "go through you" or as if trying to start a fight with a peer. These physical gestures are always accompanied by verbal threats or sarcastic, derisive comments. When given a time-out or prompted to take space, David will swing into full-scale aggression with fist swinging and kicking out with his feet.

Part IV. Final definitions of target behaviors for observation

Take behaviors from each group above and write definitions according to the following standards:

- Objectivity: Include observable, measurable characteristics of the behavior using active verbs or events in the environment caused by the behavior that are also observable.
- Clarity: Be as specific and clear as possible so that ambiguity is reduced to a minimum. Keep in mind the "stranger test"—could a new team member read the description and immediately use it to guide observation or treatment?
- Completeness: Be thorough, noting all responses that are part of the behavior and noting related behaviors or milder expressions of the behavior that are *not* included in the definition.

Example: Target behavior: DefianceThis target behavior can be observed when an adult gives the child an instruction to stop an activity in progress or to begin a new activity. It will be scored as occurring whenever there is an incident of defiance following an instruction, defined as the child responding with a raised voice and any verbal statement indicating an intention not to follow the instruction of the form "No!" or "You can't tell me what to do!" or "You're not the boss of me!" or statements including any curse words. Not scored as defiance will be silent delays in compliance (i.e., doing nothing) or overly slow compliance. Similarly, unpleasant facial expressions accompanying compliance will not be scored.

Target Behavior #1:

Verbal defiance–physical aggression
Target is defined as refusal to comply with a direction with statements like "Oh really?" and "No way!" and "Give me a break!" David will then invade the space of the other with his hands or body in a pushing motion, hitting with fists or kicking with feet when the adult moves to contain him.

Behavioral assessment planning worksheet

Baseline determination

Date:	2/18/09
Client name:	David S.

The purpose of this worksheet is to assist the team in planning the first step of behavioral assessment. It can also be used later in the treatment process to plan additional observations of target behaviors to assess the impact of intervention efforts. Because different target behaviors may implicate different behavioral variables (e.g., frequency, duration, intensity), the worksheet is organized by target behavior.

Target Behavior #1:

Physical aggression
Target is defined as refusal to comply with a direction with statements like "Oh really?" and "No way!" and "Give me a break!" David will then invade the space of the other with his hands or body in a pushing motion, hitting with fists or kicking with feet when the adult moves to contain him.

Key variable described by behavioral definition. Check appropriate box:

☒ Frequency   ☐ Duration   ☐ Latency   ☐ Intensity

☐ Qualitative dimensions or outcomes. Specify:

Assessment decisions

1. When will the assessment be carried out? What are the times of day or key settings in which the target behavior occurs?

The target behavior can happen at any time that David is given a direction, asked to stop an activity, or asked to begin an activity that he is not interested in.

2. Who will carry out observation of this target behavior? (If necessary, specify by setting.)

Residence: House staff on David's point sheet as assigned by manager
Day treatment program: Classroom staff on point sheet

3. What method will be used to assess this target behavior? Check appropriate box.

   ☒ Frequency Count   ☐ Intensity Measure   ☐ Duration Measure
   ☐ Outcome Measure   ☐ Qualitative Measure

4. How will observers be trained in the definition of this target behavior?

The definition of this behavior is very straightforward. It will be discussed in team meetings, and the definition will be printed on a recording form attached to the point sheet.

5. When will the first evaluation of this behavioral assessment be carried out?

After discussion at the next team meeting.

6. How long an observation period will be needed to get a meaningful assessment of baseline?

Based on the estimates of frequency made by the team, the observation period will need to be 2 weeks.

Functional analysis worksheet

Functional analysis: collaborative meeting worksheet

Client name:	David S.
Date of meeting:	2/28/09

(If multiple meetings are held among different groups of team members then use a new worksheet for each meeting.)

Team members present:

1. Clinician Anna F.
2. Former foster mother, Viola C.
3. House Manager, Karl B.
4. County Social Worker Melinda W.
5. Teacher Kari M.
6. Residential staff: Sally H., Mike G., Robert R., Fred J.

Note: This meeting is specifically focused on the client's target behaviors. This meeting assumes that some initial gathering of more general, often historical, information has already occurred. This might include, but is not limited to, family and developmental history, trauma history, strengths and vulnerabilities of the client, history of the target behaviors, and history of prior interventions and their results.

In focusing on behavior this meeting should be an exercise in curiosity, a collaborative sharing of information, experience, and understanding that will help us all understand what seems to cause the behavior and what seems to keep it going. We want to find out what purpose it serves. The questions provided below are offered as potentially useful prompts. Pursuing data may require more specific questions based on what emerges as the discussion proceeds.

Target Behavior 1

Definition:

Target is defined as refusal to comply with a direction with statements like "Oh really?" and "No way!" and "Give me a break!" David will then invade the space of the other with his hands or body in a pushing motion, hitting with fists or kicking with feet when the adult moves to contain him.

1. Setting questions: Are there settings in which the behavior is more likely to occur? These can include real settings—actual places—as well as activities and states of vulnerability in the client such as fatigue, hunger, or anger about some other issue. Does the problem occur only at school? Only at home? Only in transitions? Are there settings in which the behavior never occurs?

There is a consensus among all participants that this target behavior is associated with situations in which David is being asked to do something he doesn't want to do such as end a game or begin a chore, that it is more likely with adult females than males and more likely with smaller males than larger males. It is also more likely with new or less experienced, confident staff. With peers it rarely happens with much younger or much smaller children, who generally avoid or appease David. There is some evidence that it is more likely in the early evening after free time and before dinner.

2. Antecedent questions: Are there any events that often occur right before the behavior that seem to "trigger" it? These can include certain kinds of interactions, activities, and even particular people.

Most common antecedent is an adult direction to perform a task or end an activity. This usually leads to a period of defiant, verbal aggression and sarcasm; and when the adult holds his or her ground, David will escalate to aggression.

3. Consequence questions: Are there any results, consequences, or responses from the environment that seem to follow the behavior? These can include getting something, getting to do something, not having to do something, and responses from adults and peers.

Since entering this setting, it has most commonly resulted in being physically contained and then losing privileges. Internally, it seems to confirm David's view of himself as tough or indomitable.

4. Intervention questions: What responses or procedures have the adults (teachers, staff, caregivers) utilized in the past to deal with this target behavior?

There is some evidence that David has in prior placements been able to create a reputation for aggression that has afforded him a certain amount of power. At least one foster parent reported to the county worker that she was afraid of him, and in the earlier group home setting David laughingly says he "Got away with murder." Several participants noted that David has a lot of power in the peer group and that many of the other kids defer to him and have commented to staff that they are afraid of him.

5. Exception data: Are there settings (people, places, activities, etc.) in which the target behavior never occurs? Are there settings that are regularly associated with the client engaging in positive behavior?

Kevin W. (large, very physically confident school staff with a very calm, quiet demeanor) has never seen this target behavior when David has been in his activity group. One of the art therapists has had only one "near incident" of aggression and has taken the approach of taking David aside before each group and reminding him that he is in control of how the group goes and that she very much wants him to remain in the group for the whole activity.

Initial hypotheses: Given the data developed above, do the team have any initial hypotheses about the function of the behavior? A hypothesis can be stated in the form of "When x occurs or is occurring, the client does behavior y and the result is that z occurs."

This behavior has, in some form or another, been going on for a long time and must certainly have roots in David's history of witnessing violence, of being poorly regulated by a succession of caretakers, and of actually gaining some measure of power and control from this behavior in some settings.

Currently, when given a direction, David experiences some level of loss of control and safety and fears being dominated or hurt. Escalating to aggression affords him some escape from this and adds to feelings of control and power. He is also rewarded by the deference of his peers and the "walking on eggshells" of staff who want to avoid a physical confrontation.

Plan for direct observation: Given the above hypotheses, describe a plan for appropriate direct observation of the behavior, in the environment in which it occurs, to collect systematic data. Include who will be responsible for collection of the data, what forms will be used or created for the recording of the data. and for how long the data will be collected.

Staff will use a Functional Behavior Assessment Form to record data. This behavior is of sufficiently low frequency (not more than two instances per shift or school period) that any member of the team who is completing David's point sheet can fill in the relevant information. Data will be collected for 2 weeks.

Replacement behavior worksheet

Client name:	David S.
Date:	2/28/09

Team members present:

Anna F. and Karl B., Residential Counselors

Target behavior:

Target is defined as refusal to comply with a direction with statements like "Oh really?" and "No way!" and "Give me a break!" David will then invade the space of the other with his hands or body in a pushing motion, hitting with fists or kicking with feet when the adult moves to contain him.

What is the function of the target behavior? What need or purpose does it express?

The target behavior is complex and has multiple sources. The target behavior appears to provide some relief from fears of being controlled, dominated, or victimized by adults. Functional assessment in current setting does show that there is some inadvertent reinforcement by some staff. When David uses verbal defiance, they sometimes negotiate with him and end up letting him evade the direction or task. The behavior yields some real rewards in the form of reduced demands from some adults and the deference of most peers.

What replacement behavior(s) will enable the client to meet the same need and still preserve safety and continued development?

1. Using words to ask for what he wants and to gain appropriate level of personal control. Asking for greater control over his activities and tasks by, for example, requesting permission to decide on the order and timing of academic tasks and chores or by setting his own schedule for the parts of his evening schedule that staff are able to allow.
2. Asking to take space for 5 minutes when upset by a direction.
3. Compliance with adult directions within 1 minute.

Does the client already show the proposed replacement in another setting or behaviors that include components of the replacement behavior?

Yes, verbal and reasoning skills will support this replacement behavior. David has shown some instances of the replacement behavior in, for example, working out his chore schedule with the Saturday morning staff. David is able to comply with directions.

What method will the team utilize in teaching the behavior? Will it need to be broken down into teachable components (chained) or taught in successive approximations (shaped)?

No.

Is there anyone in the client's environment who is a skilled practitioner of the replacement behavior?

There are two boys in the adolescent classroom who have very similar replacement behaviors. They will be asked to work with David to develop the details of his behavior plan.

How will the team monitor the client's mastery of the replacement behavior?

By David's point sheet.

Behavioral treatment plan worksheet

Client name:	David S.
Date of plan development:	2/28/09

Team members:

Anna, Karl, Robert, Wayne, Stacy, Kevin, Dawn, Linda, and Tony.

Target behavior 1

Definition:

Target is defined as refusal to comply with a direction with statements like "Oh really?" and "No way!" and "Give me a break!" David will then invade the space of the other with his hands or body in a pushing motion, hitting with fists or kicking with feet when the adult moves to contain him.

Functional assessment information:

1. Antecedents and settings:

Clear antecedents found in functional assessment: being given a direction to stop a valued activity or to begin an undesired activity.

2. Consequences:

Currently, if David escalates to actual aggression, he is contained and loses his level. By historical report it seems that in some settings his use of violence led to actual control, escape from adult authority, and a certain level of deference from his peers.

3. Functional hypothesis:

David uses aggression to escape from fears of being dominated or controlled and has also gained in other settings some immediate reinforcement by keeping caretakers uneasy about taking him on.

Intervention planning:

1. Antecedent and setting modifications:

None.

2. Replacement behaviors:

1. Using words to ask for what he wants, to gain appropriate level of personal control. Asking for greater control over his activities and tasks by, for example, requesting permission to decide on the order and timing of academic tasks and chores or setting his own schedule for the parts of his evening schedule that staff are able to allow.
2. Asking to take space for 5 minutes when upset by a direction.
3. Compliance with adult directions within 1 minute.

3. Reinforcement procedures (be sure to specify reinforcement strategies in all relevant settings):

In all settings David should be thanked for his compliance, for asking for space when he is frustrated by staff directions, or for making a reasonable effort to exert appropriate control of his environment. Praise should be used with care as David often reacts as though he feels infantilized when he is praised.

David's replacement behaviors will also be listed on his point sheet and will be reinforced for each incident of the behaviors.

4. Reactive methods to be used:

David will be physically contained if he escalates from verbal to physical aggression. He is never to be managed physically if he limits his defiance to verbal aggression. If this happens, he should be waited out and, if possible, peers should be removed from the immediate environment, to avoid reinforcement by their attention and interest.

THE CASE OF SARAH P.

(This case example was prepared by Leticia Galyean, MSW, with the collaboration of John Sprinson.)

Sarah is a 14-year-old girl currently residing in the home of her maternal aunt, Jane M. Sarah is being served by a community-based wrap program, whose overarching goal is to avoid or shorten residential placements and to reestablish and support permanent connections with safe family members. She was recently placed with Jane after failing the fourth foster placement since her removal from the care of her mother (Mary) and father (Bill). Sarah's removal occurred at the age of 9, when her older sister (Cassandra) disclosed that their father had repeatedly sexually abused both girls and invited other men to sexually abuse them as well. This allegation was not initially taken seriously, in part because their father was a local community leader. This resulted in subsequent abuse occurring over several more years and both girls making further allegations and recanting numerous times. After Sarah was removed from the care of their parents, she spent 5 years in foster care prior to the most recent placement occurring with her aunt. During her time in care, Sarah was also hospitalized twice after writing detailed letters describing an intent, plan, and method for killing herself. Prior to placement in the home, Sarah and Jane had had a limited relationship; and possible placement with Jane was considered only after Sarah's most recent foster placement ended and an active family finding process had located Jane. As an alternative to placement in residential care, Jane offered to try to provide a home for Sarah with intensive services to support the transition. Mary, who had ultimately divorced Sarah's father, remains in regular contact with him. He continues to deny the allegations, and Mary continues to communicate feeling conflicted about the validity of the allegations. Upon emancipation from foster care at age 18, Cassandra moved into transitional-age housing and continues to refuse to see her mother—holding her primarily responsible for the abuse that occurred in the home. Sarah and Cassandra maintain regular phone and e-mail contact but, due to logistical complications, rarely have in-person visits. Sarah has had some visits with her mother since being removed from the family home, and her mother writes to her with some regularity. She has had no contact with her father and maintains that she will not ever want contact with him.

In Jane's home, Sarah is withdrawn, quiet, isolated, and noncommunicative. Jane is concerned about the behaviors Sarah has been displaying while placed in her home. Jane reports that Sarah appears depressed, she "hides in her room," "wears clothes with hundreds of safety pins," "doesn't shower or brush her teeth," "listens to Marilyn Manson," and "keeps the light out of her room." At a recent school meeting, Jane also reported that she saw scars on Sarah's thighs and stomach consistent with superficial razor blade cuts. At times in which Sarah has openly communicated her needs, she reported "feeling everything and nothing." When asked about the scars and marks on her thighs and stomach, Sarah initially denied engaging in self-mutilating behaviors; but she has just recently admitted that she cuts on a regular basis and fantasizes about "bleeding out." Though Sarah's frame and build are normal for her age, her physical presence is diminutive and slight, often leading people to assume she is smaller than she really is as well as to not notice her or forget she is present. Sarah also intentionally hides herself under what she's wearing—she will always dress in baggy, heavy clothes, with many layers and with the hood of her sweatshirt over her head, regardless of the weather.

Sarah's interactions with her aunt are primarily strained and punctuated by Jane's unsuccessful attempts to engage her and "connect with her." Jane finds herself frustrated and exhausted by the absence of Sarah's engagement in "letting her know what's going on" and communicating her needs. She wants to be able to "be a friend and a real support" for Sarah but feels ineffective and discouraged because Sarah won't reciprocate her attempts to connect. It is noteworthy that, while Sarah does not actively share her needs with Jane, she is also not actively refusing her invitations. It is better understood as an avoidance of engagement, as opposed to a refusal of engagement. Jane is also worried about Sarah's isolation at home but notes that she has been making a new group of friends at school and online.

Sarah reports having many friends and that they are her only escape. The support counselors who often spend time with her after school report that many of these "friends" seem like superficial acquaintances and that in her peer group she is often following the lead of others and is rarely initiating social interactions. In group settings, Sarah's presence often goes unnoticed and she actively attempts to divert any attention that may be directed at her. Sarah does seem to have a strong online network of friends, whose primary form of interaction is through writing and art. Though Sarah doesn't know these individuals outside of her online interactions, she considers them to be close friends and her primary support system.

With adults, Sarah presents as shy, apathetic, and withdrawn and at times she appears fearful, cautious, and suspicious. The adults in Sarah's life are often activated by this behavior and feel drawn to care for her or are put off by her outward coldness and lack of engagement and feel helpless and ineffectual. In her interactions with adults, she simultaneously demonstrates deference, while also appearing to be annoyed by their attempts to draw her out. This invites adults to experience Sarah as having needs they will never effectively meet. In this way, some adults find Sarah to be "a project to work on," while others find interactions with her exhausting and nonreciprocal.

Of note, Sarah had a significantly different relationship with an adult male in one of her previous foster homes. In this setting, the primary caregiver was a female but her ailing father also resided in the home. Though Sarah's relationship with the foster mother was strained, Sarah reported feeling very connected to the foster-grandfather, Jim. Sarah described Jim as being "harmless" and in need of someone to help him "make sense of the world." Due to a traumatic brain injury, Jim had limited cognitive faculties and spent the majority of time watching television or swimming. When Sarah moved into the home, she found him odd and avoided him. Over some months, she began to invite Jim to draw with her and started to teach him how to crochet. Jim's engagement with Sarah was limited by his cognitive capacity, but her attempts at engagement were always reciprocated.

Sarah reported enjoying her interactions with Jim and was disappointed when she was moved from that foster home.

Sarah has notable strengths that have helped sustain her through her most challenging experiences. Sarah enjoys pencil and charcoal drawing and, prior to her initial removal, reported using art as a mechanism to "tolerate the pain." Sarah is also an avid and prolific writer and documents much of her thoughts and experiences in a blog that her online community can access and comment on. Much of the content of the blog is unknown to Jane and staff as Sarah has intentionally limited access, but Sarah reports documenting "day-to-day activities" and their impact on her. Of note, Sarah reports that she "hates to write" (with paper and pencils or pens) but finds the process of blogging to be cathartic. Finally, in her online community, Sarah's personality is significantly different from in her "offline" social interactions. She is far more communicative and assumes a role of caretaker as her online persona, often seeking opportunities to identify the needs of others and then making attempts to meet those. It is important to note that although adults in her life would identify numerous strengths for Sarah, she seems unable to experience or acknowledge any of her activities as particularly positive.

When asked, Sarah is unable to identify any personal strengths and might offer "I like to draw."

Relational assessment worksheet

Client name:	Sarah P.
Date of admission:	May 1, 2009
Clinician name:	Leticia Galyean

Domains of data

Use the spaces provided to enter notes on each of the categories listed. An entry can be thought of as a key piece of data, an observation, or a discrepancy in the material as it emerges. Some categories are highly overlapping and correlated. Some are not as salient as others and some may not seem relevant at all.

For children with complex caretaker histories, provide a brief summary of their experiences. For example, "with biological parents from birth to age 3," "emergency foster care for 3 months," "long-term foster care for 3 years," "residential treatment."

I. The child's experience with caretakers.

Summary of caretaking stability: Provide a brief summary of the child's caretaking history. Include, for example, estimated numbers of placements, average length of placements, and the placements that seem to have been the longest or most important.

1. Sarah was with her mother and father from birth to age 9.
2. At the age of 9, Sarah was removed from her parents' care as a result of substantiated sexual abuse allegations. While in foster care, Sarah's only contact with her father occurred in relation to the criminal abuse hearings and trial that Sarah and Cassandra participated in. Sarah had regular but limited visits with her mother while in care, and for the first 3 years Sarah's mother delivered letters from Sarah's father, while also maintaining discussion and debate with Sarah about the legitimacy of the abuse allegations.
3. Between 9 and 14, Sarah had four foster placements and experienced two hospitalizations.
4. During the third foster placement, Sarah connected with an ailing man (Jim) in the home and was disappointed about the loss of contact with Jim when she had to move from the home. The placement ended when Sarah was hospitalized.
5. Recently, Jane was contacted after a family search for possible placement alternatives, and she expressed a willingness to care for Sarah. Prior to this she had seen Sarah only a handful of times at family gatherings. Though Sarah's input was sought in the course of developing the placement with Jane, she demonstrated little engagement in the discussion and the decision was made for her to live in Jane's home with grudging agreement from Sarah.

1. Availability:

Interviews with Mary, Sarah, and Cassandra suggest that Mary's availability to Sarah early in Sarah's development was compromised due to her own mental illness (severe depression) and prescription drug addiction. Mary's depression was episodic and not well managed, and it seems that many times she was not capable of recognizing or responding to proximity seeking from Sarah and at best was unpredictably available to Sarah. While Mary reflects on her substance use and mental illness with guilt and shame, she also observes, in a somewhat self-justifying way, that Sarah needed little and was very self-contained from an early age. Mary will tearfully hold herself responsible for not being aware of the sexual abuse and her difficulties in effectively responding to her daughters' needs. Mary describes Sarah's father as the primary caregiver for Sarah and her sister during much of their early years, that his approach was that of a "protective and doting father," and that he was reliably available. This view of Bill seems to arise, though, from Mary's sense that his rigid boundaries against the world outside the family system and his apparent "protectiveness" were evidence of his availability.

2. Attunement:

In the absence of direct observational data or reliable informants, it is difficult to assess the quality of emotional attunement from her parents in Sarah's early years.

Certainly, there is evidence that not all was well. Mary's addiction and periods of severe depression quite likely impaired her capacity for attuned connection with Sarah. The evidence of Bill's eventual sexual victimization of his daughters suggests, at the very least, that he is a man whose attention to his own needs and states takes precedence over those of others. Current interactions between Sarah and Mary during visits of several hours' duration demonstrate fairly consistent problems with attunement. Mary understands Sarah's behaviors entirely in diagnostic terms—Sarah is depressed. Mary will often bring up the history of her own struggles with depression in these conversations but seems unable to respond in an attuned fashion to the adolescent girl in front of her. Information about attunement was not known in Sarah's foster placements. In later childhood Mary misread Sarah's behavior as being driven to meet a need to "rebel" against her father since he was the primary caregiver and the authoritarian in the home.

3. Engagement:

As a result of her own substance use and mental health needs, Mary's engagement with Sarah prior to her removal from the home was intermittent and inconsistent. Sarah's father was, in a certain sense, highly engaged with his children. He was always aware of their whereabouts and the details of their activities and sharply limited their contact with peers and the families of their peers. This engagement, though, was an element in his incestuous exploitation of the girls and was intrusive and enmeshed.

4. Reflective function—mentalization

Mary's capacity to understand Sarah's motivations, needs, drives, etc. seems to have been quite limited. In current conversations about her daughter she often views her through a very egocentric lens—that of her own depression. This limits her ability to entertain other theories about Sarah's internal states. She has even attributed Sarah's emotional state to feelings of guilt for causing the disruption in their nuclear family. Sarah's mother seems incapable of thinking in terms of varied feeling states and intentions and will almost always revert to a diagnostic description of Sarah's needs and behavioral presentation. It is assumed that Bill was not capable of any sort of consistent mentalizing stance in relation to his children and was instead most focused on viewing them as available for his own gratification.

5. Regulatory function:

Sarah's mother reports that Sarah was exposed to opiates in utero but was a very healthy baby and had a relatively normal pattern of development. Mary did not breast-feed Sarah and attributes "minor" feeding problems to this. Mary describes Sarah as having frequently spit up all the formula she had just consumed after many meals. Early in her development, medical records indicate a concern with a failure to thrive, but Mary reports that when Sarah's father assumed the role of feeding Sarah her eating pattern changed and the amount she regurgitated was drastically reduced. As a child, Sarah's father was skilled at recognizing moments of emotional distress and effectively helped to downregulate Sarah and her sister. Mary was not effective at helping to regulate Sarah in her early development and lacked confidence in her ability to meet Sarah's needs after having the experience of Sarah's feeding complications.

By Mary's account, Sarah demonstrated, from a surprisingly early age, an ability to self-regulate and only rarely sought comfort and safety from her mother or father. This pattern of self-regulation continued throughout Sarah's foster placements. Sarah's aunt is anxious to help Sarah be less depressed and makes efforts to support her, cheer her up, and engage her in physical activity. She feels that she is often unsuccessful but expresses an interest in figuring out what would be helpful.

6. Tolerance of and support for autonomy:

Though Mary had little tolerance for Sarah's autonomy and independence during her early development, she was often more tolerant than Sarah's father. He was hypervigilant of Sarah's developing independence and frequently limited and controlled her exploration and opportunities out of his stated fear for Sarah's safety. For example, Sarah and her sister were never given permission to attend sleepover parties with friends and only when a parent could be present would they be allowed time with friends and peers. Upon arrival at her first foster home, the parent reported being struck by Sarah's intense need to know the schedule for the day and the structure in the home. Sarah had difficulty meeting people and developing relationships with friends and is/was most triggered in settings with a lack of clear structure. Currently, Jane is uneasy with the independence and autonomy that Sarah is seeking out and has asked the team for help with knowing what are safe activities and how much autonomy to both allow and encourage.

7. Traumatic factors:

During her own childhood Mary experienced pervasive physical and emotional abuse perpetrated by her father (Sarah's grandfather) and, similar to Sarah's experience, was not protected by her mother. Mary reports not receiving treatment for the trauma but receiving treatment for her substance abuse following an arrest for possession of a small amount of drugs. Sarah's father's upbringing is unknown, but Mary reports that he is currently estranged from his parents.

Sarah's father's authoritative parenting style, controlling home structure, sexual exploitation, and position of authority in the community ensured that Sarah's multiple exposures to abuse went undetected from the age of 5 to 9. Sarah was the victim of ongoing sexual abuse and exploitation at the hands of her father, who both perpetrated abuse as well as invited other men to perpetrate sexual abuse on Sarah. Sarah's trauma was amplified by lack of consistent support for disclosure and by pressure to retract from mother and father and inexperienced investigators who deferred to the parents. This led to a cycle, over some months, of retraction and redisclosure.

Mary's permissive parenting style, denial, and deference to Sarah's father prevented her from adequately protecting Sarah from further abuse from her father and other men.

8. Projective processes directed at the child by the caretaker:

Mary does tend to view all of Sarah's difficulties as arising from depressive illness that is the same as her own depression. She has told Sarah that "it's probably genetic."

9. Boundary function:

The boundaries in Sarah's family were regularly violated throughout her childhood and completely failed to create any protection for her and her sister. Her father demonstrated rigid and nonpermeable boundaries related to community, social, and educational systems. While Mary was unable to resist her husband's rigid boundaries between the family and the outside world, she managed to be unaware of and unable to stop his boundary violations within the family.

10. Hierarchy:

Mary was not a consistent or effective authority figure with her children. Because of substance use and depression, she was not an effective authority in the home and was seen as permissive by both her husband and her children. Mary would often assert her authority while under the influence of drugs, which would incite fear and intimidation in Sarah and lead to effusive apologizing and self-deprecation from Mary.

During her early development, a quite clear hierarchy marked Sarah's relationship with her father. Her father acted as the authority figure in the home, often delivering structure, limits, rewards, and consequences. At its most extreme, however, Sarah described her father as a "control freak," "unable to let go," and "afraid of letting us make any mistakes."

Jane, Sarah's current caretaker, appears to be an effective authority. She is not conflicted about being in charge, and in the first months of the placement Sarah has responded to her directions and limits.

II. The child's current interpersonal behavior

1. Organization and self-regulation:

The history obtained through hospital records, mental health records, and caregiver reports suggests periods of effective self-regulation with moments of critical dysregulation that include engagement in self-harming behaviors and suicidal ideation.

Sarah experiences hypersomnia, requires adult intervention to wake her every morning, and has difficulty remaining awake during the school day regardless of the activity or amount of sleep she got the night before. Current emotional self-regulation is variable and hard to assess because Sarah does not openly communicate her needs but actively and regularly engages in activities that could be assumed to be attempted coping mechanisms and tools to self-regulate. At home, Jane is often unaware of what Sarah is doing because of Sarah's frequent self-isolation in her room. Intellectual functioning is mostly intact and quite high, but Sarah suffers from lack of energy and motivation and low investment in school. Sarah reports that she doesn't enjoy or feel challenged at school and that it is "pretty silly."

2. Proximity seeking and the pursuit of relationship:

At home, at school, and in the community, proximity seeking is minimal. Sarah's fear of vulnerability and loss of safety leads to her avoidance of social interactions with adults. She is almost never experienced as seeking care, comfort, proximity, or relationship. This appearance of independence sometimes is rewarded by her peers, who then see her as a leader.

3. Exploratory capacity:

Sarah experiences a generalized fear of the world as a result of her experience that people both will exploit her and cannot protect her from the exploitation. This fear is often expressed as a generalized resistance to trying anything new or challenging. Sarah demonstrates little curiosity, and her fearfulness emerges when on outings with her support counselors. In these settings she is timid and shy and often tries to avoid new experience.

The exception to this is in Sarah's online network. While on the Internet, Sarah demonstrates curiosity, exploration, boldness, and engagement with novel experiences and opportunities. When Sarah is engaging in her social networking site, she is confident, active, and adept at connecting with others and the world.

4. Sense of self:

Sarah reports that she sometimes feels disconnected from her body and "can't tell if she's part of it or if it's just a shell." Sarah also describes that the pain "inside" that she experiences only makes sense to her when she can see a manifestation of something she understands to be painful (i.e., blood, scratches, cuts, etc.).

Sarah also invites others to experience her as hidden or invisible and actively avoids attention and focus, ensuring she doesn't create situations that could render her vulnerable to others.

Sarah's sense of self in the online world, however, is in stark contrast to her presentation in the "real" or offline world. Online, Sarah's personality and sense of self is communicated through an avatar (or pictorial representation of herself) that is confident, stylish, funny, and attention-seeking. Her personality is outgoing, positive, engaging, and supportive, often leading or supporting others in positive endeavors.

5. Boundary functions:

Sarah is overly boundaried in her relationships with peers and adults. She is cautious, skeptical, suspicious, and untrusting in most interactions and has little tolerance for overt attempts at connection by others. She makes clear attempts to protect herself from physical and emotional engagement with others in her manner of dress, personal hygiene, and relational interactions. When invitations for affection or connection are made, Sarah will act in ways to demonstrate a lack of safety and trust of the individual and will remove herself from the situation. Sarah also avoids physical contact by keeping most of her body covered at all times and avoiding close contact with anyone. When physical contact is made and advanced by someone else, she will frequently have a startle response and walk away without further interaction.

Sarah also experiences an acute fear of exploitation by everyone, especially by men in positions of authority. In order to manage this threat, Sarah makes attempts to maintain rigid boundaries with adults. Her style of dress is bulky and cumbersome, her hygiene is poor, and her communication style is neither engaging nor reinforcing. Her active avoidance of connection with adults leads them to feel frustrated and ineffectual. The exception to this is the adult male in the previous foster home, who Sarah described as "harmless." Sarah sought proximity and connection with this individual and effectively connected with him while living in the home.

6. Affective expression:

Sarah demonstrates a limited (flat) affective range. Most often, Sarah seems to function in the range of apathy, irritability, anger, sadness, and despondence. Her emotional state is often influenced by her friends and their current emotional states. Sarah rarely smiles, demonstrates enjoyment of something, or reports feeling satisfied. Similarly, she seldom demonstrates intense emotional outbursts like anger and rage. The one exception to this is when Sarah becomes irritated or irritable. At these times, Sarah may quickly escalate, startling staff and adults with the intensity of the unexpected outburst. These outbursts are followed immediately by a "shut-down" state in which Sarah looks fearful that she will now suffer retaliation.

Online, however, her avatar's personality is positive, optimistic, joyful, and full of hope and encouragement for others.

7. Emotions evoked in staff:

Adults experience Sarah as a "tough nut to crack" and as someone who has "a lot more going on than she let's on." Adults feel frustrated and exhausted by Sarah's consistent indifference to and rejection of their invitations for engagement and support. People often describe Sarah as difficult to work with because of the "walls" she puts up and the difficulty they experience connecting with her. If adults don't experience their interactions with Sarah as frustrating, they often see her as a "project" and a challenge to be problem-solved. These rejections from Sarah lead adults to feel unhelpful or harmful and to conclude that she can't be helped. In some situations, adults have forgotten that Sarah was present or was part of a group because of her lack of engagement and her unwillingness to make requests for support or resources.

8. Themes of current relationships:

In "real life," Sarah's relationship themes include being distant, removed, unapproachable, rejecting, unloving, and unlovable. Staff often use words and phrases like "remote," "aloof," "not much fun," "unresponsive," and "quiet."

The relationship themes of her online avatar include reciprocity, support, acceptance, tolerance, hope, and love.

Description of the internal working model

In providing a useful description of the child's internal working model of relationships you may organize your thinking with questions such as:

How have important experiences with caretakers influenced the child's capacity for connections with others? How have they influenced his or her own interpersonal stance as well as his or her general functioning in the world?

What are the child's implicit beliefs about how the interpersonal world works?

How does he or she seem to expect to be treated or responded to in that world? In behavioral terms, what sort of treatment does he or she seem to invite from others?

To what degree and in what way is he or she able to make use of caretakers and other important adults in his or her life? To increase feelings of safety and security? To learn about his or her environment? To comfort him or her when he or she is sick, hurt, or upset?

What are the key themes in his or her relationships with caretakers and other important adults?

Sarah's early caretaking was significantly compromised by her mother's depression and substance abuse. Her father, who took over many aspects of her care, ultimately abused her sexually. Not surprisingly, Sarah has little capacity to trust that adults will keep her safe, both because they may seek opportunities to actively exploit her and because they lack the capacity to keep her safe. Sarah avoids connection with adults and peers as it would require risking exploitation and harm. In her encounters with structure and boundaries in her daily life at school and with program staff, Sarah also demonstrates a general stance that overly rigid boundaries can lead to secrecy and exploitation and that reduced structure or permissiveness can prevent intervention and safety. Clearly, this ends up being a terrible dilemma for her.

Sarah invites her aunt, other adults, and staff to leave her alone, avoid her, and forget or not notice that she exists. Sarah experiences herself as vulnerable, unsafe, and unable to trust that adults can ensure her safety. By avoiding staff and adults she is inviting an absence of care or interaction, which allows her to ensure that she can be kept safe, leading staff to feel frustrated, incompetent, exhausted, and ineffective, further reinforcing Sarah's avoidance of engagement. Adults and staff inadvertently reinforce Sarah's internal working model when they are not able to (or miss opportunities to) prevent her from further harm, which is sometimes self-inflicted.

This avoidance of human interaction has also contributed to Sarah seeking support, engagement, and relationship online on a complex social networking Web site. The isolating behavior both contributes to feelings of unreality, to self-harming behavior, and to negative rumination as well as prevents positive peer and adult interaction.

Sarah's relationship themes include being distant, removed, unapproachable, rejecting, unloving, and unlovable. The relationship themes of her online avatar include reciprocity, support, acceptance, tolerance, and love.

Relational Treatment Plan

Client name:	Sarah S.
Date:	5/20/09

Description of the child's internal working model of relationships (from the Relational Assessment Worksheet). Give particular attention to the "interpersonal invitations" that the child seems to direct at others; what sorts or relationships does he or she seem to try to establish with others?

Sarah has developed an interpersonal stance that states that only she can keep herself safe and she can only ensure safety by avoiding human interaction and contact. Sarah's experiences have led her to expect that interactions with adults can lead to harm and that safety cannot be ensured by anyone except herself. Sarah expects that others will either exploit her, put her in harm's way, or be harmless and in need of her help.

Sarah invites her aunt, other adults, and staff to leave her alone, avoid her, and forget or not notice that she exists. Sarah experiences herself to be vulnerable, unsafe, and unable to trust that adults can ensure her safety. By avoiding staff and adults she is inviting an absence of care or interaction, which allows her to ensure that she can be kept safe, leading staff to feel frustrated, incompetent, exhausted, and ineffective, further reinforcing Sarah's avoidance of engagement. Adults and staff inadvertently reinforce Sarah's internal working model when they are not able to (or miss opportunities to) prevent her from further harm, which is sometimes self-inflicted.

Describe the responses that seem to be invited from or evoked in adults who are working with this child. In other words, how might staff members or other adults find themselves inadvertently confirming the child's implicit beliefs about the world? Try to be detailed and include descriptions of unsuccessful interactions in which the child's functioning declined. Information about the failure of prior placements is often useful in this regard; that is, what sorts of responses to the child seemed to lead to declines in functioning and, in turn, to placement failure?

1. Sarah is working to transmit a message that she is self-contained and needs no support or resonant engagement with others. This may result in adults and staff to experience the following:

   a. Not knowing how to engage and respond to Sarah
   b. Finding themselves avoiding opportunities for engagement and interaction
   c. Literally forgetting or not noticing her presence
   d. Allowing Sarah to isolate herself and inadvertently reinforcing her experience that she is on her own and adults can't effectively protect her

2. Sarah is working to avoid connection with others and the risks that engagement can carry with it. People in relationships with her may feel or do the following:

   a. Overestimate her independence and capacity for self-management because she will not actively seek support or comfort from others
   b. Assume that she needs nothing in the way of support or nurturing because of her active attempts to reject that
   c. Forget that she is present
   d. Forget to protect her when others become unsafe
   e. Feel hopeless, frustrated, or exhausted by her overt rejection of attempts at engagement

3. Sarah is making exaggerated efforts to avoid connection and possible exploitation. The resulting states/actions in others might include the following:

   a. Efforts to disengage and maintain distance, followed by frustration, hopelessness, exhaustion, and the experience of not "reaching" Sarah
   b. Avoidance of contact and opportunities for engagement
   c. Feelings of inadequacy, inexperience, and incompetence because of the inability to engage and help her

Describe a disconfirming stance for staff to use in working with this child. This should include a general posture staff should take in response to the "interpersonal invitations" detailed above, as well as specific statements and behaviors that can be directed at the child in specific situations that are repeatedly encountered in the work. Try to include scenarios from all the settings in which staff engage the child.

Generally, adults and staff should resist the pull to avoid Sarah. Specifically, the goal is to create engagement by always remembering that she is a girl who needs nurturing and support in spite of her efforts to keep people away from her. For example, create opportunities of mutual engagement that don't require face-to-face interaction but can facilitate mutual participation in a nonthreatening manner. This can be done by engaging her in art and writing projects while sitting diagonal or next to her—ensuring that adults do not initiate physical contact. This interaction should not appear planned but, instead, spontaneous or should be presented as needed for the benefit of the staff person or someone else since Sarah will resist engagement in an activity that she perceives to be about her and that might bring attention to her. In the classroom and at home, do not wait for her to seek adult help or engagement but, instead, prompt questions and feedback from her. This should be done in a neutral, nonthreatening way that doesn't draw attention to Sarah. For example, Sarah should not be called on if the teacher is leading class but, instead, approached by an adult at her desk during a time in which others would be least likely to notice as she will have little tolerance for engagement if attention is focused on her by the entire class.

Sarah avoids asking for one-to-one engagement with staff members and peers. The team should resist this avoidance of connection by creating opportunities for one-to-one activities with key staff members and peers. Creating opportunities in which Sarah can help others she experiences as "harmless" has had the most success. Engagement in art projects or activities with younger students could be scheduled into her regular school day. Any adults that have made a connection with Sarah should create distinct opportunities to check in with her throughout the school day during neutral activities and during points in the school day in which Sarah would not experience the interaction to be planned or forced.

In the home, Jane should resist allowing Sarah to isolate for long periods of time in her room and should create natural opportunities that allow her to act in the role of a nurturer to Sarah. Since Sarah has little tolerance for activities that are perceived as attempts to connect with her, these opportunities should be experienced as spontaneous and natural. For example, Jane could solicit Sarah's favorite meals and ensure that those are intermittently provided, with the offer to cook them together. Jane could also provide Sarah with her favorite hygiene products (soap, lotions, shampoo, conditioner, etc.), which would both reinforce good hygiene practices and create the opportunity for Jane to act in a nurturing role.

1. In working to connect to Sarah, keep in mind the value of helping others—especially those Sarah experiences as nonthreatening. Sarah cannot tolerate being cared for, but she enjoys helping others.

   • Mutual self-care activities or engagement/utilization of replacement behaviors could be made into structured activities to help reinforce her own utilization of replacement behaviors as well as create opportunities for her to be a caretaker to others who are more vulnerable than herself.

- She and Jane doing each other's hair, Jane asking for Sarah's help with the computer and online research or setting up her own social-networking page.
- Situations in which she has to "show off" her own work or completed activity should be avoided as she may have little tolerance for the attention brought upon her.
- Involvement in some form of community service that would build on her openness to engagement with her foster grandfather.

2. Construct a list of critical behaviors that staff must intervene on. This list would describe all the avoidance behaviors that have been sometimes passed over in the interest of preventing the experience of feeling incompetent. Some of the most important of these will be fairly subtle and may involve her readiness to defer to others (to avoid engaging), silence, nonresponsiveness, and the absence of initiating contact/communication.

3. Contain with flexible structure. When Sarah is contained, either in the general sense of limit setting or in the specific sense of seclusion or restraint, it is her expectation that the interaction will be an attempt to exploit and harm her and that adults won't be able to keep her safe or protect her from more powerful/controlling individuals.

- Even as she strives to give the interaction this quality, it is critical that every effort be made to offer her opportunities for autonomy, independence, and control, emphasizing her empowerment in the situation.
- Generally, prompts are more successful than moving rapidly to time-outs for noncompliance—as this will be experienced as rigid and inflexible.

Functional analysis worksheet

Functional analysis: Collaborative meeting worksheet

Client Name:	Sarah S.
Date of Meeting:	5/18/09

(If multiple meetings are held among different groups of team members then use a new worksheet for each meeting.)

Team members present:

1. Sarah
2. Mary
3. Jane
4. Sarah's day treatment staff
5. Sarah's community-based team
6. Sarah's social worker

Note: This meeting is specifically focused on the client's target behaviors. This meeting assumes that some initial gathering of more general, often historical, information has already occurred. This might include, but is not limited to, family and developmental history, trauma history, strengths and vulnerabilities of the client, history of the target behaviors, and history of prior interventions and their results.

In focusing on behavior this meeting should be an exercise in curiosity, a collaborative sharing of information, experience and understanding that will help us all understand what seems to cause the behavior and what seems to keep it going. We want to find out what purpose it serves. The questions provided below are offered as potentially useful prompts. Pursuing data may require more specific questions based on what emerges as the discussion proceeds.

Target behavior 1

Definition:

Cutting (self-harmful behaviors)—Sarah engages in self-harmful behaviors that include cutting on her stomach, thighs, and/or arms, using metal pieces of pencils, broken CDs, pieces of glass, or razor blades. The cutting behaviors present in Sarah's home and school with varied frequency, intensity, and duration and include scratching her arms, legs, or stomach, resulting in minor abrasions that don't require first-aid or medical attention; making superficial cuts on her arms, legs, and stomach that result in breaking skin and that require minor first-aid or medical attention; and making deep cuts on her arms, legs, and stomach that are life-threatening, cause significant injury and scarring, and/or require immediate medical attention.

1. Setting questions: Are there settings in which the behavior is more likely to occur? These can include real settings—actual places—as well as activities and states of vulnerability in the client such as fatigue, hunger, or anger about some other issue. Does the problem occur only at school? Only at home? Only in transitions? Are there settings in which the behavior never occurs?

Sarah reports feeling most triggered at times when she is alone (e.g., isolated in her room) and when she's between classes or at breaks in school. Sarah is most vulnerable and at risk of cutting on herself when she is not being supervised or not engaging in other activities (i.e., connecting with friends on her social-networking site, with friends, or closely watched by adults.) It has been reported that Sarah is also most likely to engage in the cutting behavior when she experiences herself to be invisible. This occurs when staff or adults forget about her presence and expose Sarah to vulnerability or risk (whether intentionally or not).

2. Antecedent questions: Are there any events that often occur right before the behavior that seem to "trigger" it? These can include certain kinds of interactions, activities, and even particular people.

Sarah has a complex routine associated with her cutting behavior. If this routine is disrupted at any time, she can be prevented from engaging in the target behavior. Most frequently, Sarah will retreat to her room or a bathroom, reduce the light as much as possible, clean and sanitize the instrument that she'll utilize for the cutting, and then engage in the cutting behavior.

3. Consequence questions: Are there any results, consequences, or responses from the environment that seem to follow the behavior? These can include getting something, getting to do something, not having to do something, and responses from adults and peers.

Most frequently, staff and adults aren't aware of the times when Sarah engages in the cutting behavior, so there are no externally (and immediately) imposed consequences. When adults and staff become aware of the behavior, they often respond with great concern, first ensuring that the cuts have been attended to and that Sarah doesn't require immediate medical attention. After assessing for immediate safety, staff and adults engage Sarah in a discussion that seeks to answer why Sarah is engaging in this behavior, as opposed to seeking to understand the function of the behavior or the need that is being met. Sarah experiences this extra attention as uncomfortable and has difficulty tolerating any discussion in the moment about why she engages in this behavior.

4. Intervention questions: What responses or procedures have the adults (teachers, staff, caregivers) utilized in the past to deal with this target behavior?

Staff and adults were previously unaware of Sarah's engagement in this behavior, and this behavior has only recently been brought to staff and adult attention. Like the ways in which Sarah becomes invisible to staff, they were unaware of this behavior, which only served to reinforce Sarah's internal working model that adults can't keep her safe from herself even.

5. Exception data: Are there settings (people, places, activities, etc.) in which the target behavior never occurs? Are there settings that are regularly associated with the client engaging in positive behavior?

Sarah doesn't engage in the target behavior when she is with her peers, when adults and her aunt are supervising or monitoring her, when she is engaging with her online community, and when she is helping others—especially those she considers harmless and benefiting from her attention.

Initial hypotheses: Given the data developed above, does the team have any initial hypotheses about the function of the behavior? A hypothesis can be stated in the form of "When x occurs or is occurring, the client does behavior y and the result is that z occurs."

Sarah reports that she feels "nothing" and that she wants desperately to "feel something, anything." She reports not knowing or feeling like her body is her own at times and that cutting seems to reconnect her to her body and restore a feeling of reality. This behavior allows her to see, feel, and experience what she understands to be pain and allows her a sensory experience of the pain and "torture" she describes feeling inside. To summarize the function of the target behavior: Sarah uses cutting to obtain relief from intense feelings of distress.

Plan for direct observation: Given the above hypotheses, describe a plan for appropriate direct observation of the behavior, in the environment in which it occurs, to collect systematic data. Include who will be responsible for collection of the data, what forms will be used or created for the recording of the data, and for how long the data will be collected.

The cutting behavior that Sarah engages in is private and, hence, difficult to observe directly. The observations therefore will necessarily focus on the tracking of antecedent behavior and observable marks left by cutting. Adults in Sarah's life will be asked to track and monitor the times in which Sarah isolates herself as this is an antecedent to the behavior and is directly observable. The schedule and responsible parties for the data collection will include the following:

- Sarah will be a key participant in the tracking process to the degree she is able to be effectively engaged: She will be asked to complete a daily behavior tracking log that documents the ABC's of the behavior (refer to Appendix L), reporting on the behavior in school, in the community, and at home.
- Sarah's aunt will be trained in and responsible for completing the frequency and intensity tracking form (refer to Appendices E and F) relating to Sarah's cutting behavior as she is most likely the person to observe the cuts on Sarah's body. Sarah's aunt will also be trained and responsible for completing the duration tracking form (refer to Appendix H) for isolating behavior with the intention of gaining information about correlations with length of isolation and engagement in cutting. Sarah's aunt will also complete the ABC tracking form, which will be compared with Sarah's to assess accuracy of information collected and ensure the team is accurately understanding the behavior.

    In school, the classroom counselors will complete the frequency and duration tracking form for the isolating behavior. Classroom counselors will also complete a weekly ABC tracking form to compare with Sarah's ABC form, again ensuring that the team is understanding the behavior accurately. Classroom counselors, with the collaboration of the entire team, will complete/update the functional analysis on a monthly basis to ensure that the team continues to accurately understand the behavior and is responding in ways that are effectively meeting Sarah's needs.

Client variables form

Functional assessment of behavior: Client variables

Client name:	Sarah S.
Date:	5/20/09

Target behaviors:

Cutting (self-harmful behaviors)—Sarah engages in self-harmful behaviors that include cutting on her stomach, thighs, and/or arms, using metal pieces of pencils, broken CDs, pieces of glass, or razor blades. The cutting behaviors present in Sarah's home and school with varied frequency, intensity, and duration and include scratching her arms, legs, or stomach, resulting in minor abrasions that don't require first-aid or medical attention; making superficial cuts on her arms, legs, and stomach that result in breaking skin and that require minor first-aid or medical attention; and making deep cuts on her arms, legs, and stomach that are life-threatening, cause significant injury and scarring, and/or require immediate medical attention.

Client variables: Describe how any of the skills, life circumstances, and states are related to any of the target behaviors. If an entry is related to only target behavior in particular, then refer to that behavior by its number above.

Health issues or problems:

Sarah has no presenting health needs or problems at this time.

Academic abilities:

Intellectual functioning is high, but Sarah suffers from lack of energy and motivation to excel in school.

Cognitive skills/learning disabilities:

Sarah has not been diagnosed with any learning disabilities.

Emotional states (e.g., "vulnerability states" such as fear, anxiety, anger, etc.):

Sarah is most vulnerable when she feels "invisible" and/or when she is isolating herself from peers, adults, and staff. Sarah reports cutting to make real the pain that she feels inside. At the times that she is most likely to cut, she is most frequently experiencing apathy, despondence, irritability, and sadness.

Substance use:

There is no known substance use at this time.

Expressive or receptive language skills:

While Sarah is an effective communicator on her blog (online journal), prior to, while, and after engaging in the target behavior, she does not communicate her needs or seek support of staff. She is also not open to or engaging when staff invite her to communicate her needs.

Immediate physical states (e.g., hunger, fatigue, etc.):

There are no physical states that have been found to correlate with engagement in the target behavior.

Medication:

Sarah is not prescribed medication at this time.

Cognitive states (e.g., beliefs, "thought disorders"):

There are no known thought disorders at this time. Sarah does believe and experience cutting to be an effective mechanism for coping with the "internal pain" she experiences.

Social skills:

Sarah does not demonstrate strong social skills in her interactions with peers and adults. She avoids connection and engagement with most adults and staff and doesn't initiate social interactions with peers. In her online interactions, however, Sarah demonstrates strong social skills by seeking out and offering support to peers and actively engaging peers in "social interactions."

Preoccupations (e.g., fairness or justice, worries about resources, etc.):

Sarah reports that she constantly thinks about cutting herself and she is preoccupied with planning her next opportunity for cutting.

Other client variables:

N/A

This form is adapted from Watson and Steege (2003).

Replacement Behavior Worksheet

Client name:	Sarah S.
Date:	5/19/09

Team members present:

Mary
Jane
Sarah
Sarah's day treatment team
Sarah's community-based services team
Sarah's social worker

Target behavior:

Cutting (self-harmful behaviors)—Sarah engages in self-harmful behaviors that include cutting on her stomach, thighs, and/or arms. When Sarah engages in cutting behaviors, she uses metal pieces of pencils, broken CDs, pieces of glass, or razor blades. Sarah engages in a range of cutting behaviors that include scratching her arms, legs, or stomach, resulting in minor abrasions that don't require first-aid or medical attention; making superficial cuts on her arms, legs, and stomach that result in breaking skin and that require minor first-aid or medical attention; and making deep cuts on her arms, legs, and stomach that are life-threatening, cause significant injury and scarring, and/or require immediate medical attention.

What is the function of the target behavior? What need or purpose does it express?

Sarah reports that she feels "nothing" and that she wants desperately to "feel something, anything." She reports not knowing or feeling like her body is her own at times and that cutting seems to reconnect her to her body and restore a feeling of reality. This behavior allows her to see, feel, and experience what she understands to be pain and allows her a sensory experience of the pain and "torture" she describes feeling inside. To summarize the function of the target behavior: Sarah uses cutting to obtain relief from intense feelings of distress.

What replacement behavior will enable the client to meet the same need and still preserve safety and continued development?

Sarah experiences cutting to provide a sensory experience of the pain she feels inside, so replacement behaviors that will be taught and reinforced will include sensory experiences for her. The treatment team will also teach and reinforce communication skills with Sarah to create another mechanism for Sarah to "make real" her internal experience. These replacement behaviors may include journaling, art, writing stories, rubbing ice or applying lotion to the areas that she otherwise would cut, and writing on a blog. The communication techniques that Sarah is taught may be verbal, written, or drawn but will include a clear cue that will indicate to the staff or adult the severity and immediacy of the need for extra support.

Does the client already show the proposed replacement in another setting or behaviors that include components of the replacement behavior?

On her blog Sarah is a strong communicator and utilizes that forum as a journal, so this replacement behavior can be utilized early on to help Sarah experience immediate success and reinforcement while other replacement behaviors are taught and rehearsed.

What method will the team utilize in teaching the behavior? Will it need to be broken down into teachable components (chained) or taught in successive approximations (shaped)?

Because Sarah avoids almost all attempts at engagement with adults and staff, she may find it particularly challenging to initiate and increase her communication with them. This replacement behavior will be shaped by defining each step that leads to the full presentation of the behavior and reinforcing each successive step as it is mastered. Similarly, in the teaching of the ice and lotion replacement behavior, the team will identify the steps necessary to fully utilize the ice and lotion and will reinforce each approximation of the behavior.

Is there anyone in the client's environment who is a skilled practitioner of the replacement behavior?

The team identified a school staff team member and community-based support counselor who demonstrate strength in utilizing and teaching these replacement behaviors. These two individuals also have demonstrated a low-level connection with Sarah over many months, and their invitations and offers of engagement are less likely to be ignored or avoided by Sarah.

How will the team monitor the client's mastery of the replacement behavior?

The team will utilize a daily and weekly replacement behavior tracking log to monitor her progress and engagement in the target behavior. This will help to ensure that Sarah receives reinforcement immediately and that the reinforcement schedule is neither too frequent nor too infrequent.

Behavioral treatment plan worksheet

Client name:	Sarah S.
Date:	5/19/09

Team members:

Sarah's mother, Mary; Sarah's aunt (and caregiver), Jane; Sarah's day treatment team; Sarah's community-based services team; and Sarah's social worker

Target behavior 1

Definition:

Cutting (self-harmful behaviors)—Sarah engages in self-harmful behaviors that include cutting on her stomach, thighs, and/or arms, using metal pieces of pencils, broken CDs, pieces of glass, or razor blades. The cutting behaviors present in Sarah's home and school with varied frequency, intensity, and duration and include scratching her arms, legs, or stomach, resulting in minor abrasions that don't require first-aid or medical attention; making superficial cuts on her arms, legs, and stomach that result in breaking skin and that require minor first-aid or medical attention; and making deep cuts on her arms, legs, and stomach that are life-threatening, cause significant injury and scarring, and/or require immediate medical attention.

Functional assessment information:

1. Antecedents and settings:

Sarah reports feeling most triggered at times when she is alone and isolating in her room and when she's at school during breaks between classes. It has also been reported that Sarah is most likely to engage in the cutting behavior when she experiences herself to be invisible. This can occur for several reasons but frequently comes up when staff or adults forget about her presence or expose Sarah to vulnerability or risk (whether intentionally or not). Sarah is most vulnerable and at risk of cutting on herself when she is not being supervised or not engaging in other activities (i.e., connecting with friends on her social-networking site, with friends, or closely watched by adults). Sarah has a complex routine associated with her cutting behavior. If this routine is disrupted at any time, she can be prevented from engaging in the target behavior. Most frequently, Sarah will retreat to her room or a bathroom, reduce the light as much as possible, clean and sanitize the instrument that she'll utilize for the cutting, and then engage in the cutting behavior.

2. Consequences:

Most frequently, staff and adults aren't aware of the times when Sarah engages in the cutting behavior, so there are no externally imposed consequences. When adults and staff become aware of the behavior, they often respond with great concern, first ensuring that the cuts have been attended to and that Sarah doesn't require immediate medical attention. After assessing for immediate safety, staff and adults engage Sarah in a discussion that seeks to answer why she is engaging in this behavior, as opposed to seeking to understand the function of the behavior or the need that is being met. Sarah experiences this extra attention as uncomfortable and has difficulty tolerating any discussion in the moment about why she engages in this behavior.

3. Functional hypothesis:

Sarah reports that she feels "nothing" and that she wants desperately to "feel something, anything." She reports not knowing or feeling like her body is her own at times and that cutting seems to reconnect her to her body and restore a feeling of reality. This behavior allows her to see, feel, and experience what she understands to be pain and allows her a sensory experience of the pain and "torture" she describes feeling inside. To summarize the function of the target behavior: Sarah uses cutting to obtain relief from intense feelings of distress.

Intervention planning:

1. Antecedent and setting modifications:

Sarah experiences internal processes that are difficult for her to understand, manage, cope with, and expel and has found cutting to be an effective mechanism for coping with and managing this behavior. Sarah also has a complex routine related to the behavior that requires her to have specific tools and privacy. In order to help manage the impact of Sarah's trigger and antecedents, the treatment team will target interventions in three ways:

1. Develop predictive intervention from staff/adults when a known trigger is presenting or to avoid the trigger altogether (i.e., reduce the time when Sarah is unsupervised and not allow her to have long periods of privacy and isolation).
2. Skill building for Sarah to help her manage the experience of being triggered and reduce her engagement in the target behavior.
3. Create and prompt opportunities for Sarah to "expel" or externalize what she's feeling internally.

In order to do this, the team will identify the typical times and locations that Sarah will seek privacy and not be monitored and those that can be mitigated or eliminated will be. For example, Sarah has a computer and television in her room. These are both activities that can be moved to a public area without making them unavailable to Sarah. This will increase Jane's ability to monitor Sarah and create more opportunities for engagement with Sarah. At school, if Sarah is allowed to spend more time in the bathroom because staff forget she's there, a mechanism for creating a structure around bathroom visits (since she self-identified bathrooms as locations for cutting) can be created and implemented to reduce the length of unsupervised time that Sarah has in the classroom. If Sarah is also allowed to wander campus after school while waiting for the bus, the team will create a plan that creates a structure for her time as she waits for the bus. This plan will balance Sarah's independence and natural desire to build mastery and independence but should also ensure that staff are able to keep her in view whenever possible.

The team will then provide targeted skill-building and distress-tolerance interventions to help Sarah effectively externalize the overwhelming feelings she is currently internalizing. These may include somatic recognition activities to help Sarah create a definition and vocabulary for what she's experiencing as well as to build insight about her physiological and emotional responses to this trigger. Behavior logs and tracking will be utilized to help Sarah increase and build her awareness of the internal process she is experiencing as well as how she manages the behavior (by cutting) and the consequences of cutting. Once Sarah has built a vocabulary and gained insight about the behavior and her response to feeling triggered, skills will be developed to help her gain mastery and control over her physiological responses (like deep breathing, biofeedback techniques, and self-talk that includes utilizing the vocabulary to define her current state) and distress-tolerance activities will be taught so that she experiences success in building awareness and defining, modulating, and regulating her internal processes and emotions (like structured distractions, thought stopping, and focusing/

mindfulness activities). Experience and success in modulating and regulation can be practiced with less triggering and more benign behaviors to allow Sarah the opportunity to initially experience success.

In order to help Sarah replace the target behavior when she is actively and currently seeking to cut herself, the treatment team will consider Sarah's strengths and develop specific replacement behaviors that she can utilize instead of engaging in the target behavior (see replacement behavior section below).

The treatment team will identify, create, and prompt engagement in opportunities for Sarah to help others and be in a positive leadership role with her peers (like a volunteer activity).

When staff and adults begin to observe the presentation of the antecedent behavior or Sarah verbalizes a triggering internal process, early intervention will be implemented to help minimize the impact of the triggering event. Only interventions that have efficacy with Sarah will be utilized to help mitigate the impact and will be implemented with consistency across all settings and by all caregivers. For example, it is known that Sarah will not engage in the cutting behavior while others are around, so neutral, nonthreatening opportunities for engagement will be prompted and utilized to eliminate the opportunity for Sarah to isolate herself and engage in the behavior. As Sarah begins to gain insight and a vocabulary for her internal experience, staff and adults will be more explicit in their invitations for engagement, helping to name and identify for her their observation of a potentially risky or unsafe situation (antecedent) that could contribute to her engagement in the target behavior.

Finally, Jane will be taught how to develop her own avatar and online personality to monitor Sarah's online activity. In that it is thought that Sarah's online activity is a positive outlet for her and the behaviors she engages in are supportive, engaging, emotionally connected, etc., Jane will also have the opportunity to positively reinforce Sarah in this virtual world and Sarah will have the experience of receiving positive feedback and having positive interactions with her aunt in a safe and neutral environment.

2. Replacement behaviors:

Sarah will utilize the following alternative and noncompatible externalizing replacement behaviors to reduce her engagement of cutting while increasing her understanding, vocabulary, and communication of the internal experience she is having: journaling, art, writing stories, rubbing ice or applying lotion to the areas that she otherwise would cut, and writing on a blog. Sarah will also be taught, role-play, and rehearse communicating to staff her internal experiences when she is feeling triggered to engage in the target behavior. This communication may be verbal, written, or drawn but should include a clear (and previously agreed upon) cue that will indicate to the staff or adult the severity and immediacy of the need for extra support.

3. Reinforcement procedures (be sure to specify reinforcement strategies in all relevant settings):

The treatment team will implement a schedule of positive reinforcement when Sarah engages in desired behaviors. The schedule of reinforcement and specific rewards will be determined by the treatment team each time a distinct contract is set up but should utilize a combination or both predictive as well as intermittent reinforcement schedules. Staff and adults who act as caregivers for Sarah will utilize reinforcement strategies in the following ways:

- Because Sarah has difficulty initiating engagement with peers and adults, she will receive consistent reinforcement from staff and adults when there is any observed or experienced initiated contact. Sarah will receive reinforcement for sustained engagement with peers and staff, and duration tracking will ensure staff and adults are able to monitor improvement in length of interaction. Sarah already experiences helping others who are considered "harmless" to be enjoyable, so she will receive reinforcement for that as well as any invitation to help people that Sarah doesn't experience as threatening. Finally, any approximation or utilization of a replacement behavior will be reinforced.
- The treatment team will take extra care to ensure that the reinforcement will begin with approximations of behavior, moving progressively toward the full presentation of the desired replacement behavior. Whenever possible, the reinforcement will be provided by the adult who observed the desired behavior immediately after the presentation of the behavior.

4. Reactive methods to be used:

- When Sarah engages in the target behavior, staff and adults will respond in ways that are consistent, do not inadvertently reinforce the target behavior, and do reinforce desired behaviors.
- Sarah does not engage in cutting behaviors when she is with someone else, in a public area, or able to externalize her internal processes, so staff and adults will be trained to respond to her in ways that reinforce positive replacement behaviors, that ensure her invitations to avoid engagement are not reinforced by staff or adults. They will be trained and helped to understand the behavioral pattern, triggers, antecedents, and escalation phase to identify the most effective point of intervention. This redirection will include naming the presentation of behavior (without drawing undo attention to the behavior), asking/encouraging Sarah to utilize a replacement behavior, and reinforcing any approximation of the desired behavior. Focus (for staff and adults) on maintaining consistency, neutrality, and nonreactivity will be emphasized and reinforced.

- Staff and adults will also be helped to understand how to manage their own experience of frustration, inadequacy, and incompetence to ensure that does not get communicated to Sarah in the course of responding to her behavior. Natural supports or staff resources will be utilized (both in school and at home) as the team builds confidence and expertise in this reactive stance. Predicting that Sarah may experience the shift in staff and adults' behavior as triggering in and of itself, extra care will be utilized when intervening during the first opportunities that present. For example, staff and adults that Sarah feel particularly connected to may be accessed to help support the individuals implementing the new intervention plan.

5. Provision for next behavioral assessment (specify timeline and measurement approach):

It is expected that Sarah will be utilizing her replacement behaviors and have reduced her engagement in the target behavior within 12 weeks. The treatment team will complete daily and weekly behavior tracking logs and will utilize the monitoring tools to track Sarah's progress toward her goal. These will be assessed on a weekly and monthly basis, and adjustments to the treatment plan will be made according to the effectiveness of the interventions, replacement behaviors, and reinforcement schedule stated above.

A Note Regarding Values

Having detailed at some length the ways in which treatment of vulnerable children and families is informed by learning theory, attachment theory, and an understanding of the social–environmental contexts in which these families must operate, it is now necessary to introduce an additional ingredient in the treatment mix. This element is not present in treatment plans in an explicit way. Instead, it is, like unconditional care, an element of treatment that is implicit, that operates in the background. Nonetheless, it has a very significant impact on final outcomes for clients and for the job satisfaction of clinicians and staff members who are doing this difficult work. This element is concerned with organizational values.

Why introduce values to a discussion of intervention with vulnerable children and families? Indeed, the following thoughts about values and their role in treatment are presented with some uneasiness about alienating the reader. After all, shouldn't a set of key concepts for working with troubled children and their families be based on research, careful clinical observation, and thoughtful reflection on social policy? What do values have to do with any of that? Aren't values a personal matter that should remain apart from professional activities? Certainly, one finds few explicit discussions of values in professional journals or in the literature concerned with treatment and intervention.

Nevertheless, after some reflection, a very conscious decision was made to end this discussion with an account of some values that, when present in work with vulnerable children, make one's efforts more satisfying and more effective. What are referred to here as "values" are also emotional states that can create and animate connections with clients. Calling attention to the role of values in this work is also a powerful way to engage the energy and passion of an organization's staff. When newly hired staff members begin their orientation to an organization with a discussion of values, they are connected to the work they will do in a different way. As new staff members begin their first day of a preservice training program, a discussion of organizational values engages them and connects them to their work with clients in a new and more vital way.

It is, of course, the case that many practices and interventions have sound scientific underpinnings and clear connections to current thinking about social policy. Being explicit about organizational values and working intentionally to keep them active and present, however, give any intervention a particular emotional coloring or resonance that is very important. When practices are connected to values, the worker is personally implicated in what he or she does every day in a different way. The activities that are performed on the job are no longer just "being at work" but become the same as who one is. A different sense of responsibility is experienced for what happens each day. This responsibility is felt in relation to the children and their families, as well as to coworkers.

Throughout this book the importance of unconditional care as a basis for work with vulnerable children has been repeatedly emphasized. This idea is conceptually simple but operationally challenging. It arises from a simple recognition that in order to succeed children and families who have undergone repeated treatment failures must experience the feeling of safety that comes from knowing that they will not, once again, be ejected for doing what they have always done or for being who they have always been. While a commitment to unconditional care has an intellectual rationale that can be articulated, it also has an emotional or values-based dimension that arises from the importance of such nonscientific (or at least not traditionally scientific) concepts as love, compassion, and joy.

LOVE AND COMPASSION

Any discussion of the values that can enliven this challenging work must begin with the related ideas of love and compassion. Loving concern is at the heart of the connections workers regularly make with children and families. Compassion is not the same as pity or a detached recognition of another's suffering and struggles. Instead, it must be an engaged, active participation in the efforts of clients to master their troubling life experiences and to resume the tasks of healthy development. This loving concern begins with heartfelt curiosity, genuine interest in clients' lives and experiences, an appreciation of their strengths and resources, and a realistic acknowledgment of their vulnerabilities and the risk factors present in their environments. This curiosity makes possible the first step in loving concern: an authentic seeing of the client that will make active engagement possible.

Love and compassion should be visible in engagement with clients and families in several ways. First, it should be visible in a commitment to working with clients to help them establish healthy relationships with the workers themselves and with others in their lives. Real change for children and families can arise only in the context of relationships. The most fundamental expression of this belief in real practice is a commitment to unconditional care. This basic operating principle is a commitment to maintain relationships with clients in the face of their most difficult and troubling behavior. Children and youth who have faced great struggles in development and who have confronted very difficult life circumstances have experienced failure and exclusion as a regular part of their encounters with other agencies and helpers. A simple but profound antidote to this history is provided by striving to never discharge clients for showing the behavior that brought them to placement or to treatment in the first place. Love and compassion should also be evident in the emotional tone that is present in work with clients. This tone should convey a posture of respectful interest and curiosity, an acceptance of the client's experience, and an attitude of warmth, nurturance, and caring. When a child becomes a client of an intensive program of any kind, he or she should have the experience of being cherished and nurtured. Finally, this tone should reflect the staff's delight and joy in the clients' successes and growth.

RESPECT

Closely related to the values of love and compassion is the belief in the importance of respect in all dealings with the children and families. This means that all relationships with clients begin with the default assumption that they have been doing the very best they can with the resources they have available. Workers do not blame, look for faults, or assume that they know best. Instead, an attempt is made to listen without judgment and create a situation in which the client's experience can emerge and unfold. Respect can be shown in many ways, some quite obvious and others more subtle. Respect is shown by communicating openly with clients about their treatment. Respect is shown by involving clients in a collaborative dialogue about their needs and goals. Respect is shown by honoring appropriate boundaries. Respect is shown by recognizing the difficult work clients do in treatment and by realizing that at times they may need to stop or even retreat from this work. Similarly, respect is shown by pushing clients hard when they can accomplish more, learn more, and feel more.

When respect is held as a core value, it is also important to be prepared to encounter and work with differences, including differences of gender, culture, sexual orientation, class, and race. Workers have a responsibility to be sensitive to these differences and to always be aware of the ways in which their individual views and understanding may be skewed or influenced by who they are and what their own life experiences have been. It is easy to see differences of gender, culture, race, sexual orientation, and class as barriers to engagement and collaboration; but in fact, it is vital that knowledge of such differences be woven into a total understanding of clients and their families. Recognition of these differences can then enrich the workers' understanding of how a parent sees a child, the family, his or her own life, and, ultimately, the organization and the various individuals involved in trying to help. This will expand empathy for the parent and the child and greatly support a vital, effective connection with the family. It is also true that recognition of differences and vigilance about their effects do not place the worker outside the problems created by inequalities of power and privilege.

The value of respect is critical not only to relationships with clients but also to relationships with others within the agency. An organization's staff is its greatest asset. The quality of services depends most of all on the skill and compassion of staff members, who must be mentored, nurtured, and trained in order to be effective. This process of training and staff development should yield a certain kind of respect among coworkers in which a responsibility is felt to communicate with directness and clarity and to hold each other to the very highest standards.

CURIOSITY

Inevitably, in working with very vulnerable children who have experienced repeated placement failures, it emerges that some of the prior efforts to understand them have been helpful but some have not. If these earlier formulations of the child's difficulties had been completely adequate, then it would be unlikely that he or she would come to need more intensive services. Because of this, it is important to cultivate and sustain an attitude of curiosity about the client and his or her experience. While a great deal of data may be available when work begins with a child, it is useful to assume that very little is known with confidence and that a "start from scratch" approach must be taken. This stance often involves a skeptical review of prior formulations of the child and then must move into a careful inquiry into the child's and the family's history, their situation, and the context of the child's development. Curiosity about these issues can then function as a barrier against the pull of easy assumptions and received ideas. As work with the client unfolds, this curiosity continues to be of great importance: One needs to be curious about the real effects of interventions, about the client's experience of these interventions, and about the play of thoughts and feelings that are evoked for the client and the team in the course of work together. Often, the very difficult and provocative symptoms of the child, the challenges faced by their families, the weight of years of assessments and treatment summaries, and the urgency of bureaucratic demands can push staff in the direction of assessments that are reactive or incomplete. Holding to the value of curiosity is an important safeguard against such thinking. Finally, when clients are engaged with respect and settings are provided that foster safety and security, a natural result is that they can become collaborators or coparticipants in this attitude of curiosity. Their own curiosity will inevitably lead to an enlarged understanding of their lives and their experience and create the conditions for greater resilience, richer and more accurate views of the world, and developmental progress.

HOPE AND COURAGE

Another critical pair of values that supports and drives an organization's mission is hope and courage. These twin values are especially important to providing unconditional care to very troubled children and their families. Passion and intensity of purpose about avoiding premature discharge rely on hope and courage. Hope and courage are present in the determination to find ways to help clients succeed. Hope and courage can also be seen in the dogged search for strengths and for the conditions that will allow real engagement with clients, as well as in the thoughtfulness, optimism, and tenacity of all staff. Finally, hope and courage are demonstrated in a resolve to find strengths and resources in the children and their families that can be supported and built upon.

Courage is also about taking risks. In serving children and youth who have struggled greatly, an organization must sometimes risk investing great amounts of energy and resources to address situations that initially appear terribly bleak. By holding hope and courage as values, workers may confidently and optimistically confront the histories of failure and exclusion that clients bring to new placements or interventions. Optimism gives clients a sense of possibility, of having a new and different story that is available for their lives.

JOY

Sustaining hope and courage would often be terribly difficult without also regularly finding moments of humor and celebration in work with clients. Such moments should not be diminished by viewing them as lucky by-products of staff efforts. Instead, it is believed that these experiences represent a core value, which can be summarized simply as joy. This feeling of joy should be seen in the strength of staff engagement with clients, in a vivid sense of pleasure in the children's exuberance and playfulness, and in a conviction that the settings provided for clients must be filled with opportunities for pleasure, satisfaction, and just plain fun. If one goes on a hunt for joy in an organization, one should find it in the food that is served, in the outings the kids go on, in dances held for older children at summer camp, in the laughter at meetings, in the dancing at parties, in the pleasure felt by both children and staff at mastering new skills, in the smiles and hugs given to children, in the stories read at bedtime, in the hilarious kickball games on the playground, and in a shared delight at a client's and family's gains. Joy also comes from doing a very hard job very well. Having joy as a value means that staff members are able to think and act with presence and vitality, which may create a new experience for clients who have so often met with tired, familiar interventions.

Appendices

Appendix A: Relational assessment worksheet

Client name: _____

Date of admission: _____

Clinician name: _____

Domains of data

Use the spaces provided to enter notes on each of the categories listed. An entry can be thought of as a key piece of data, an observation, or a discrepancy in the material as it emerges. Some categories are highly overlapping and correlated. Some are not as salient as others and some may not seem relevant at all.

For children with complex caretaker histories, provide a brief summary of their experiences. For example, "with biological parents from birth to age 3," "emergency foster care for 3 months," "long-term foster care for 3 years," "residential treatment."

_____

_____

_____

I. The child's experience with caretakers.

Summary of caretaking stability: Provide a brief summary of the child's caretaking history. Include, for example, estimated numbers of placements, average length of placements, and the placements that seem to have been the longest or most important.

_____

_____

1. Availability:

_____

_____

_____

2. Attunement or contingent responsiveness:

_____

_____

_____

3. Engagement:

_____

_____

_____

4. Reflective function—mentalization:

_____

_____

_____

5. Regulatory function:

_____

_____

_____

6. Tolerance of and support for exploration and autonomy:

_____

_____

_____

7. Traumatic factors:

_____

_____

_____

8. Projective processes directed at the child by the caretaker:

_____

_____

_____

9. Boundary function:

_____

_____

_____

10. Hierarchy:

_____

_____

_____

II. The child's current interpersonal behavior

1. Organization and self-regulation:

_____
_____
_____

2. Proximity seeking and the pursuit of relationship:

_____
_____
_____

3. Exploratory capacity:

_____
_____
_____

4. Sense of self:

_____
_____
_____

5. Boundary functions:

_____
_____
_____

6. Affective expression:

_____
_____
_____

7. Emotions evoked in staff:

_____
_____
_____

8. Themes of current relationships:

_____
_____
_____

Description of the internal working model

In providing a useful description of the child's internal working model of relationships you may organize your thinking with questions such as:

How have important experiences with caretakers influenced the child's capacity for connections with others? How have they influenced his or her own interpersonal stance as well as his or her general functioning in the world?

What are the child's implicit beliefs about how the interpersonal world works?

How does he or she seem to expect to be treated or responded to in that world? In behavioral terms, what sort of treatment does he or she seem to invite from others?

To what degree and in what way is he or she able to make use of caretakers and other important adults in his or her life? To increase feelings of safety and security? To learn about his or her environment? To comfort him or her when he or she is sick, hurt, or upset?

What are the key themes in his or her relationships with caretakers and other important adults?

_____

_____

_____

Appendix B: Relational Treatment Plan

Client name: _____

Date: _____

Description of the child's internal working model of relationships (from the Relational Assessment Worksheet). Give particular attention to the "interpersonal invitations" that the child seems to direct at others; what sorts of relationships does he or she seem to try to establish with others?

_____

_____

_____

Describe the responses that seem to be invited from or evoked in adults who are working with this child. In other words, how might staff members or other adults find themselves inadvertently confirming the child's implicit beliefs about the world? Try to be detailed and include descriptions of unsuccessful interactions in which the child's functioning declined. Information about the failure of prior placements is often useful in this regard; that is, what sorts of responses to the child seemed to lead to declines in functioning and, in turn, to placement failure?

_____

_____

_____

Describe a disconfirming stance for staff to use in working with this child. This should include a general posture staff should take in response to the "interpersonal invitations" detailed above, as well as specific statements and behaviors that can be directed at the child in specific situations that are repeatedly encountered in the work. Try to include scenarios from all the settings in which staff engage the child.

_____

_____

_____

Appendix C: Target Behavior Definition Form

Date: _____

Client name: _____

Note: Input to this form may occur across several different meetings of the various participants in the treatment team. Please date each entry as it is added for each participant in the planning process. If necessary, use more than one form.

Part I. Areas of concern

List all behaviors/issues/concerns that each participant feels is important for the team, the client, and the family to address together. These initial entries may be of any form—this is a no-fault brainstorming process. (Please enter names of all participants in this planning process.)

(Example: "Defiance.")

Family:

_____

_____

_____

Current caregivers (if other than the family):

_____

_____

_____

Client:

_____

_____

_____

Referral source (if relevant):

_____

_____

_____

Treatment team partners:

_____

_____

_____

Seneca team members:

_____

_____

_____

Behaviors known to have contributed to difficulties in prior placements:

_____

_____

_____

Other notes, thoughts, reflections, objections, or concerns:

_____

_____

_____

Part II. Prioritize behaviors

Among the various concerns raised by participants, what are the most important areas for the team to begin to address in their initial efforts? The following considerations might be important: risk of injury to self or other, disruptiveness in important settings in which the child must function. Try to focus on three areas of concern and give a brief "headline" summary of each one, such as "running away" or "losing temper" or "has a bad attitude."

1. _____

2. _____

3. _____

Part III. Moving from concerns to target behaviors

Here, we are going to bring a sharper focus on actual behavior—we want to move from what may be fairly general areas of concern to specific behaviors that are observable and measurable. For each area of concern listed above, ask the question "What does the child actually do that makes this a good description of him or her? Try to think in terms of verbs, not adjectives (e.g., out of seat and talking out rather than "hyper"). For each area of concern, there may be several (or even more) specific behaviors that the child has that make the items above good descriptions of things to work on. Some of the areas of concern may already be expressed in terms of pretty specific, concrete behaviors. If so, that's fine, just write them below. Examples of the level of focus that we're looking for here might be "doesn't complete homework," "steals food from the kitchen," "calls out for staff at bedtime," or "shouts angrily when given an instruction."

(Example: "Defiance." Shouts curses when given an instruction, puffs up chest and moves into the personal space of the adult, balls up hands into fists, tries to negotiate the instruction by pointing out that peers are not being given the same instruction.)

1. _____

2. _____

3. _____

Part IV. Final definitions of target behaviors for observation

Take behaviors from each group above and write definitions according to the following standards:

- Objectivity: Include observable, measurable characteristics of the behavior using active verbs or events in the environment caused by the behavior that are also observable.
- Clarity: Be as specific and clear as possible so that ambiguity is reduced to a minimum. Keep in mind the "stranger test"—could a new team member read the description and immediately use it to guide observation or treatment?
- Completeness: Be thorough, noting all responses that are part of the behavior and noting related behaviors or milder expressions of the behavior that are *not* included in the definition.

Example: Target behavior: Defiance.

This target behavior can be observed when an adult gives the child an instruction to stop an activity in progress or to begin a new activity. It will be scored as occurring whenever there is an incident of defiance following an instruction, defined as the child responding with a raised voice and any verbal statement indicating an intention not to follow the instruction of the form, "No!" or "You can't tell me what to do!" or "You're not the boss of me!" or statements including any curse words. Not scored as defiance will be silent delays in compliance (i.e., doing nothing) or overly slow compliance. Similarly, unpleasant facial expressions accompanying compliance will not be scored.

Target Behavior #1:

_____
_____
_____

Target Behavior #2:

_____
_____
_____

Target Behavior #2:

_____
_____
_____

Appendix D: Behavioral Assessment Planning Worksheet

Baseline determination

Date: _____

Client name: _____

The purpose of this worksheet is to assist the team in planning the first step of behavioral assessment. It can also be used later in the treatment process to plan additional observations of target behaviors to assess the impact of intervention efforts. Because different target behaviors may implicate different behavioral variables (e.g., frequency, duration, intensity, etc.), the worksheet is organized by target behavior.

Target Behavior #1:

_____

_____

_____

Key variable described by behavioral definition. Check appropriate box:

    ☐ Frequency   ☐ Duration   ☐ Latency   ☐ Intensity

    ☐ Qualitative dimensions or outcomes. Specify:

_____

_____

_____

Assessment decisions

1. When will the assessment be carried out? What are the times of day or key settings in which the target behavior occurs?

_____

_____

_____

2. Who will carry out observation of this target behavior? (If necessary, specify by setting.)

_____

_____

_____

3. What method will be used to assess this target behavior? Check appropriate box.

    ☐ Frequency Count   ☐ Intensity Measure   ☐ Duration Measure

    ☐ Outcome Measure   ☐ Qualitative Measure

4. How will observers be trained in the definition of this target behavior?

_____

_____

_____

5. When will the first evaluation of this behavioral assessment be carried out?

_____

_____

_____

6. How long an observation period will be needed to get a meaningful assessment of baseline?

_____

_____

_____

Target Behavior #2:

_____

_____

_____

Key variable described by behavioral definition. Check appropriate box:

☐ Frequency   ☐ Duration   ☐ Latency   ☐ Intensity
☐ Qualitative dimensions or outcomes. Specify:

_____

_____

_____

Assessment decisions

1. When will the assessment be carried out? What are the times of day or key settings in which the target behavior occurs?

_____

_____

_____

2. Who will carry out observation of this target behavior? (If necessary, specify by setting.)

_____

_____

_____

3. What method will be used to assess this target behavior? Check appropriate box.

    ☐ Frequency Count   ☐ Intensity Measure   ☐ Duration Measure
    ☐ Outcome Measure   ☐ Qualitative Measure

4. How will observers be trained in the definition of this target behavior?

_____

_____

_____

5. When will the first evaluation of this behavioral assessment be carried out?

_____

_____

_____

6. How long an observation period will be needed to get a meaningful assessment of baseline?

_____

_____

_____

Target Behavior #3:

_____

_____

_____

Key variable described by behavioral definition. Check appropriate box:

    ☐ Frequency   ☐ Duration   ☐ Latency   ☐ Intensity
    ☐ Qualitative dimensions or outcomes. Specify:

_____

_____

_____

Assessment decisions

1. When will the assessment be carried out? What are the times of day or key settings in which the target behavior occurs?

_____

_____

_____

2. Who will carry out observation of this target behavior? (If necessary, specify by setting.)

_____

_____

_____

3. What method will be used to assess this target behavior? Check appropriate box.

   ☐ Frequency Count   ☐ Intensity Measure   ☐ Duration Measure
   ☐ Outcome Measure   ☐ Qualitative Measure

4. How will observers be trained in the definition of this target behavior?

_____

_____

_____

5. When will the first evaluation of this behavioral assessment be carried out?

_____

_____

_____

6. How long an observation period will be needed to get a meaningful assessment of baseline?

_____

_____

_____

Appendix E: Observation Form–Frequency

Frequency of target behavior

Date: _____

Client name: _____

Target behavior (definition from Target Behavior Definition Form)

_____

_____

_____

Explanatory notes/special instructions (e.g., specify observation periods)

_____

_____

_____

(Instructions: This form can be used for continuous interval frequency counts by dividing the day into equal or naturally occurring observation intervals and entering a mark each time the behavior occurs in that interval. It may also be used for selected briefer observation periods that are then divided into equal shorter intervals in which the behavior is simply scored as having occurred or not occurred.)

Observer	Date	Duration (in minutes)/ Frequency							F = total # of duration entries	D = total duration

Appendix F: Observation Form–Intensity

Intensity of target behavior

Client name: _____

Definition of target behavior: _____

Provide specific behavioral anchoring scale for assigning an intensity rating (e.g., 1 = low, 4 = high).

1. _____ 2. _____ 3. _____ 4. _____

Rater	Date	Intensity Ratings									Average Intensity

Record level of intensity by placing the appropriate number in the cell each time the behavior occurs. Calculate average level of intensity by dividing the total of ratings for that date by the number of ratings.

Appendix G: Observation Form–Frequency/Duration

Frequency and duration of target behavior

Client name: _____

Target behavior (definition from Target Behavior Definition Form. Please note: To obtain reliable duration data, it is essential that the definition of the target behavior has very clear, explicit guidelines for judging the starting and stopping of the behavior.)

_____

_____

_____

(Instructions: Enter a duration for each occurrence of the target behavior.)

Observer	Date/Time of Observation	1	2	3	4	5	6	7	8	Daily Total All
		☐	☐	☐	☐	☐	☐	☐	☐	
		☐	☐	☐	☐	☐	☐	☐	☐	
		☐	☐	☐	☐	☐	☐	☐	☐	
		☐	☐	☐	☐	☐	☐	☐	☐	
		☐	☐	☐	☐	☐	☐	☐	☐	
		☐	☐	☐	☐	☐	☐	☐	☐	
		☐	☐	☐	☐	☐	☐	☐	☐	

Appendix H: Observation Form–Duration

Duration of target behavior

Client name: _____

Target behavior (definition from Target Behavior Definition Form. Please note: To obtain reliable duration data, it is essential that the definition of the target behavior has very clear, explicit guidelines for judging the starting and stopping of the behavior.)

_____

_____

_____

(Instructions: Enter start and stop times for each incidence of the behavior, go to next line if necessary for a particular day.)

Observer	Date	Start	Stop	Start	Stop	Start	Stop	Start	Stop	Daily total and average

Appendix I: Functional Assessment Worksheet

Functional analysis: Collaborative meeting worksheet

Client name: _____

Date of meeting: _____

(If multiple meetings are held among different groups of team members, then use a new worksheet for each meeting.)

Team members present:

1. _____ 4. _____
2. _____ 5. _____
3. _____ 6. _____

Note: This meeting is specifically focused on the client's target behaviors. This meeting assumes that some initial gathering of more general, often historical, information has already occurred. This might include, but is not limited to, family and developmental history, trauma history, strengths and vulnerabilities of the client, history of the target behaviors, and history of prior interventions and their results.

In focusing on behavior, this meeting should be an exercise in curiosity, a collaborative sharing of information, experience, and understanding that will help us all understand what seems to cause the behavior and what seems to keep it going. We want to find out what purpose it serves. The questions provided below are offered as potentially useful prompts. Pursuing data may require more specific questions based on what emerges as the discussion proceeds.

Target behavior 1

Definition:

_____

_____

_____

1. Setting questions: Are there settings in which the behavior is more likely to occur? These can include real settings—actual places—as well as activities and states of vulnerability in the client such as fatigue, hunger, or anger about some other issue. Does the problem occur only at school? Only at home? Only in transitions? Are there settings in which the behavior never occurs?

_____

_____

_____

2. Antecedent questions: Are there any events that often occur right before the behavior that seem to "trigger" it? These can include certain kinds of interactions, activities, and even particular people.

_____

_____

_____

3. Consequence questions: Are there any results, consequences, or responses from the environment that seem to follow the behavior? These can include getting something, getting to do something, not having to do something, and responses from adults and peers.

_____

_____

_____

4. Intervention questions: What responses or procedures have the adults (teachers, staff, caregivers) utilized in the past to deal with this target behavior?

_____

_____

_____

5. Exception data: Are there settings (people, places, activities, etc.) in which the target behavior never occurs? Are there settings that are regularly associated with the client engaging in positive behavior?

_____

_____

_____

Initial hypotheses: Given the data developed above, do the team have any initial hypotheses about the function of the behavior? A hypothesis can be stated in the form of "When x occurs or is occurring, the client does behavior y and the result is that z occurs."

_____

_____

_____

Plan for direct observation: Given the above hypotheses, describe a plan for appropriate direct observation of the behavior, in the environment in which it occurs, to collect systematic data. Include who will be responsible for collection of the data, what forms will be used or created for the recording of the data, and for how long the data will be collected.

_____

_____

_____

Target behavior 2

Definition:

_____

_____

_____

1. Setting questions: Are there settings in which the behavior is more likely to occur? These can include real settings—actual places—as well as activities and states of vulnerability in the client such as fatigue, hunger, or anger about some other issue. Does the problem occur only at school? Only at home? Only in transitions? Are there settings in which the behavior never occurs?

_____

_____

_____

2. Antecedent questions: Are there any events that often occur right before the behavior that seem to "trigger" it? These can include certain kinds of interactions, activities, and even particular people.

_____

_____

_____

3. Consequence questions: Are there any results, consequences, or responses from the environment that seem to follow the behavior? These can include getting something, getting to do something, not having to do something, and responses from adults and peers.

_____

_____

_____

4. Intervention questions: What responses or procedures have the adults (teachers, staff, caregivers) utilized in the past to deal with this target behavior?

_____

_____

_____

5. Exception data: Are there settings (people, places, activities, etc.) in which the target behavior never occurs? Are there settings that are regularly associated with the client engaging in positive behavior?

_____

_____

_____

Initial hypotheses: Given the data developed above, does the team have any initial hypotheses about the function of the behavior? A hypothesis can be stated in the form of "When x occurs or is occurring, the client does behavior y and the result is that z occurs."

Plan for direct observation: Given the above hypotheses, describe a plan for appropriate direct observation of the behavior, in the environment in which it occurs, to collect systematic data. Include who will be responsible for collection of the data, what forms will be used or created for the recording of the data, and for how long the data will be collected.

Target behavior 3

Definition:

---

1. Setting questions: Are there settings in which the behavior is more likely to occur? These can include real settings—actual places—as well as activities and states of vulnerability in the client such as fatigue, hunger, or anger about some other issue. Does the problem occur only at school? Only at home? Only in transitions? Are there settings in which the behavior never occurs?

---

2. Antecedent questions: Are there any events that often occur right before the behavior that seem to "trigger" it? These can include certain kinds of interactions, activities, and even particular people.

---

3. Consequence questions: Are there any results, consequences, or responses from the environment that seem to follow the behavior? These can include getting something, getting to do something, not having to do something, and responses from adults and peers.

_____

_____

_____

4. Intervention questions: What responses or procedures have the adults (teachers, staff, caregivers) utilized in the past to deal with this target behavior?

_____

_____

_____

5. Exception data: Are there settings (people, places, activities, etc.) in which the target behavior never occurs? Are there settings that are regularly associated with the client engaging in positive behavior?

_____

_____

_____

Initial hypotheses: Given the data developed above, does the team have any initial hypotheses about the function of the behavior? A hypothesis can be stated in the form of "When x occurs or is occurring, the client does behavior y and the result is that z occurs."

_____

_____

_____

Plan for direct observation: Given the above hypotheses, describe a plan for appropriate direct observation of the behavior, in the environment in which it occurs, to collect systematic data. Include who will be responsible for collection of the data, what forms will be used or created for the recording of the data and for how long the data will be collected.

_____

_____

_____

Appendix J: Client Variables Form

Functional Assessment of Behavior: Client Variables

Client name: _____

Date: _____

Target behaviors

_____

_____

_____

Client variables: Describe how any of the skills, life circumstances, and states are related to any of the target behaviors. If an entry is related to only target behavior in particular, then refer to that behavior by its number above.

Health issues or problems:

_____

_____

_____

Academic abilities:

_____

_____

_____

Cognitive skills/learning disabilities:

_____

_____

_____

Emotional states (e.g., "vulnerability states" such as fear, anxiety, anger, etc.):

_____

_____

_____

Substance use:

_____

_____

_____

Expressive or receptive language skills:

_____

_____

_____

Immediate physical states (e.g., hunger, fatigue, etc.):

_____

_____

_____

Medication:

_____

_____

_____

Cognitive states (e.g., beliefs, "thought disorders"):

_____

_____

_____

Social skills:

_____

_____

_____

Preoccupations (e.g., fairness or justice, worries about resources, etc.):

_____

_____

_____

Other client variables:

_____

_____

_____

This form is adapted from Watson and Steege (2003).

Appendix K: Functional Behavior Assessment Form

Client name: _____

Target behaviors: _____

1. _____
2. _____
3. _____

Date/ Time	Staff Involved	Setting Events	Antecedent	Behavior (1/2/3)	Consequence	Effect

This form is adapted from Watson and Steege (2003).

Appendix L: ABC Observation Form

Antecedent–Behavior–Consequence Form (ABC)

Client name: _____

Target behaviors:

_____

_____

_____

Date	Antecedents: People involved/ place/activity/ academic subject, etc.	Behavior: Key to target behaviors above or describe what you observed	Consequences: What actions followed the behavior on the part of adults, peers

Appendix M: Behavior Log

Client name: _____

Target behaviors:

_____

_____

_____

_____

Date	Time/Activity	Behavior	Outcome/Result

Appendix N: Replacement Behavior Worksheet

Client name: _____

Date: _____

Team members present:

_____

_____

_____

Target behavior:

_____

_____

_____

What is the function of the target behavior? What need or purpose does it express? What replacement behavior will enable the client to meet the same need and still preserve safety and continued development?

_____

_____

_____

Does the client already show the proposed replacement in another setting or behaviors that include components of the replacement behavior?

_____

_____

_____

What method will the team utilize in teaching the behavior? Will it need to be broken down into teachable components (chained) or taught in successive approximations (shaped)?

_____

_____

_____

Is there anyone in the client's environment who is a skilled practitioner of the replacement behavior?

_____

_____

_____

How will the team monitor the client's mastery of the replacement behavior?

_____

_____

_____

Appendix O: Behavioral Treatment Plan Worksheet

Client name: _____

Date of plan development: _____

Team members:

_____

_____

_____

Target behavior 1

Definition:

_____

_____

_____

Functional assessment information:

1. Antecedents and settings:

_____

_____

_____

2. Consequences:

_____

_____

_____

3. Functional hypothesis:

_____

_____

_____

Intervention planning:

1. Antecedent and setting modifications:

_____

_____

_____

2. Replacement behaviors:

_____

_____

_____

3. Reinforcement procedures (be sure to specify reinforcement strategies in all relevant settings):

_____

_____

_____

4. Reactive methods to be used:

_____

_____

_____

5. Provision for next behavioral assessment (specify timeline and measurement approach):

_____

_____

_____

Target behavior 2

Definition:

_____

_____

_____

Functional assessment information:

1. Antecedents and settings:

_____

_____

_____

2. Consequences:

_____

_____

_____

3. Functional hypothesis:

_____

_____

_____

Intervention planning:

1. Antecedent and setting modifications:

_____

_____

_____

2. Replacement behaviors:

_____

_____

_____

3. Reinforcement procedures (be sure to specify reinforcement strategies in all relevant settings):

_____

_____

_____

4. Reactive methods to be used:

_____

_____

_____

5. Provision for next behavioral assessment (specify timeline and measurement approach):

_____

_____

_____

Target behavior 3

Definition:

_____

_____

_____

Functional assessment information:

1. Antecedents and settings:

_____

_____

_____

2. Consequences:

_____

_____

_____

3. Functional hypothesis:

_____

_____

_____

Intervention planning:

1. Antecedent and setting modifications:

_____

_____

_____

2. Replacement behaviors:

_____

_____

_____

3. Reinforcement procedures (be sure to specify reinforcement strategies in all relevant settings):

_____

_____

_____

4. Reactive methods to be used:

_____

_____

_____

5. Provision for next behavioral assessment (specify timeline and measurement approach):

_____

_____

_____

Notes

Chapter 2

1. The original format of these tables was developed and refined by Dr. Tony Stanton. They are one of many of Dr. Stanton's contributions to work with very vulnerable children. As an aid to assessment and case formulation, they are invaluable. The use of these tables as a method for organizing initial assessment information and for communicating key issues of historical context to the treatment team will be discussed later.

Chapter 3

1. "2000" changed to "2002" as listed in ref section. Please check. check

Chapter 4

1. It is worth noting that a table of life events can often function as a valuable support to more reflective responses to a child's provocative behavior. In the absence of the historical context and narrative that such a table provides, it is all too easy for beleaguered direct care staff to arrive at reactive, often negative or blaming attributions about behavior. In this light it is interesting to watch new staff attend a team meeting and read a child's table for the first time. Having been on the receiving end of startling, provocative behavior but lacking any sense of history or context, they have ended up feeling completely off balance. As they read the table, they will often begin to smile and nod; the light bulb is going on over their heads and suddenly the child is starting to make sense to them.

Chapter 7

1. Appendix G, Observation Form—Frequency/Duration, is also included in the appendices.

References

Abrams, K. Y., Rifkin, A., and Hesse, E. (2006) Examining the role of parental Frightened/frightening subtypes in predicting disorganized attachment within a brief observational procedure. *Development and Psychopathology* 18:345–361.

Ainsworth, M. D. S. (1979) Infant–mother attachment. *American Psychologist* 34(10): 932–937.

Ainsworth, M. D. S., Blehar, M. C., Waters, E., and Wall, S. (1978) *Patterns of attachment: a psychological study of the strange situation.* Hillsdale, NJ: Erlbaum.

Alexander, F., and French, T. (1946) *Psychoanalytic therapy: principles and application.* New York: Ronald Press.

Allen, J. G., Fonagy, P., and Bateman, A. W. (2008) *Mentalizing in clinical practice.* Arlington, VA: American Psychiatric Press.

American Psychiatric Association (1994) *Diagnostic and statistical manual of mental disorders,* 4th ed. Washington, DC: American Psychiatric Association.

Axelrod, S., and Hall, R. (1999) *Behavior modification: basic principles.* Austin, TX: Pro-Ed.

Baer, D. M. (1999) *Plan for generalization.* Austin, TX: Pro-Ed.

Baker, A. and Curtis, P. (2006) Prior placements of youth admitted to therapeutic foster care and residential treatment centers: the odyssey project population. *Child and Adolescent Social Work Journal* 23(1):38–60.

Bambara, L. M., and Kern, L. E. (eds.) (2005) *Individualized supports for children with problem behaviors.* New York: Guilford Press.

Beck, A. T. (1976) *Cognitive therapy and the emotional disorders.* New York: International University Press.

Beebe, B., and Lachmann, F. M. (2002) *Infant research and adult treatment.* Hillsdale, NJ: Analytic Press.

Berg, I. K. (1994) *Family based services.* New York: W.W. Norton.

Berger, L. M. (2004) Income, family structure, and child maltreatment risk. *Children and Youth Services Review* 26:725–748.

Berger, L. M. (2005) Income, family characteristics, and physical violence toward children. *Child Abuse and Neglect* 29:107–133.

Bion, W. R. (1962) *Learning from experience.* New York: Jason Aronson.

Bleiberg, E. (2001) *Treating personality disorders in children and adolescents.* New York: Guilford Press.

Bleiberg, E. (2003) Treatment of dramatic personality disorders in children and adlescents. In J. J. Magnavita (ed.), *Handbook of personality disorders.* Hoboken, NJ: Wiley.

Bolger, K. E., Patterson, C. J., Thompson, W. W., and Kupersmidt, J. B. (1995) Psychosocial adjustment among children experiencing persistent and intermittent family economic hardship. *Child Development* 66: 1107–1129.

Bowlby, J. (1969) *Attachment,* vol. 1 of *Attachment and loss.* New York: Basic Books.

Bowlby, J. (1973) *Separation: anxiety and anger,* vol. 2 of *Attachment and loss.* New York: Basic Books.

Bowlby, J. (1977) The making and breaking of affectional bonds. *British Journal of Psychiatry* 130:421–431.

Bowlby, J. (1980) *Loss: sadness and depression,* vol. 3 of *Attachment and loss.* New York: Basic Books.

Bowlby, J. (1988) *A secure base.* New York: Basic Books.

Bretherton, I., and Munholland, K. (2008) Internal working models in attachment relationships—a construct revisited. In J. Cassidy and P. R. Shaver (eds.), *Handbook of attachment: theory, research and clinical applications,* 2nd ed. New York: Guilford Press, pp. 102–127.

Brooks-Gunn, J. and Duncan, G. J. (1997) The effects of poverty on children. *Children and Poverty* 7(2):55–71.

Bruner, J. (1996) *The Culture of Education.* Cambridge, MA: Harvard University Press.

Carlson, E. A. (1998) A prospective, longitudinal study of attachment disorganization/disorientation. *Child Development* 69:1107–1128.

Carr, J. E., and LeBlanc, L. A. (2003) Functional analysis of problem behavior. In W. O'Donohue, J. E. Fisher, and S. C. Hayes (eds.), *Cognitive behavior therapy: applying empirically supported techniques in your practice.* Hoboken, NJ: Wiley, pp. 167–175.

Cassidy, J. (1994) Emotion regulation: influence of attachment relationships. In N. A. Fox (ed.), The development of emotion regulation: biological and behavioral considerations. *Monographs of the Society for Research in Child Development,* vol. 59, no. 2/3, serial no. 240, pp. 228–250.

Cassidy, J. (2008) The nature of the child's ties. In J. Cassidy and P. R. Shaver (eds.), *Handbook of attachment: theory, research and clinical applications,* 2nd ed. New York: Guilford Press, pp. 3–20.

Cassidy, J., and Shaver, P. R. (2008) *Handbook of attachment: theory, research and clinical applications,* 2nd ed. New York: Guilford Press.

Chamberlain, P. (2003) *Treating chronic juvenile offenders: advances made through the Oregon multidimensional treatment foster care model.* Washington, DC: American Psychological Association.

Ciccheti, D., and Toth, S. L. (1987) The application of a transactional risk model to intervention with multi-risk maltreating families. *Zero to Three* 7(5):1–8.

Collins, B., and Collins, T. (1990) Parent–professional relationships in the treatment of seriously emotionally disturbed children and adolescents. *Social Work* 35:522–526.

Cook, A., Blaustein, M., Spinazzola, J., and van der Kolk, B. (2003) *Complex trauma in children and adolescents.* White Paper from the National Child Traumatic Stress Network. www.NCTSNet.org.

Crittenden, P. M. (1990) Internal representational models of attachment relationships. *Infant Mental Health Journal* 11(3):259–277.

DeKlyen, M., and Greenberg, M. T. (2008) Attachment and psychopathology in childhood. In J. Cassidy and P. R. Shaver (eds.), *Handbook of attachment: theory, research and clinical applications*, 2nd ed. New York: Guilford Press, pp. 637–665.

Esveldt-Dawson, K., and Kazdin, A. E. (1998) *How to maintain behavior*. Austin, TX: Pro-Ed.

Fonagy, P. (1998) The transgenerational transmission of holocaust trauma: lessons learned from the analysis of an adolescent with obsessive compulsive disorder. Paper presented at the Annual Conference of the Institute of Contemporary Psychoanalysis, Los Angeles, California.

Fonagy, P., Gergely, G., Jurist, E. L., and Target, M. (2002) *Affect regulation, mentalization and the development of the self.* New York: Other Press.

Fonagy, P., and Target, M. (1997) Attachment and reflective function: their role in self-organization. *Development and Psychopathology* 9:679–700.

Fraiberg, S., Adelson, E., and Shapiro, V. (1980) Ghosts in the nursery: a psychoanalytic approach to impaired infant-mother relationships. In S. Fraiberg and L. Fraiberg (eds.), *Clinical studies in infant mental health: the first year of life*. New York: Basic Books, pp. 164–194.

Freud, S. (1955) *Beyond the pleasure principle*. In J. Strachey (ed., trans.), *The standard edition of the complete psychological works of Sigmund Freud*, vol. 18. London: Hogarth Press, pp. 7–64 (original work published 1920).

Gergely, G., and Unoka, Z. (2008) Attachment and mentalization in humans: the development of the affective self. In E. L. Jurist, A. Slade, and S. Bergner (eds.), *Mind to mind: infant research, neuroscience, and psychoanalysis*. New York: Other Press.

Gianino, A., and Tronick, E. Z. (1988) The mutual regulation model: the infant's self and interactive regulation coping and defense. In T. Field, P. McCabe, and N. Schneiderman (eds.), *Stress and coping*. Hillsdale, NJ: Erlbaum, pp. 47–68.

Greenberg, J. R. and Mitchell, S. A. (1983) *Object Relations in Psychoanalytic Theory*. Cambridge, MA: Harvard University Press.

Greenberg, M. T., Cicchetti, D., and Cummings, E. M. (1990) *Attachment in the preschool years: theory, research and intervention*. Chicago: University of Chicago Press.

Gross, J. J., and Thompson, R. A. (2006) Emotion regulation: conceptual foundations. In J. J. Gross (ed.), *Handbook of emotion regulation*. New York: Guilford Press.

Hall, R. V., and Hall, M. L. (1998a) *How to use systematic attention and approval*. Austin, TX: Pro-Ed.

Hall, R. V., and Hall, M. L. (1998b) *How to select reinforcers*. Austin, TX: Pro-Ed.

Hall, R. V., and Hall, M. L. (1998c) *How to use planned ignoring (extinction)*. Austin, TX: Pro-Ed.

Halle, J., Bambara, L. M., and Reichle, J. (2005) Teaching alternative skills. In L. M. Bambara and L. E. Kern (eds.), *Individualized supports for children with problem behaviors*. New York: Guilford Press.

Harter, S. (1999) *The construction of the self: A developmental perspective*. New York: Guilford Press.

Harter, S., Bresnick, S., Bouchey, H. A., and Whitsell, N. R. (1997) The development of multiple role-related selves during adolescence. *Development and Psychopathology* 9:835–853.

Hawkins, R. P., and Dobes, R. W. (1975) Behavioral definitions in applied behavior analysis: explicit or implicit. In B. C. Etzel, J. M. LeBlanc, and D. M. Baer (eds.),

New developments in behavioral research: theory, methods and applications. In honor of Sidney W. Bijou. Hillsdale, NJ: Erlbaum, pp. 167–188.

Heider, F. (1958) *The psychology of interpersonal relations.* New York: Wiley.

Hesse, E. (1999) The adult attachment interview: historical and current perspectives. In P. R. Shaver and J. Cassidy (eds.), *Handbook of attachment: theory, research and clinical applications,* 1st ed. New York: Guilford Press, pp. 395–433.

Hesse, E. (2008) The adult attachment interview: protocol, method of analysis and empirical studies. In P. R. Shaver and J. Cassidy (eds.), *Handbook of attachment: theory, research and clinical applications,* 2nd ed. New York: Guilford Press, pp. 552–598.

Hesse, E., and Main, M. (2000) Disorganized infant, child and adult attachment: collapse in behavioral and attentional strategies. *Journal of the American Psychoanalytic Association* 48(4):1097–1127.

Hesse, E., Main, M., Abrams, K. Y., and Rifkin, A. (2003) Unresolved states regarding loss or abuse can have "second generation" effects: disorganization, role inversion, and frightening ideation in the offspring of traumatized, non-maltreating parents. In M. F. Solomon and D. J. Siegel (eds.), *Healing trauma: attachment, mind, body and brain.* New York: W.W. Norton.

Hofer, M. A. (2006) Psychobiological roots of early attachment. *Current Directions in Psychological Science* 15(2):84–88.

Horowitz, M. J. (1987) *States of mind: configurational analysis in individual psychology,* 2nd ed. New York: Plenum Press.

Hurst, N. C., Sawatzky, D. D., and Pare, D. P. (1996) Families with multiple problems through a Bowenian lens. *Child Welfare* 75:693–708.

Jacobvitz, D. and Hazen, N. (1999) Developmental pathways from infant disorganization to childhood peer relationships. In J. Solomon, and C. George (eds.), *Attachment Disorganization.* New York: Guilford Press, pp. 127–159.

Kaplan, J. S., and Carter, J. (1995) *Beyond behavior modification,* 3rd ed. Austin, TX: Pro-Ed.

Karen, R. (1994) *Becoming attached.* Oxford: Oxford University Press.

Kazdin, A. E. (1995) *Conduct disorders in childhood and adolescence.* Thousand Oaks, CA: Sage.

Kazdin, A. E. (2001) *Behavior modification in applied settings.* Belmont, CA: Wadsworth.

Kern, L. (2005) Developing hypothesis statements. In L. M. Bambara and L. E. Kern (eds.), *Individualized supports for children with problem behaviors.* New York: Guilford Press, pp. 165–200.

Lewis, T., Amini, F., and Lannon, R. (2000) *A general theory of love.* New York: Random House.

Lieberman, A. F. (1997) Toddlers' internalization of maternal attributions as a factor in quality of attachment. In L. Atkinson and K. J. Zucker (eds.), *Attachment and psychopathology.* New York: Guilford Press, pp. 277–291.

Lieberman, A. F. (1999) Negative maternal attributions: effects on toddlers' sense of self. *Psychoanalytic Inquiry* 19:737–756.

Lieberman, A. F., Padron, E., Van Horn, P., and Harris, W. W. (2005) Angels in the nursery: the intergenerational transmission of benevolent parental influences. *Infant Mental Health Journal* 26(6):504–520.

Lieberman, A. F., and Pawl, J. H. (1990) Disorders of attachment and secure base behavior in the second year of life. In M. T. Greenberg, D. Cicchetti, and E. M. Cummings (eds.), *Attachment in the preschool years: theory, research and intervention.* Chicago: University of Chicago Press.

Lieberman, A. H., and Van Horn, P. (1998) Attachment, trauma, and domestic violence. Implications for child custody. Child and Adolescent Psychiatric Clinics of North America 7(2):423–443, viii–ix.

Linehan, M. (1993) *Cognitive-behavioral treatment of borderline personality disorder.* New York: Guilford Press.

Lyons-Ruth, K. (1996) Attachment relationships among children with aggressive behavior problems: the role of disorganized early attachments. *Journal of Consulting and Clinical Psychology* 64(1):64–73.

Lyons-Ruth, K., Bronfman, E., and Atwood, G. (1999) A relational-diathesis model of hostile-helpless states of mind: expressions in mother–infant interaction. In J. Solomon and C. George (eds.), *Attachment disorganization.* New York: Guilford Press, pp. 33–70.

Lyons-Ruth, K., and Jacobvitz, D. (1999) Attachment disorganization: unresolved loss, relational violence and attentional strategies. In J. Cassidy and P. R. Shaver (eds.), *Handbook of attachment: theory, research and clinical applications.* New York: Guilford Press, pp. 520–554.

Lyons-Ruth, K., and Jacobvitz, D. (2008) Attachment disorganization: genetic factors, parenting contexts and developmental transformation from infancy to adulthood. In J. Cassidy and P. R. Shaver (eds.), *Handbook of attachment: theory, research and clinical applications,* 2nd ed. New York: Guilford Press, pp. 666–697.

Madsen, W. C. (2007) *Collaborative therapy with multi-stressed families,* 2nd ed. New York: Guilford Press.

Main, M., and Cassidy, J. (1988) Categories of response to reunion with the parent at age 6: predicted from infant attachment classifications and stable over a 1-month period. *Developmental Psychology* 24:415–426.

Main, M., and Hesse, E. (1990) Parents' unresolved traumatic experiences are related to infant disorganized attachment status: is frightened and/or frightening parental behavior the linking mechanism? In M. T. Greenberg, D. Cicchetti, and E. M. Cummings (eds.), *Attachment in the preschool years: theory, research and intervention.* Chicago: University of Chicago Press, pp. 161–182.

Main, M., Kaplan, N., and Cassidy, J. (1985) Security in infancy, childhood and adulthood: a move to the level of representation. In I. Bretherton and E. Waters (eds.), Growing points of attachment theory and research. *Monographs of the Society for Research in Child Development,* vol. 50, no. 1/2, serial no. 209, 66–104.

Main, M., and Solomon, J. (1986) Discovery of a new, insecure-disorganized/disoriented attachment pattern. In T. B. Brazelton and M. W. Yogman (eds.), *Affective development in infancy.* Norwood, NJ: Ablex, pp. 95–124.

Main, M., and Solomon, J. (1990) Procedures for identifying infants as disorganized/disoriented during the Ainsworth strange situation. In M. T. Greenberg, D. Cicchetti, and E. M. Cummings (eds.), *Attachment in the preschool years: theory, research and intervention.* Chicago: University of Chicago Press, pp. 121–160.

Main, M., and Weston, D. (1981) The quality of the toddler's relationship to mother and father: related to conflict behavior and the readiness to establish new relationships. *Child Development* 52:932–940.

Martin, G., and Pear, J. (1999) *Behavior modification: what it is and how to do it.* Upper Saddle River, NJ: Prentice Hall.

Masten, A. S., Best, K. M., and Garmezy, N. (1991) Resilience and development: contributions from the study of children who overcame adversity. *Development and Psychopathology* 2:425–444.

Masten, A. S., and Powell, J. L. (2003) Resilience framework for research, policy, and practice. In S. S. Luthar (ed.), *Resilience and vulnerability: adaptation in the context of childhood adversities.* Cambridge: Cambridge University Press, pp. 1–28.

Masters, J. C., Burish, T. G., Hollon, S. D., and Rimm, D. C. (1987) *Behavior therapy.* New York: Harcourt Brace Jovanovich.

Mayers, H., and Siegler, A. L. (2004) Finding each other using a psychoanalytic–developmental perspective to build understanding and strengthen attachment between teenaged mothers and their babies. *Journal of Infant, Child and Adolescent Psychotherapy* 3(4):444–465.

McGoldrick, M. and Gerson, R. (1985) *Genograms in Family Assessment.* New York: W.W. Norton.

Miles, P. and Franz, J. (2006) *The Collaborative Toolkit: A Handbook for Family Team Facilitators.* Paperboat.com.

Miller, A. L., Rathus, J. H., Linehan, M. M., Wetzler, S., and Leigh, E. (1997) Dialectical behavior therapy adapted for suicidal adolescents. *Journal of Practical Psychiatry and Behavioral Health* 3:78–86.

Miltenberger, R. G. (2005) Strategies for measuring behavior change. In L. M. Bambara and L. E. Kern (eds.), *Individualized supports for children with problem behaviors.* New York: Guilford Press, pp. 107–128.

Minuchin, S. (1977) *Families and family therapy.* New York: Routledge.

Nader, P. (2008) *Understanding and assessing trauma in children and adolescents: measures, methods, and youth in context.* New York: Routledge.

Ogden, P., and Minton, K. (2000) Sensorimotor psychotherapy: one method for processing traumatic memory. *Traumatology* 6(3):149–173.

Oppenheim, D., and Goldsmith, D. F. (2007) *Attachment theory in clinical work with children.* New York: Guilford Press.

Ornish, D. (1998) *Love and survival: the scientific basis for the healing power of intimacy.* New York: Harper Collins.

Patterson, G. R. (1982) *Coercive family process.* Eugene, OR: Castalia Press.

Patterson, G. R. (2002) The early development of coercive family process. In J. B. Reid, G. R. Patterson, and J. Snyder (eds.), *Antisocial behavior in children and adolescents: a developmental analysis and a model for intervention.* Washington, DC: American Psychological Association.

Patterson, G. R., DeBaryshe, B. D., and Ramsey, E. (1989) A developmental perspective on antisocial behavior. *American Psychologist* 44:329–335.

Pawl, J. (1995) The therapeutic relationship as human connectedness. *Zero to Three* 15(4):2–5.

Perry, B. D., Pollard, R. A., Blakley, T. L., Baker, W. L., and Vigilante, D. (1995) Childhood trauma, the neurobiology of adaptation, and use-dependent development of the brain: how states become traits. *Infant Mental Health Journal* 16(4):271–291.

Persons, J. B. (2008) *The case formulation approach to cognitive-behavior therapy.* New York: Guilford Press.

Persons, J. B., Davidson, J., and Tompkins, M. A. (2001) *Essential components of cognitive-behavior therapy for depression.* Washington, DC: American Psychological Association.

Piaget, J. (1954) *The construction of reality in the child.* New York: Basic Books.

Plunkett, J. W., Meisels, S. S., Stiefel, G. S., Pasick, P. L., and Roloff, D. W. (1986) Patterns of attachment in infants of varying biological risk. *Journal of the American Academy of Child Psychiatry* 25(6):794–800.

Premack, D. (1959) Toward empirical behavioral laws. I: Positive reinforcement. *Psychological Review* 66:219–233.

Reid, J. B., Patterson, G. R., and Snyder, J. (2002) *Antisocial behavior in children and adolescents: a developmental analysis and a model for intervention.* Washington, DC: American Psychological Association.

Renken, B., Egeland, B., Marvinney, D., Mangelsdorf, S., and Sroufe, L. A. (1989) Early childhood antecedents of aggression and passive-withdrawal in early elementary school. Journal of Personality 58:257–281.

Robertson, J. (1953) Some responses of young children to the loss of maternal care. *Nursing Times* 49:382–386.

Rushton, J. P., and Teachman, G. (1978) The effects of positive reinforcement, attributions, and punishment on model induced altruism in children. *Personality and Social Psychology Bulletin* 4(2):322–325.

Schaffer, H. R., and Emerson, P. E. (1964) The development of social attachments in infancy. *Monographs of the Society for Research in Child Development*, vol. 29, no. 3, serial no. 94, pp. 3–77.

Schore, A. N. (1994) *Affect regulation and the origin of the self: the neurobiologuy of emotional development.* Hillsdale, NJ: Erlbaum.

Schore, A. N. (2003a) *Affect dysregulation and disorders of the self.* New York: W.W. Norton.

Schore, A. N. (2003b) *Affect regulation and the repair of the self.* New York: W.W. Norton.

Siberschatz, G. (2005) The control-mastery theory. In G. Silberschatz (ed.), *Transformative relationships: the control-mastery theory of psychotherapy.* New York: Routledge, pp. 3–24.

Siegel, D. J. (1999) *The developing mind: how relationships and the brain interact to shape who we are.* New York: Guilford Press.

Siegel, D. J., and Hartzell, M. (2003) *Parenting from the inside out: how a deeper self-understanding can help you raise children who thrive.* New York: Tarcher/Putnam.

Silverman, R. C., and Lieberman, A. F. (1999) Negative maternal attributions, projective identification, and the intergenerational transmission of violent relational patterns. *Psychoanalytic Dialogues* 9:161–186.

Slade, A. (2008) Mentalization as a frame for working with parents. In E. L. Jurist, A. Slade, S. Bergner (eds.), *Mind to mind: infant research, neuroscience and psychoanalysis.* New York: Other Press.

Snyder, J. (2002) Reinforcement and coercion mechanisms in the development of antisocial behavior: peer relationships. In J. B. Reid, G. R. Patterson, and J. Snyder (eds.), *Antisocial behavior in children and adolescents: a developmental analysis and a model for intervention.* Washington, DC: American Psychological Association, pp. 101–122.

Solomon, M. F., and Siegel, D. J. (2003) *Healing trauma: attachment, mind, body and brain.* New York: W.W. Norton.

Sorce, J. F., Emde, R. N., Campos, J. J., and Klinnert, M. D. (1985) Maternal emotional signaling: its effect on visual cliff behavior of one-year-olds. *Developmental Psychology* 21:195–200.

Spitz, R. A. (1946) Anaclitic depression. *Psychoanalytic Study of the Child* 2:313–342.

Sroufe, L. A. (1995) *Emotional development: the organization of emotional life in the early years.* Cambridge: Cambridge University Press.

Sroufe, L. A., Carlson, E. A., Levy, A. K., and Egeland, B. (1999) Implications of attachment theory for developmental psychopathology. *Development and Psychopathology* 11:1–13.

Stern, D. N. (1985) *The interpersonal world of the infant.* New York: Basic Books.

Stern, D. N. (1994) One way to build a clinically relevant baby. *Infant Mental Health Journal* 15(1):9–25.

Thomas, A., and Chess, S. (1977) *Temperament and development.* New York: Brunner-Mazel.

Sullivan, H. S. (1953) *The interpersonal theory of psychiatry.* New York: W.W. Norton.

Sutton, C. (2001) Resurgence of attachment (behaviours) within a cognitive-behavioural intervention: evidence from research. *Behavioural and Cognitive Psychotherapy* 29, 357–366.

Thompson, R. A. (1999) Early attachment and later development. In J. Cassidy and P. R. Shaver (eds.), *Handbook of attachment.* New York: Guilford Press, pp. 265–286.

Tronick, E. Z. (1989) Emotions and emotional communication in infants. *American Psychologist* 44(2):112–119.

van der Kolk, B. A. (1989) The compulsion to repeat the trauma: reenactment, revictimization and masochism. *Psychiatric Clinics of North America* 12(2):389–411.

van der Kolk, B. A. (1994) The body keeps the score. *Harvard Review of Psychiatry* 1:253–265.

van der Kolk, B. A. (2005) Developmental trauma disorder. *Psychiatric Annals* 35: 401–408.

van der Kolk, B.A, MacFarlane, A. C., and Weisaeth, L. (eds.) (1996) *Traumatic stress.* New York: Guilford Press.

Van Houten, R. (1998) *How to motivate others through feedback,* 2nd ed. Austin, TX: Pro-Ed.

Van IJzendoorn, M. H. (1995) Adult attachment representations, parental responsiveness, and infant attachment: a meta-analysis of the predictive validity of the Adult Attachment Interview. *Psychological Bulletin* 117:387–403.

Walsh, F. (2002) Clinical views of family normality, health, and dysfunction: from deficit to strengths perspective. In F. Walsh (ed.), *Normal family processes: growing diversity and complexity,* 3rd ed. New York: Guilford Press, pp. 24–53.

Watson, T. S., and Steege, M. W. (2003) *Conducting school-based functional behavioral assessments: a practitioner's guide.* New York: Guilford Press.

Weinfeld, N. S., Sroufe, L. A., and Egeland, B. (2000) Attachment from infancy to early adulthood in a high-risk sample. *Child Development* 71:528–543.

Weiss, J. (1993) *How psychotherapy works.* New York: Guilford Press.

Weiss, J., and Sampson, S. (1986) *The psychoanalytic process: theory, clinical observation, and empirical research.* New York: Guilford Press.

Werner, E. (1995) Resilience in development. *Current Directions in Psychological Science* 4:81–85.

Winnicott, D. (1964) *The child, the family, and the outside world.* Harmondsworth, UK: Penguin Books.

Young, J. E. (1990) *Cognitive therapy for personality disorders: a schema-focused approach* (rev. ed.). Sarasota, FL: Professional Resources Press.

Young, J. E., Klosko, J. S., and Weishaar, M. E. (2003) *Schema therapy: a practioner's guide.* New York: Guilford Press.

Zeanah, C. H., and Scheeringa, M. (1998) The experience and effects of violence in infancy. In J. D. Osofsky and P. Scharf (eds.), *Children in a violent society.* New York: Guilford Press, pp. 97–123.

Zelenko, M., Lock, J., Kraemer, H. C., and Steiner, H. (2000) Perinatal complications and child abuse in a poverty sample. *Child Abuse and Neglect* 24(7):939–950.

Index